USBORNE
SOCCER SCHOOL

Gill Harvey, Richard Dungworth,
Jonathan Miller and Clive Gifford

Illustrations by Bob Bond • Photographs by Chris Cole
Designed by Stephen Wright and Neil Francis
Edited by Cheryl Evans, Felicity Brooks and Gill Harvey
Cover design by Stephen Wright and Zöe Wray

Consultant: John Shiels, Bobby Charlton International Soccer Schools Ltd.

Photographic manipulation by John Russell
Additional photographs by Shaun Botterill, Allsport

With thanks to Phil Darren and Peter Bonetti

Contents

PART ONE
BALL CONTROL

CONTENTS

GETTING STARTED

Good ball control is the first thing that any soccer player needs to work on. It means being able to receive the ball quickly and effectively and then keep control of it, too. This part of the book shows you how to develop these skills. It covers many techniques, and there are plenty of exercises and challenges to try.

A loose shirt with short or long sleeves is good for training in.

WHAT DO I NEED?

All you need to train with are a soccer ball and some markers. Special sports markers are shown here, but you can use bags or sweaters. Wear loose, comfortable clothing such as a tracksuit or shorts and T-shirt. On most surfaces trainers are fine, but soccer boots are best if you are playing on muddy ground.

Don't wear shorts or tracksuit bottoms that are tight. They will slow you down.

Shinpads protect you against hard tackles.

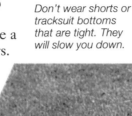

Sports marker.

WARMING UP

To have good ball control, you need to be able to move your whole body well. Being able to twist, turn and keep your balance are key skills for many control techniques.

Do this exercise in pairs. More than one pair can play at once. It is a good warm-up exercise which will improve your balance and movement.

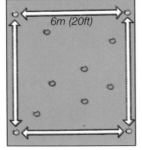

6m (20ft)

Mark out a 6m (20ft) square. Scatter six or seven markers inside it. Decide who will be attacker and who will be defender.

The attacker dribbles forward, weaving around the markers. The defender tries to stop him reaching the other side.

You cannot touch each other or leave the square. If the defender forces the attacker off the square, he has won.

GETTING THE FEEL OF THE BALL

If you are used to playing around with a soccer ball you will probably already have some idea of how the ball responds when you touch it in different ways. This is what it means to have a feel for the ball. This page looks more closely at how this works and how you can use the different parts of your foot to do different things.

This exercise helps you to get a feel for the parts of your foot that you use most often – the inside, outside and instep (see left).

Lay out seven markers 2m (6ft) part in a zigzag line. Push the ball from the first to the second with the outside of your foot.

The inside of your foot is used most often. Use it for controlling, dribbling and passing.

The outside of the foot tends to tap the ball away from you. To keep it in control you need a gentle touch.

At the second marker, start using the inside of your foot.

This is the easiest way to push the ball, as it naturally rolls in front of you.

The outside of your foot is useful for turning, dribbling and passing the ball to the side.

Your instep is the most powerful part of your foot. It is best for kicking, especially shooting.

Your heel is not often used, but it is good for flicking the ball backwards or a quick reverse pass.

This is basic 'juggling', which you can do without letting the ball bounce. Find out more about juggling on page 4.

At the next marker, use your instep. Tap the ball into the air, let it bounce once, then tap it up again.

At the following marker, start the sequence again. Try to get used to using both your left and your right foot.

It is very difficult to control the ball with the tips of your toes. You should hardly ever use them.

It is risky to use the sole of your foot to control the ball, but you use it for some trick moves.

CHALLENGE

When you see this trophy, you will find an idea for a challenge. Soccer is very competitive, so you need to keep pushing yourself to improve your personal best for every exercise. Get into the habit of giving yourself new targets each time you practise so that you can tell how fast your skills are growing.

MOVING ON

Once you have a basic feel for the ball you are on the way to developing good control. The next stage is to do plenty of practice to develop your skills. Things like juggling the ball are good for this, but you also need to work on special control methods. Here you can find out about the basic techniques that will help you.

JUGGLING

Although you rarely use juggling in an actual game, it helps you to develop the quick reactions, tight ball control and concentration that you need in order to play well.

To get the ball into the air, roll your foot back over the top of the ball, then hook it under and flick the ball up.

Keep the ball in the air by bouncing it off your foot. Hold your foot out flat. If you point your toes up, you will probably lose control.

As you develop your control, pass from one foot to the other, or bounce it up further into the air so that you juggle it on your knee.

Keep your eye on the ball all the time.

You could try juggling the ball on your shoulder and with your head.

JUGGLING GAME

Work on your juggling with a group of friends. Choose someone to be a caller. All of you dribble until the caller shouts 'Up!'

Everyone flicks the ball up and juggles. The last one to keep the ball in the air wins. When he drops it, you all start dribbling again.

RECEIVING THE BALL

Controlling the ball as you receive it is one of the most important skills you can learn. Everything else you do depends on this, so it's well worth spending plenty of time on it. These are the main points to remember.

FIRST TOUCH

This player is demonstrating good first touch. The ball is moving and in a good position to be played away.

1. To get your timing right, you need to judge the flight of the ball carefully.

2. Don't just hope the ball will come straight to you. Move into line with it.

3. Decide early which part of your body you will use to control the ball.

4. Once you have the ball, don't hesitate. Decide on your next move quickly.

The moment you make contact with the ball is called the 'first touch.' A good first touch keeps the ball moving and places it a short distance from your feet. To develop this skill, you need to 'cushion' the ball.

WHAT IS CUSHIONING?

Cushioning means taking the speed out of the ball, just as a cushion would if it was attached to your body. It slows the ball down without making it bounce away. Here you can see how cushioning works in practice.

As the ball travels towards you, position your foot in line with it to receive it.

On making contact, relax your foot and let it travel back with the ball.

The speed of the ball is absorbed. It slows down and you can play it away.

FOOT CONTROL

Your feet are the parts of your body that you use most often to receive the ball. Remember that a good first touch keeps the ball moving, so use the inside, outside or instep of your foot rather than your sole. Try to slow the ball down and position it in one smooth movement.

USING THE INSIDE OF YOUR FOOT

If you use the inside of your foot, you will be in a good position to play the ball away when you have cushioned it.

Watch the ball as it approaches and place your foot in line with it. Balance on one leg with your receiving foot turned out.

As you receive the ball with the inside of your foot, relax your leg and foot so that they travel back with it.

The ball should drop just in front of your feet. Look around you and play it away to the left or right as quickly as possible.

This player is balanced and in line with the ball.

Make sure you work on receiving with your left and your right foot.

USING THE OUTSIDE OF YOUR FOOT

If you are going to use the outside of your foot, decide to do so quickly and turn so that your side faces the ball.

Lift your leg to receive the ball with the outside of your foot. Relax your foot back and down to the ground.

Push the ball to the outside with the same foot, as you can see here, or across your body with either foot.

USING YOUR INSTEP

To control the ball with your instep, make sure you are facing the ball with your arms out for balance.

Lift your foot, but keep it flat. If you point your toes up the ball will probably bounce off them.

Just as you receive the ball, lower your foot to the ground, letting the ball drop off it in front of you.

THINGS TO AVOID

Try not to stop the ball dead. If you do, you have to touch it again before you can play your next move.

If the ball bounces off your foot and ends up a long way from you, you waste time chasing it.

PASS AND CONTROL EXERCISE

Do this exercise with a friend. Make a 'gate' with two markers and stand with the gate between you. Pass the ball through the gate so that your partner has to control it.

He turns and passes the ball down the outside of the gate. Control it, turn and pass it back through the gate or down the other side of it. Carry on passing and receiving like this.

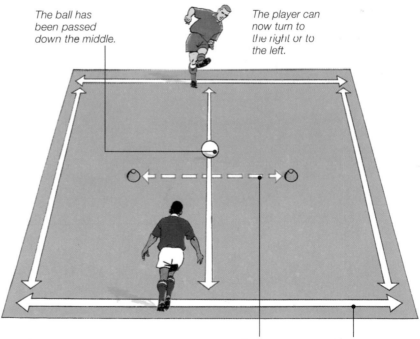

The ball has been passed down the middle.

The player can now turn to the right or to the left.

Try to vary your passes as much as possible, but keep them low.

Anticipate which way the ball will come and run for it.

The gate is about 2m (6ft) wide.

Your pitch is about 5m (16ft) wide.

HIGHER BALLS

When a ball comes at you from a higher angle, there are several things you can do. Depending on where you position yourself and how high the ball is, you can receive it with your foot, thigh or chest. Whichever you decide upon, you still use a cushioning technique to take the pace out of the ball.

USING YOUR THIGH

If you cushion the ball properly it shouldn't sting your leg.

Watch the ball carefully so that you can judge where it will land.

Bend your knee to meet the ball, using your arms for balance. On making contact, straighten your leg gradually so that the ball drops off your thigh in front of your feet.

USING YOUR FOOT

Keeping your arms out for balance, lift your leg to meet the ball. Catch it with the inside of your foot.

Without hooking your foot completely under the ball, drop it down to the ground, dragging the ball down with it.

USING YOUR CHEST

Your chest is good for cushioning because it is bigger than any other part of your body. Keep your hands open, because clenching your fist makes your chest muscles tighten and they need to relax. Keep your arms out of the way, too, to avoid handling the ball.

Put your arms back and open up your chest as the ball approaches you.

As the ball makes contact with you, cushion it by letting yourself relax.

Bring your shoulders in and hollow your chest, so that the ball rolls off you.

The ball drops to the ground gently and you are able to play your next move.

HIGH BALL PRACTICE

Throw the ball over your head, as you would for a throw-in, to make it bounce high.

Try to judge how the ball will land as it comes towards you.

Vary the angle and height of the throws.

Run into the best position to receive the ball.

Do this practice in pairs. One of you throws the ball to the other so that it bounces once. The other person decides which part of the body to control it with, controls it as quickly as possible and passes it back. Swap after ten throws. After ten throws each, repeat the exercise, this time without letting the ball bounce.

CHALLENGE

When you are doing the high ball practice, build up to controlling at least eight out of ten throws with no more than three touches. When both you and your partner can do this, compete with each other. Score out of ten.

HEADING THE BALL

Controlling the ball with your head is not very easy until you are sure of your heading technique, so these pages show you how to develop a range of heading skills. The main points to remember are to keep your eyes open and to use your forehead, not the top of your head. You may find it easier to begin with a fairly light, soft ball.

BASIC HEADING TECHNIQUE

Put yourself in line with the ball. With one foot in front of the other, bend your knees and lean back.

As the ball comes close, try to keep your eyes open. Stay relaxed right up to the last minute.

Attack the ball with your forehead. If you use any other part of your head it can be painful.

Push the ball away, keeping your neck muscles firm so that your head can direct the ball.

POWER HEADING

Put one foot in front of the other for balance and bend your legs as the ball comes towards you.

Keep your eyes fixed on the ball and take off on one foot. This gives you more power and height.

Drive forward as powerfully as you can with your forehead, keeping your eyes open.

Watch where the ball goes as you land so that you are ready to carry out your next move.

CONTROL HEADING

Use a control header to cushion the ball if you want to play the next move yourself instead of passing.

Don't lean quite as far back as the ball approaches. Stay relaxed to provide a cushion for the ball.

Hold your position as you receive the ball. Bend your knees and lean back slightly further.

Push the ball forward gently, so that it drops and lands not far from your feet.

HEADING PRACTICE

Basic heading

Control heading

Power heading

Work with a partner. Stand about 4m (13ft) apart. Your partner throws the ball for you to head back. Have five goes at each of these techniques, then swap.

First, cushion the ball with a control header. Let it drop to the ground. Pass it back.

Next, head the ball so that your partner can catch it easily.

Finally, power the ball away, heading it over your partner.

CHALLENGE

Set distance targets. For power headers, try to head the ball more than 6m (20ft). For control headers, try to head it no more than 1m (3ft) from your feet.

TURNING

Once you have received the ball and controlled it, you need to move off with it as fast as possible before an opponent can challenge you. You improve your chances of doing this effectively if you can turn quickly and sharply, so it is worth learning several turns to outwit your opponents.

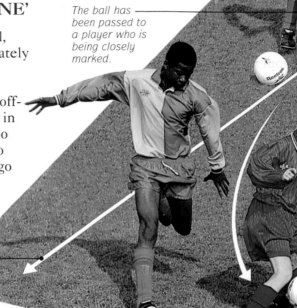

Marker

TURNING 'OFF-LINE'

When you receive the ball, always try to turn immediately and take it off in another direction. This is what is meant by taking the ball 'off-line'. If you keep running in the same direction, it is too easy for your opponents to guess where the ball will go next. They will quickly be able to reach you and tackle you.

The ball has been passed to a player who is being closely marked.

This line shows the 'on-line' route that the player must try to avoid taking.

Instead of taking the on-line route, the player reaches the ball and turns off-line.

DOING AN INSIDE HOOK

As you receive the ball, watch out for approaching opponents and lean in the direction you want to go.

Drop your shoulder so that you are partly turned. Hook the inside of your foot around the ball.

Move off at a sharp angle, dragging the ball around with the inside of your foot. Accelerate away.

DOING AN OUTSIDE HOOK

To begin the turn, reach across your body and hook the ball at the bottom with the outside of your foot.

Sweep the ball around to the side with the same foot. Lean in the direction you want to go.

Turn to follow the path of the ball and accelerate away from your opponent as quickly as possible.

CONTROL AND TURNING EXERCISE

This exercise helps you to develop the different skills of controlling the ball and turning with it into one smooth movement. You will need three or more people.

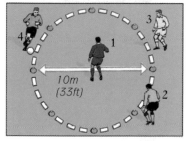 

1. Mark out a circle 10m (33ft) wide. Number the players. The highest (Player 4 here) has the ball and the lowest stands in the middle.

2. Player 4 begins the game by passing the ball into the middle. Player 1 controls it and turns with it. He can turn in any direction.

3. Player 1 dribbles the ball to the edge of the circle and Player 2 runs to the middle. Player 1 turns and passes the ball back to Player 2.

4. Player 2 controls the ball, turns and runs to the edge. Player 3 takes his place in the middle. After Player 3, Player 4 runs in, and so on.

STAR TURN

Here, Swiss player Georges Bregy uses an inside hook to pull the ball away from Leonel Alvarez (Columbia).

 ## CHALLENGE

Touching the ball lots of times slows you down, so try to touch it as little as possible. Count the number of touches you need to control the ball and turn it, then reduce this number to four or less.

TURNING TRICKS

Basic turns are useful for speed, but they do not disguise your movements very much. In many situations, a slightly more complicated turn can help you to fool your opponents. Be flexible, and experiment. You may prefer to develop your own way of doing a particular turn.

THE DRAG BACK TURN

This turn is ideal if you are being closely marked. Once you have mastered it, you can adapt it, depending on your position or that of your opponent.

Think about where to go next.

Spin quickly on your standing foot.

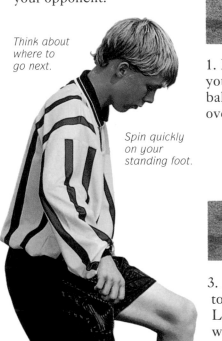

1. Draw your leg back as if you are about to kick the ball, but swing your foot over it instead.

2. As you bring your leg back again, catch the top of the ball with your foot and drag it back.

3. As you drag back, begin to spin on your other foot. Lean in the direction you want to go.

4. When you have pulled the ball all the way back, complete the turn. Accelerate past your opponent.

VARIATIONS

Instead of dragging the ball back, step to the inside. Push it away with the outside of your foot.

You can also step to the outside of the ball. Turn, pushing the ball with the inside of your foot.

THE CRUYFF TURN

This turn was named after the Dutch player Johan Cruyff. Try to exaggerate the movements. You can give the turn extra disguise by pretending to kick the ball first.

As you are about to do the turn, swing one foot around the ball so that it is in front of it. Keep this foot firmly on the ground.

Leaning away from the ball, push it back and then behind you with the other foot. Turn quickly and follow the ball.

Try to develop a quick flick of your foot to push the ball around.

Watch where the ball goes so that you can follow it

TURNING PRACTICE

Work with a partner. Place four markers in the pattern shown and stand at the end ones. One person is the leader and the other person mirrors what he does.

Both dribble to the middle. Just before the marker, the leader turns. The other tries to mirror his turn.

Run out to the side marker, round it and back to the end ones. Try not to bump into each other as you cross.

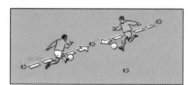

Start toward the middle again and turn at the marker. The leader will now be the other player.

CHALLENGE

Compete with each other. Score a point for mirroring a turn correctly, or for fooling your opponent with a turn. Race back to your markers and score a point for winning. The first to ten points wins.

DRIBBLING

Once you have possession of the ball, you may want to pass or shoot, but one of the most exciting parts of playing soccer is keeping the ball under your control and dribbling it up the field. If you watch a good dribbler, the ball seems almost stuck to his feet as he runs. This is what you should aim for.

BASIC TECHNIQUE

You can use your instep to dribble, especially for the first few touches. Be careful not to kick the ball very far.

You are free to run faster if you use the outside of your foot, but try not to tap the ball too far out to the side.

The inside of your foot may feel the most comfortable to use.

Be careful not to let the ball get under your feet.

MOVEMENT AND BALANCE

You need to be flexible and balanced to dribble well. To develop these skills, dribble around a slalom. Lay ten markers about 4m (13ft) apart in a zigzag line. Start to dribble down the line, weaving around the markers.

4m (13ft)

Try dribbling with different parts of your feet to see which feels most comfortable.

Keep the ball close to your feet. Try to exaggerate the twists and turns, leaning as far as you can as you run.

Keep as close to the path of the slalom as possible. Turn sharply at the markers.

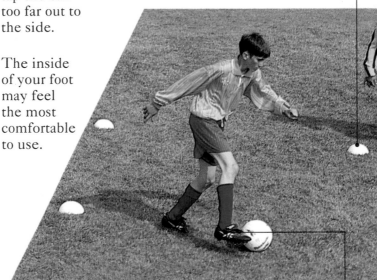

In a game, you would need to look out for other players, so try to look around as you dribble.

Gradually increase your speed. If you find that you cannot lean as far, slow down again until you improve.

Try to run lightly on your toes, so that you can change direction quickly and easily.

TAG DRIBBLE

This game is for up to four people, though more people can play if you make the square bigger.

1. Lay out a 6 x 6m (20 x 20ft) square with four markers. Each player has a ball and stands in the square.

2. Dribble around the square. Try to 'tag' other players without being tagged yourself and without losing control of the ball.

3. Keep a score. You gain a point each time you tag someone, and if you are tagged, you lose a point.

6m (20ft)

Try to play an attacking game. Don't just avoid being tagged.

Keep an eye out for other players all the time.

Be careful not to lose control of your own ball when you tag someone.

You cannot run outside the square to avoid being tagged.

IDEAL TECHNIQUE

Good dribbling should combine tight control with freedom of movement. Some people think that you should dribble with the outside of your foot as much as possible, because it gives you freedom to run and makes it easier for you to turn to the outside.

Here you can see Roberto Baggio of Italy dribbling with the ball at an ideal distance from his feet.

CHALLENGE

The best way to measure how you improve at dribbling is by timing yourself. When you dribble down a slalom, time yourself, then try to beat your record. Try to keep the ball close to your feet. Remember that there is no point in going faster unless the ball is under your control.

WORKING ON PACE

One of the things which will make your dribbling skills more effective is being able to vary your speed. If you can slow down or sprint away suddenly without losing control of the ball, you add disguise to your game and increase your chances of keeping possession.

CHANGES OF PACE

Keep an eye out for opponents and opportunities to pass.

Be ready to slow down and do something different if someone challenges you.

Take long strides so that you cover as much ground as possible.

1. Fool opponents by slowing down. This gives you time to take them by surprise.

2. To dodge around someone, watch for an opportunity to change pace suddenly.

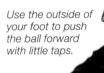

Use the outside of your foot to push the ball forward with little taps.

3. Sprint as fast as possible when you have just dodged around your opponent.

4. When you are clear of opponents, choose the pace that gives you most control.

RUNNING WITH THE BALL

Running with the ball is different from dribbling. It means sprinting up the field with a clear path ahead, pushing the ball quite a long way in front of you. When you dribble you keep the ball under closer control, beating opponents as you go.

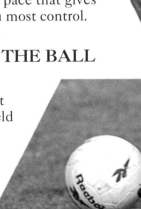

SLALOM AND SPRINT

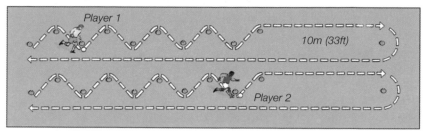

Player 1

10m (33ft)

Player 2

You can play this with as many people as you like. You each need a ball. Lay down ten markers in a zigzag line (see page 16), then place an extra marker 10m (33ft) from the last one. Make one course like this for each person.

At the shout of 'Go!', everyone starts to dribble in and out of the slalom.

At the end of the slalom, accelerate. Run with the ball to the last marker.

Turn, then race back to the starting point with the ball. The first one back wins.

SPRINT AND STOP GAME

This game is for three or more players. Lay out a circle about 3m (10ft) wide and a bigger circle around it. There should be about 10m (33ft) between them. All of you begin to dribble around the inside circle.

Take turns shouting 'Go!' The player who shouts has an unfair advantage, so he cannot be the winner of that game.

To keep the ball close to the circle, use the outside of your foot. Brush the ball along with the foot nearest the circle.

This player has reached the outer circle and stopped with his foot on the ball, so he wins.

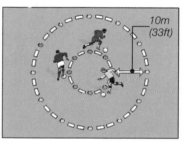

10m (33ft)

On the shout of 'Go!', turn and sprint out from the circle. The first person to reach the outer circle and put a foot on their ball is the winner. Dribble back to the inner circle and start the game again.

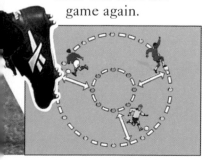

FEINTING

Feinting means fooling your opponents while you are dribbling. It is also called 'selling a dummy'. Two things will make your opponent move in a particular direction, either the movement of your body or the movement of the ball. Feinting uses the movement of your body.

A SIMPLE DUMMY

The simplest dummy or feint is pretending to go one way, then swerving and going the other. Here, Player 1 dribbles up the field as Player 2 comes to challenge him.

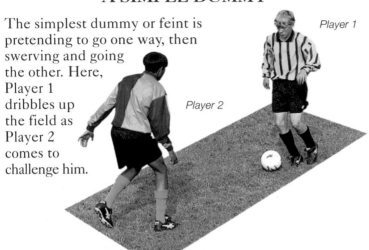

Player 1

Player 2

Player 1 drops his right shoulder, making Player 2 think that he is going to turn to the right.

Player 2 moves to the right, but Player 1 now swerves back to the left. He dodges around Player 2 and accelerates past him.

KEY FACTORS

Exaggerate your dropped shoulder and body swerve to fool your opponent.

Accelerate past your opponent before he has time to recover.

Be confident when you try to sell a dummy, or you risk losing the ball.

A STAR FEINT

Here, Alberto Garcia Aspe of Mexico drops his shoulder to sell a dummy to Paul McGrath of Ireland.

BASIC FEINTING PRACTICE

Work with a partner. Try to dribble past him, using a feint – you are not allowed to just push the ball past him and run.

If you get past him, turn and try again. If you don't, he dribbles past you instead. Score a point each time you get past.

GUESS AND DODGE GAME

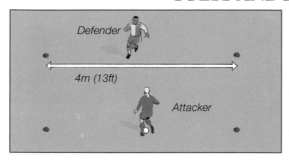

Defender

4m (13ft)

Attacker

The attacker dodges to the left, so the defender also turns to the left.

1. This is a game for two people with one ball. Both of you stand between two markers placed about 4m (13ft) apart.

2. Decide who will attack and who will defend. The attacker has the ball. The aim is for the attacker to reach a marker.

3. If the defender has his foot on one marker, the attacker has to go the other way. He cannot touch the matching marker.

4. Keep on playing until the attacker reaches a marker, then swap over so that you both have a turn at being attacker.

You need to be able to switch your balance from one foot to the other.

Once you see that your opponent is off balance, run for your marker quickly.

Here, the attacker has quickly turned to the right to reach the other marker.

A good defender tries to watch the ball, not your movements. This game helps you to develop the speed and anticipation you need to beat him.

FEINTING TRICKS

If you are trying to sell a dummy while you are dribbling, you stand a better chance of succeeding if you know a few trick moves. On these pages there are different ways to change direction and unbalance your opponent, which you can use as part of your feinting technique.

THE STOP MOVE

1. This move relies on a change of pace. Use it if someone is chasing you.

2. Accelerate slightly. As your opponent speeds up to follow, stop suddenly.

3. You should now be in a good position to use a drag back turn (see page 14).

4. You will be able to carry out the turn while your opponent is still off balance.

5. Finish the turn and start to move away at right angles to your original direction.

6. Your opponent is now facing the wrong way to chase you as you speed off.

THE STOP-START GAME

20m (66ft)

Work with a partner. Mark out a line about 20m (66ft) long. Dribble along it with your partner behind you.

Your partner can come alongside, but he cannot overtake you. Try to 'lose' him by stopping suddenly.

Your partner is thrown off balance.

You may confuse him more if you pretend to stop, then accelerate. Keep the ball on the side farthest from him.

CHALLENGE

Allow tackling in the stop-start game. Overtaking and sliding tackles are not allowed, but you can try to hook the ball away from the side. Score a point each time you succeed.

THE ZIGZAG MOVE

Try to exaggerate the move.

You don't need to rush.

1. Drop your shoulder and lean left to make it look as though you will push the ball across your body that way.

2. As your opponent gets closer, 'show' him the ball. This confuses him into thinking he can intercept it.

You can reverse this move and turn to the left.

3. Just before he tries to tackle you, slide your right foot around the ball and hook it with the outside of your foot.

4. Pull the ball away to the right and push it past your opponent. Turn to follow it quickly and accelerate away.

SOLO PRACTICE

To gain confidence in using these moves, try doing them on your own with a marker. Pretend the marker is one of your opponents and dodge past it when you get close to it. Try using different moves.

THE SCISSORS MOVE

Dribble forward with the outside of your right foot. Make it look as though you will swerve out to the right.

Lift your foot suddenly and swing it around the front of the ball, taking a big stride as you do so.

Hook the outside of your other foot around the ball. Push it away as fast as you can to the left.

SHIELDING THE BALL

Shielding is a way of keeping control of the ball by preventing other players from getting at it. It is also known as 'screening'. You position yourself so that you become a shield between your opponent and the ball. Try to develop the habit of shielding whenever an opponent challenges you.

HOW TO SHIELD

As soon as you are challenged, turn so that you are between the ball and your opponent.

The ball is now protected. Your opponent can only reach it from behind.

The challenger risks giving away a foul if he tries to kick the ball from behind. He is more likely to kick you accidentally instead.

Keep the ball close to your feet.

The challenger has to try to get in front of you. This gives you time to pass the ball or accelerate away.

SHIELDING WHILE YOU ARE RUNNING

When you are running with the ball or dribbling, keep your head up to watch out for opponents coming up on your left or right side.

Be ready to change your body position from one side of the ball to the other. For example, if someone is coming up on the right, keep the ball on your left side.

IMPEDING OTHER PLAYERS

One of the laws of football is that you cannot 'impede the progress' of another player. This means that you cannot stop someone from reaching the ball unless you can play it yourself, or shield another player from the ball while you are still running for it. You cannot push or hold anyone either, so be careful to use your arms only as a shield.

This player is not breaking the rules, as he has possession of the ball. He is using his body and arms as a shield, but he is not holding or pushing the other player.

Here, the player is impeding. He has not yet reached the ball and is holding the other player back. He is also pushing with his arms, which is not allowed.

A STAR SHIELDING

Some players are known for shielding the ball more than others. It is important not to be afraid of making physical contact while you are playing, but this is never an excuse for giving away a foul.

Here you can see Dutch player Dennis Bergkamp using his arms and body correctly to shield the ball from an opponent.

TRUCK AND TRAILER

The trailer is not allowed to tackle.

Play this game in pairs. The player with the ball is the 'truck'. The other is the 'trailer'. The truck dribbles the ball while the trailer tries to get in front of him.

The truck has to twist and turn so that he is always shielding the ball. When the trailer gets in front of the truck, he becomes the truck instead.

 ## CHALLENGE

When you are the trailer, make a real effort to dodge around the truck. If you are the truck, aim to protect the ball successfully for at least one minute before losing control of it.

TRICKS FOR FUN

Learning tricks can give your game a lot of extra flair and disguise. Some of the tricks on these pages are just for fun but others add an extra element to your control and dribbling skills, too. Learning any of them is worth the effort because you are still improving your control of the ball.

THE BEARDSLEY TRICK

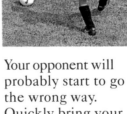

This is a feinting trick. When an opponent comes near, decide quickly on a pretend direction.

Lift your knee in the pretend direction. Really exaggerate the twist of your hips and body.

Your opponent will probably start to go the wrong way. Quickly bring your knee back down.

Before he recovers, push the ball across your body in the opposite direction. Accelerate away.

THE MARADONA MOVE

This move is sure to confuse your opponent. As the ball rolls towards you, step on it to stop it.

Step off the ball again, taking a big stride around it so that you begin to turn around the ball.

Finish turning so that your back is facing the direction you want to go. Put your other foot on top of the ball.

Drag the ball back behind you and quickly spin around again to follow it. Accelerate away.

THE FLICK OVER

This juggling trick is very spectacular, but don't use it in a game because you are almost certain to give the ball away to the other team. Learn it for fun and compete with your friends to see who can flick it highest.

You can try flicking the ball out to the side rather than over you.

Try not to look round at the ball as you do the flick.

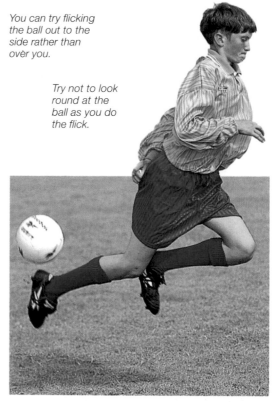

Step in front of the ball with one foot. Trap the ball between the toes of one foot and the heel of your other foot.

Roll the ball up your heel, then flick up backwards with your front foot as hard and high as you can so that it goes over you.

THE HEEL CATCH

This is another trick to try while you are juggling. Move in front of the ball, then lean forward and flick your heel up to catch it.

The ball should come round to the front of you again. Spin round to play it back into the air with your instep or knee.

THE NUTMEG

To nutmeg someone you push the ball between his legs. Don't try it unless his legs are far apart. Watch your opponent carefully and time it for when he least expects it. You can then run around him to collect the ball.

PLAYING IN A TEAM

As you build up your control skills, you will find it gradually easier to put them into practice when you are playing in matches. However, when you are playing in a team you need to think carefully about how to make the best use of your skills. Always think of the whole team, not just your own game.

KEEPING POSSESSION

Once your team has possession of the ball, it can control the whole game and create opportunities to score. Whatever you do, you should be helping your team to keep possession. You can do this by remembering these things:

Supporting player

This player is creating a chance to pass.

This player is marking a defender.

This player can see he is in a good position to dribble.

Support your team-mates by backing them up. Let them know you are there by calling to them.

Think ahead. Run into space so that other players can pass to you, or mark an opponent.

If someone passes to you, take the initiative and run for the ball. Don't wait for it to come to you.

When you receive the ball, look around to decide what to do next, then do it as quickly as possible.

DIRECTION

Change direction before opponents can reach you.

This player is passing the ball for his team member to collect.

To support another player, run into space so that he can pass forward to you.

When you are dribbling, it is fine to change direction as long as you are still moving up the field.

If you are being forced to turn back on yourself, you risk wasting time and space. Pass the ball instead.

If you need to pass the ball out of danger, try to pass it forward. Only pass back if you really have to.

WHEN TO DRIBBLE

When you receive the ball, check to see if you are in a good position to dribble. If you are heavily marked but one of your team-mates is free, it makes more sense to pass to him. If you try to dribble, you will probably lose possession.

This player is in a better position to play the ball.

Dribbling is safest when the ball is in your opponents' half of the field. Never try to dribble out of your own penalty area, because it is far too risky. Get the ball out of the danger area quickly by passing it up the field instead.

TEAM DUMMIES

Here, the player with the ball can see a supporting player to his right as he dribbles up the field.

When you are dribbling, keep your head up and watch out for other players who are moving with you to give you support.

The player with the ball sells his opponent a dummy and pretends to pass to the right.

When you sell a dummy, pretend to pass to a member of your team. This will make your dummy more realistic.

As the player with the ball dodges round his opponent, the supporting player moves up with him.

You still have support, so be ready to make a real pass if you come under too much pressure.

IMPROVING CONTROL

To keep on improving, you can play games which develop particular skills. Here, one game helps you to concentrate on your first touch control and the other on your dribbling skills. Try to remember everything you have learned and put it into practice as you play.

TWO TOUCH

'Two touch' is an excellent game for improving your first touch of the ball. It also improves your anticipation, as you have to run into space to play it well.

Make things difficult for the other team by marking closely.

Control the ball with your first touch and pass it with your second.

Mark out a pitch and two goals. Divide into teams. Play as you would in a normal game, but each player is only allowed to touch the ball twice before another player touches it.

If a player makes a third touch, the ball passes to the other team.

Try this variation if there are five or less of you. Play with just one goal, so that the goalkeeper opposes both teams.
   To keep the game moving fast, pass as much as possible before shooting.

REMINDER TIPS

★ Look for space and run into it, so that other players can pass to you.

★ Don't just hope the ball will come directly to you. Run to meet it.

★ Watch the flight of the ball carefully. Get in line with it to receive it.

★ Decide quickly which part of the body you will use to control the ball.

★ Cushion the ball with as few touches as possible. Try to cushion with your first touch.

★ Play your next move quickly before an opponent can reach you.

PINBALL DRIBBLE

This game will help you with your dribbling, feinting and shielding skills. Lay out a line of boxes, one for each person playing. In the game shown there are four.

If you find it difficult to get past a particular player, try something different each time you have to pass him.

If the ball goes out of the box, this counts as losing it and the player goes into the second box.

The player in the first box tries to dribble through the next box. The player there tries to tackle him.

If he gets through this box, he scores a point and moves on. He scores a point for each box he dribbles through.

When he loses the ball or gets to the end, he goes into the second box. Everyone else moves back a box.

The player in the last box runs to the first and starts to dribble. Continue playing like this, keeping a note of each player's score. The first person to score five points is the winner.

REMINDER TIPS

★ Keep your head up so that you can see what your opponent is doing.

★ Keep the ball close to you as you dribble, using different parts of your feet.

★ Drop your shoulder and make use of body swerve to trick your opponent.

★ Try out different trick moves and feints to unbalance your opponent.

★ Keep your body between the ball and your opponent to shield it from him.

★ Accelerate away from opponents as fast as you can.

WORLD SOCCER QUIZ

Every four years, countries from all over the world compete for the greatest soccer prize of all – the World Cup. Try this quiz to find out how much you know about the history and stars of the World Cup competition. There are questions on other worldwide soccer tournaments as well, including the Olympic Games and the Women's World Championship. The quiz continues on pages 64, 96, 128, 160, 192 and 224, and you can find answers to all the questions on page 256.

1. Which country hosted the first ever World Cup tournament, in 1930?

a. Brazil
b. Uruguay
c. Italy

2. In which American stadium was the 1994 World Cup Final held?

a. Pontiac Silverdome
b. Pasadena Rose Bowl
c. New York Giants Stadium.

3. Which one of these international teams usually plays in red and green kit?

a. Portugal
b. Croatia
c. Brazil

4. Which player missed the decisive penalty shoot-out kick to put Italy out of the 1994 World Cup Final?

a. Franco Baresi
b. Salvatore Schillaci
c. Roberto Baggio

5. Which country is the only one to have taken part in every World Cup?

a. Brazil
b. Italy
c. France

6. 13 countries took part in the 1930 World Cup. How many entered the 1998 championship?

a. 50-100
b. 100-150
c. over 150

7. Who is the only player to have been in the winning World Cup squad three times?

a. Giuseppe Meazza
b. Pele
c. Roberto Rivelino

8. When was soccer first included in the Olympic Games?

a. 1908
b. 1952
c. 1980

9. Who were the 1995 Women's Soccer World Champions?

a. Norway
b. USA
c. Germany

10. Which was the last host nation to win the World Cup?

a. England
b. Italy
c. Argentina

11. Who is England's most capped goalkeeper?

a. Peter Shilton
b. Gordon Banks
c. David Seaman

12. Who won the Golden Ball award as Player of the Tournament in the 1994 World Cup?

a. Roberto Baggio
b. Romario
c. Marco van Basten

13. Mexican goalkeeper Antonio Carbajal played in a record number of World Cups. How many?

a. 3
b. 4
c. 5

14. What was the name of the official mascot for the 1994 World Cup?

a. Ball Boy
b. Striker
c. Stripes

15. Which player was involved in the 'hand of God' incident in the 1986 World Cup in Mexico?

a. Diego Maradona
b. Paul Gascoigne
c. Lothar Matthäus

SOCCER QUIZ

PART TWO

PASSING AND SHOOTING

CONTENTS

BEFORE YOU START

This part of the book looks at the kicking, heading and team skills that you need to pass or shoot well. As before, there are plenty of games and exercises to help you improve. Here you can find out about the soccer terms that you'll come across as you read.

PARTS OF THE FOOT

These are the parts of your feet you use most often for passing and shooting. You rarely use your heel or sole.

The **inside** of your foot is from your big toe back to your ankle.

Your **instep** is the area over your laces. It doesn't include your toes.

The **outside** of your foot is from your little toe back to your ankle.

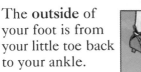

'OVER THE BALL'

Your position 'over the ball' refers to how far forward or back you are leaning. It is important because it affects how powerful and how high your kick will be. If your head is over the ball, your kick is more likely to stay low, and it may be more accurate, too.

This player is well balanced, with his head over the ball.

WHERE TO KICK THE BALL

You make the ball go in different directions by knowing which part of it to kick. To work out which part is which, think of it as having two sides, a top and a bottom. The diagrams below show you how this will be illustrated.

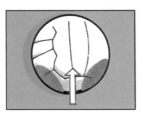

When you are told to kick one side of the ball, you see a diagram of it as it looks from above when you kick. Kick to the left or right.

Diagrams like this show the top or bottom of the ball by looking at it side on, so imagine what it would look like from the side as you kick.

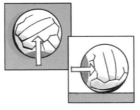

When you are told to kick the ball through the middle, this means both the middle from above and the middle from the side.

From above, you see the right side.

From the side, you see the middle.

If you are told just one part of the ball to kick, for example the right side, you can assume you kick through the middle from the other angle.

BACKSWING AND FOLLOW-THROUGH

Your **backswing** means the action of swinging your leg back before kicking.

Your **follow-through** is when you swing your leg forward and up after kicking.

The backswing

The follow-through

USING BOTH FEET

Just as you need to be able to control the ball with either foot, you need to practise all passing and shooting techniques with both feet. If you can only play well with one foot, you have to waste time moving the ball into a good position before playing it away. This can mean that you miss good chances to pass or shoot.

This left-footed pass sends the ball to the right.

SOCCER TERMS

This book uses a handful of special soccer terms to describe parts of the pitch and different types of player. The **attacking third** means the final third of the pitch, where you approach your opponents' goal. The **defending third** is where you protect your goal from opponents.

This is the red team's defending third.

In this part of the book, an **attacker** is any player in a team which has the ball. A **defender** is any player in a team which doesn't have the ball.

DISGUISE, PACE AND TIMING

Giving a kick **disguise** means making it difficult to guess which way it will go.

The **pace** of the ball is how fast it is going. If a ball 'has pace', it is going fast.

Good **timing** means judging the best time to hit the ball when you pass or shoot.

This is the red team's attacking third and the yellow team's defending third.

INSIDE FOOT KICKS

The inside of your foot is the area you use most often for kicking. It has a larger kicking surface than any other part of your foot. This makes it easier for you to judge how the ball will respond when you kick it, so it is ideal for accurate passes.

THE PUSH PASS

This is a low kick for short distances. It is called a pass, but you can use it to shoot at close range. It is easy to learn, and accurate.

1. Swing your foot back, turning it out so that it is almost at right angles to your other foot.

2. Keep your ankle firm and your body over your feet. Make contact with the middle of the ball.

3. Follow through in a smooth, level movement, keeping your eye on the ball the whole time. Keep your foot low – try not to sweep it upwards, as this will make the ball rise.

ACCURACY PRACTICE

Work with a friend. Place two markers 60cm (2ft) apart. One of you stands 1m (3ft) in front of them, the other 1m (3ft) behind. Try to pass to each other through the gap. Score a point for each success.

After five passes each, move another 1m (3ft) apart and start again. Carry on until you are 10m (33ft) apart. The player with the most points wins.

2m (6ft)

HOW TO MEASURE

The measurements for the exercises and games in this book are given in metres (m) and feet (ft). Think of 1m (3ft) as about one big stride. You can then measure out the correct distances easily in strides.

THE INSIDE FOOT SWERVE

Swerving the ball is really useful when passing or shooting. You have more control with the inside of your foot than the outside, so it is best to learn the inside foot swerve first.

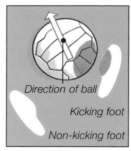

Direction of ball

Kicking foot

Non-kicking foot

The ball should swerve out, then swing back in again.

Follow through freely, your foot rising to follow the direction of the ball.

1. Keep your eyes on the ball as you swing your leg back. Your non-kicking foot should be well out of the way of the ball.

2. Use the side of your foot to kick. The secret is to kick the ball in the right place. (See above).

PIG IN THE MIDDLE

Play this game with two friends. Stand in a line with 10m (33ft) between you. The player in the middle cannot move more than 60cm (2ft) to either side. The players at each end try to bend the ball around the player in the middle. If he is able to intercept it, the player who kicked it takes his place.

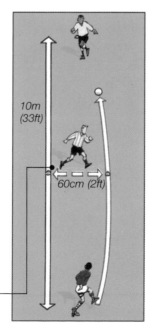

10m (33ft)

60cm (2ft)

Mark out your positions so that you can't cheat.

STAR PUSH PASS

This picture shows Romanian player Dan Petrescu following through a push pass. See how his foot is still level and low, and how his weight is balanced over his knees.

OUTSIDE FOOT KICKS

When you use the outside of your foot to kick the ball, you can disguise your movements very well. Also, because the ball is to one side of you, you are able to move freely and pass or shoot as you run. However, accuracy and control can be difficult, so you will need to practise hard.

FLICKING THE BALL TO THE SIDE

This move is particularly useful when you are under pressure and you receive a fast pass from the side which you do not have time to control. The trick is to let the ball bounce off the outside of your foot, while at the same time directing it to a team-mate with a flick of your ankle.

Make contact with little toe area

You don't need any backswing.

1. Keep your back to anyone marking you. Turn the outside of your foot towards the ball.

2. Don't cushion the ball as it makes contact. Direct it out to the side with a flick of your foot.

3. If the ball has been kicked through the middle, it should stay low but fast. Try to direct it into the path of another player.

This player can see a team-mate out of the corner of his eye.

This player has no chance of reaching the ball.

FLICK GAME

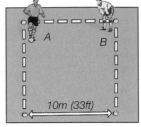

10m (33ft)

This is for two players (A and B). Mark out a 10m (33ft) square. Start in the two top corners.

B runs across the square as A passes the ball into his path. B returns it with a flick pass.

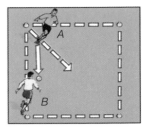

A pushes the ball to B, then starts to run. B feeds the ball for him to flick back. Carry on like this.

OUTSIDE FOOT SWERVES

This kick makes the ball swerve away to the side. It is a difficult kick to master, and you need to be quite strong to make it go a long way. However, you don't need to control the ball before you kick it and you can do it as you run, so it is an ideal kick to use for shots at goal.

Hit the ball half-way up if you want it to stay low.

Non-kicking foot

1. Swing your leg back. As you swing your foot back towards the ball, turn the toes of your kicking foot in slightly towards your other foot. Kick the inside of the ball with the area around your little toe.

2. Give the kick plenty of follow-through, sweeping your leg across your body. The ball should swerve out away from you.

Your non-kicking foot should be well out of the way of your kicking foot.

LOFTED SWERVES

A 'lofted' kick means a high kick. If you want an outside foot swerve to go higher and clear other players, kick the ball through its lower half and not through the middle.

Kicking foot swings under the ball

PAIRS PRACTICE

Pass the ball down a straight line. Try to make it swing out from the line and back in again by using outside foot swerves.

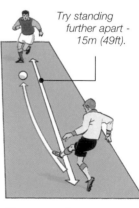

Try standing further apart - 15m (49ft).

You can also practise outside foot swerves by playing 'Pig in the Middle' (see page 37).

USING YOUR INSTEP

Your instep is the area over your laces. It is the most powerful part of your foot, so use it if you want to kick the ball a long way or kick it very hard. At first you may accidentally use your toes, but this will improve with practice.

THE LOW INSTEP DRIVE

You can use this kick as you are running to send it a long way. It is quite difficult to make it accurate, but the secret of success is to hit the ball right through the middle.

Toes

Non-kicking foot (alongside ball)

Place your non-kicking foot close to the ball.

1. Swing your kicking leg well back, so that your heel almost reaches up to your behind.

2. Point your toes toward the ground and make contact with the middle of the ball.

3. Swing your foot onwards in the direction of the ball, but make sure your ankle is still stretched out towards the ground as you follow through. This is the key to keeping the kick low.

INSTEP PASS GAME

Use this game to help you develop your basic instep kicking technique. It is best with four people, but you could play with any number above two – change the shape of the pitch to make a corner for each player.

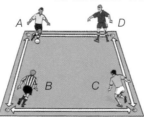

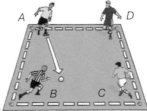

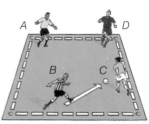

Mark out a 30m (98ft) square. Label yourselves A, B, C and D and stand at its four corners.

A passes to B at an angle so that he has to run on to it. B receives it and passes it at an angle to C.

After passing, B stays where he is. C runs on to the ball and passes to D, and so on around the square.

THE LOFTED DRIVE

The lofted drive is a long, high kick. The technique for doing it is similar to the technique for low instep kicks, but you kick the ball in a different place and let your foot swing right up when you follow through.

Kicking the ball on its lower half makes it rise.

1. Approach the ball from a slight angle. Swing your leg back, looking down at the ball as you do so.

2. Make contact with the lower half of the ball, so that your instep reaches slightly under it.

3. Follow through with a sweeping movement, letting your leg swing up across your body.

GAINING POWER AND HEIGHT

You will find that your drives will be higher and more powerful if you lean back as you swing your leg towards the ball. This usually happens naturally, though you may find it easier if you kick from slightly further away.

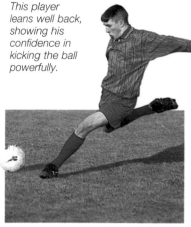

This player leans well back, showing his confidence in kicking the ball powerfully.

PERFECTING YOUR TECHNIQUE

To improve your lofted drives you may think you just need to kick the ball harder, but it is more important to develop your technique. In this game you practise drives that need to be accurate as well as powerful to reach their target.

Four of you (A, B, C, D) can work at this by marking out a row of four boxes, all 10m (33ft) square. Each of you stands in a box, which you cannot move out of.

A and B try to lob the ball over C and D. Score a point for each success. If C or D manages to intercept the ball, he takes the place of the player who kicked it.

D intercepts the ball and takes the place of A.

VOLLEYING

Volleying means kicking the ball before it has hit the ground. It is a fast and exciting way to play the ball, because you don't spend time controlling it before playing it. This gives the ball pace and makes it harder for your opponents to guess where it is going to go.

FRONT VOLLEY

Front volleys are probably the easiest volleys to do, but you still need quick reactions to do them well. You use your instep to receive the ball, so you need to be facing it. If you are not, it can be difficult to keep your balance and the volley may go out of control.

Kick through the lower half of the ball.

The ball makes contact with your instep.

If you make contact later, your non-kicking foot should be closer to the ball.

1. Lift your knee as the ball approaches. Point your toes and stretch out your ankle.

2. As you direct the ball away, try to keep your head forward over your knee.

LEARNING TO VOLLEY

Work with a friend. Stand 3m (10ft) apart. Drop the ball onto your foot and volley it to him gently for him to catch.

3m (10ft)

VARYING THE HEIGHT

If you want to send the ball high, perhaps to clear a defender, get your foot right under the ball.

To stop the ball rising too much, lift your foot up over the ball slightly after making contact.

SIDE VOLLEY

Side volleys are more difficult than front volleys. You need quick reactions, as you do for any volley, but the leg movement that you have to do is also quite tricky – you need to be able to balance on one leg while you are leaning sideways.

1. Watch the ball as it comes towards you so that you can judge the right angle to meet it.

2. As you lift your outside leg up, make sure that the shoulder nearest the ball isn't in the way.

3. Swing your leg up and round in a sideways movement so that your instep makes contact.

4. Follow through in the direction of the ball by swinging your leg right across your body.

HIGHER AND LOWER

If you want to keep the ball low, try to make contact with the ball just above the middle.

To make the ball rise over the heads of other players, kick it just below the middle.

SIDE ACTION PRACTICE

Because the leg movement is the most difficult part of this volley, you may find it helps to practise over an obstacle. Make or find something that is almost as high as your hip, and try swinging your leg over it. You can put the ball on top of it if you want. If it is too high to reach, begin with a lower obstacle.

TRIO VOLLEY GAME

When you can do the leg movement, play this with two friends. A throws the ball to B, who volleys to C. C throws the ball for A to volley, and so on.

Score a point each time you volley accurately. The player with the most points after ten volleys each is the winner.

MORE ABOUT VOLLEYING

Much of the skill in volleying depends on having the confidence to strike the ball early. If you take the initiative and go for the ball instead of waiting for it to reach you, you will find it easier to control its direction. All the volleys on these pages are most effective if you act quickly and decisively.

THE HALF-VOLLEY

To do a half-volley, you kick the ball just as it bounces. If you kick it correctly, it should stay low and also be quite powerful. Point your toes, stretch out your ankle, then kick the ball with your instep. Your knee should make a firm snapping action.

Once it is kicked, the ball shoots off very fast.

Your non-kicking foot is alongside the ball and a little behind it.

1. Judge the flight of the ball and position yourself just behind where it will land. Take a short backswing.

2. Keeping your head forward so that it is in line with your knee, kick the ball as soon as it hits the ground.

VOLLEYS IN THE AIR

If the ball is very high, you may need to jump for it and volley it in the air.

Use a front or side volley technique, depending on the angle of the ball.

Your timing has to be especially good, so keep your eye on the ball all the time.

Watch the flight of the ball as you land. Get ready to follow the ball forward.

THE 'LAY-OFF' VOLLEY

'Laying the ball off' means playing the ball to another player when you don't have much time to play it yourself. To play a 'lay-off' volley, take the ball early and direct it out to the left or right with your first touch.

Here, a defender is in a position to challenge the player receiving the ball. He can see that a team-mate is in a better position to play the ball forward, so he lays it off to him.

Instead of using your instep, turn your foot to use the inside or outside of it.

Make contact with the middle of the ball, or slightly above the middle to send the ball down.

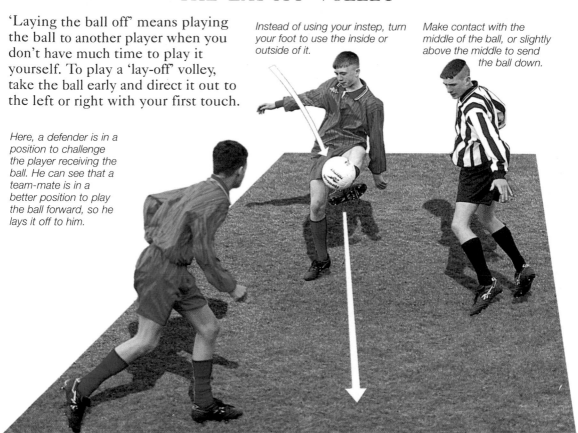

ONE BOUNCE GAME

In this game, you can make use of all the volleys you have learned. It is for three or more players, though it is best with about six. Each player begins with five lives.

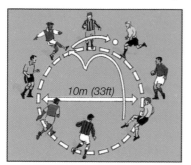

Stand in a circle 10m (33ft) across. One player kicks the ball high to another player, who lets it bounce once then volleys it to someone else. Use any type of volley.

You lose a life for missing or mis-hitting a volley. The winner is the last with any lives left. Next, play without letting the ball bounce (apart from half-volleys).

STAR VOLLEY

Here, Alessandro del Piero of Italy jumps for a volley. Even though he is at full stretch, he is balanced and has his eye on the ball.

CHIPPING

The chip is a kick which makes the ball rise very quickly into the air. It is not very powerful, but it is ideal for lifting the ball over opponents' heads, especially the goalkeeper's.

Here, the player watches the ball as it rises up away from him.

BASIC TECHNIQUE

The secret of the chip is to stab at the ball without following through. The area just below your instep acts like a wedge which punches the ball into the air.

Direction of ball

1. Face the ball straight on. It is almost impossible to chip from the side. Take a short backswing.

2. Bring your foot down with a sharp stabbing action, aiming your foot at the bottom of the ball.

3. Your foot kicks into the ground as it hits the ball, which is why there is no follow-through. This should happen naturally – it doesn't really matter if your leg does swing up as long as the ball flies into the air.

TECHNIQUE TIPS

Your non-kicking foot should be alongside the ball and close to it, only about 20cm (8in) away.

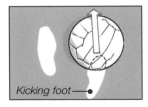

Kicking foot

Vary your chips by leaning forward or back. If you lean back, the chip will not fly as high, but it may go further.

CHIPPING PRACTICE

You can chip the ball when it is still or when it is moving. It is probably easiest to do if you run on to the ball as it is moving towards you. This exercise allows you to practise your basic technique with the ball coming towards you.

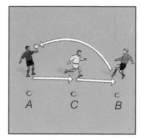

The exercise is for three players. Lay out three markers 10m (33ft) apart.

C passes along the ground to A. A chips it over C to B, who plays it back to C.

C plays the ball along the ground to B, who chips it to A. A passes it to C.

If A or B mis-hits a chip, he goes into the middle and C takes his place.

COMPARING HIGH KICKS

It is difficult to chip very far, so use a lofted drive for longer kicks. Here, you practise both types of kick. You need two or more players. Divide into two groups. Put six markers in a row, 5m (16ft) apart, and mark out a 5m (16ft) area around each one.

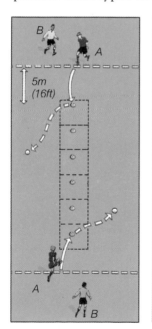

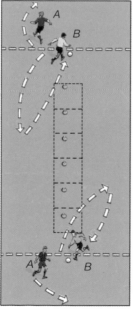

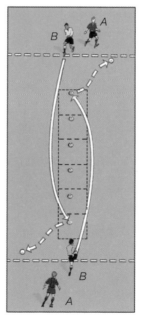

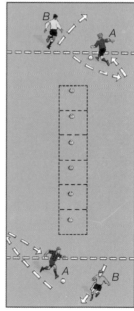

Stand 5m (16ft) from each end of the row. The first player tries to chip into the first area, aiming for the marker in the middle.

Score 10 for hitting the area, 20 for the marker. The next player gets the ball while you go to the back of the queue.

All of you try hitting the first area, then move on to the next. Use lofted drives for the last three areas, instead of chips.

To save running to collect the ball, pick up the opposite group's long drives. Keep playing, making a note of the score.

TRICK MOVES

Sometimes a trick move is just what you need to take your opponents by surprise. Some of them can be quite risky, though, so only use them in the attacking third of the field where losing the ball does not put your team in too much danger. Some of these tricks are easy to perform and others need quite a lot of practice.

THE BACKHEEL PASS

To do a backheel pass, you kick the ball back with your heel, or sometimes your sole. You can completely surprise your opponents if you do it quickly, and if there is a team-mate behind you to receive it.

For a basic backheel pass, keep your foot level as you kick so that it doesn't jab down at the ball.

To get a different angle or to disguise your movements, you can cross one leg over the other.

You can roll the ball back with your sole. Point your toes down and kick the middle of the ball.

THE CHEST PASS

Sometimes, when the ball comes at you from a high angle, you have very little time to control it before passing it. You can use your chest to redirect it, but only if the ball is travelling fast – your chest will tend to cushion a slow ball.

Tense your chest muscles and stick your chest out to make a hard surface for the ball to bounce off. Redirect it to a team-mate by turning quickly to the left or right as it reaches you.

This player cannot step back to receive the ball at a lower angle.

This team-mate is not as closely marked, so he is in a good position to receive the ball and play it away.

THE OVERHEAD KICK

This is a spectacular and exciting kick, but it is also very risky. Never try it in the defending third of the field, or in a crowded area where you might kick someone. Also, remember that if you fall you cannot follow up your pass, so make sure other players can follow it up instead.

1. The ball should be at about head height. Take off on one leg, jumping backwards.

2. Keep your eye on the ball and swing your kicking foot up over head height.

At the highest point of the kick, your foot is at other players' head height. This means you need to be especially careful not to kick someone.

3. At the highest point of your jump, strike the ball with your instep.

Try to kick the ball through the middle.

4. Cushion your fall by relaxing and rolling on your shoulder. This will stop you from hurting your wrists.

VARIATIONS

If the ball is not quite as high, you can do overhead kicks while keeping your non-kicking foot on the ground. Lift your kicking foot up to reach the ball, keeping your arms out for balance.

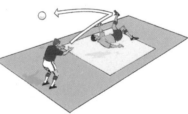

If the ball is further away from you, try the 'scissors' kick. It is a bit like the side volley (see page 43), but you jump and kick while you are sideways on in the air.

HOW TO PRACTISE

Practise on soft grass or a cushioned mat. Get a friend to help you and stand about 5m (16ft) apart. Your friend throws the ball to you for you to kick.

At first, work on landing safely. Once you are sure about this, work on timing your jump, because timing is the main secret of success.

WHAT MAKES A GOOD PASS?

Good passing is not just about mastering clever passes or trick moves. A good pass has to be useful to your team. This means that you need to look around you and think before you pass, then use a pass that is best for the situation – even if it is the simplest one you know.

ACCURACY

Accurate passing between team-mates makes it much more difficult for opponents to intercept the ball. It also saves time, because the player receiving it can take it forward straight away.

This acute angle pass reaches a player on the wing.

Direction is the first key to accuracy. Try to place the ball where it can be easily collected by your team-mate.

A defender has managed to intercept this short pass.

Pace is important, too. If your pass is too soft an opponent will intercept it. Make sure it is hard enough.

This pass has gone out of play.

Try not to pass the ball too hard, either. If you do, it will be difficult to control and may go too far.

CHOOSING YOUR KICK

There is no such thing as the 'right' kick to use, because each situation is different. However these are some general points to bear in mind before you pass.

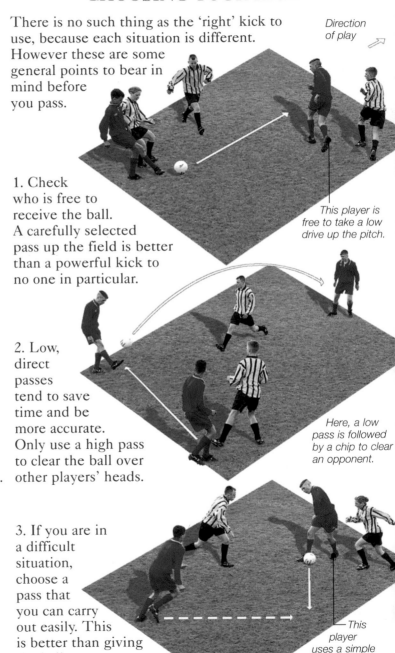

Direction of play

This player is free to take a low drive up the pitch.

Here, a low pass is followed by a chip to clear an opponent.

This player uses a simple push pass.

1. Check who is free to receive the ball. A carefully selected pass up the field is better than a powerful kick to no one in particular.

2. Low, direct passes tend to save time and be more accurate. Only use a high pass to clear the ball over other players' heads.

3. If you are in a difficult situation, choose a pass that you can carry out easily. This is better than giving the ball away.

FOOLING YOUR OPPONENTS

You can create opportunities for your team by distracting or confusing your opponents, and by making it difficult for them to guess where the ball will go.

1. Disguise your intentions by pretending to kick the ball in a different direction before you pass.

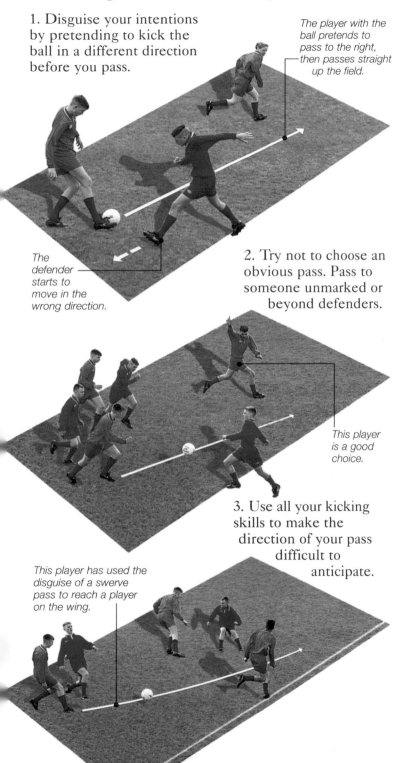

The player with the ball pretends to pass to the right, then passes straight up the field.

The defender starts to move in the wrong direction.

2. Try not to choose an obvious pass. Pass to someone unmarked or beyond defenders.

This player is a good choice.

3. Use all your kicking skills to make the direction of your pass difficult to anticipate.

This player has used the disguise of a swerve pass to reach a player on the wing.

TIMING

Even if you manage to pass accurately, you can miss your team-mate altogether if you pass at the wrong time. Also, your team-mate is more likely to be able to collect a slightly inaccurate pass if your timing is good.

This player can intercept the pass.

Passing the ball too early gives your opponents the opportunity to run and intercept it.

This defender has caught up with the player in space.

If you wait too long before passing, an opponent may start marking the team-mate who was free.

TIPS FOR SUCCESS

★ Practise all the different kicks so that you are confident enough to try any of them.

★ Look around you as you play so that you can make the best use of any opportunities to pass.

★ Communicate with your team-mates. Shout to each other or use hand signals to attract attention.

PASSING TACTICS

Tactics can mean the special team formations that you plan out before a game. They can also be the moves and decisions you make because of the position you are in on the field, or the ways that you work with other players to get the ball away from your opponents.

PLAYING IN DEFENCE

As a defender, your priority is keeping the ball out of danger. This often means passing it forward, using long drives and volleys to send the ball up the pitch or over attackers' heads.

Defender A has two options. He can pass forward to B or across to C. He chooses to pass to B, which is the best thing to do. If he had passed to C, the ball would not be any further up the field.

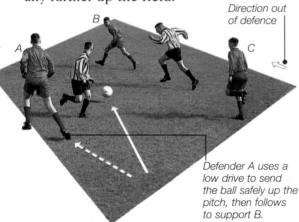

Direction out of defence

Defender A uses a low drive to send the ball safely up the pitch, then follows to support B.

A good defender only passes the ball back when he has no alternative. Here, A is surrounded. He passes back to a supporting player (B) who is in a better position to play the ball up the field to C.

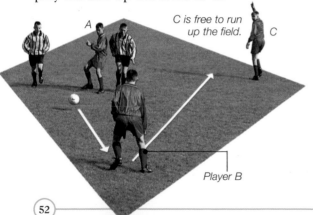

C is free to run up the field.

Player B

ATTACKING PLAY

If you are playing further up the field, you can take more risks. You need to play quickly to confuse defenders, using all the tricks and different passes possible to cut a path through to the goal.

Direction of play

Here, very rapid play using short push passes and volleys gets the ball past defenders.

Play in the middle of the field can get very cramped. Spread the play by passing out to the wing.

Try to pass the ball beyond defenders, especially to players who are in a good position to shoot.

Take defenders by surprise by turning to pass the ball in an unexpected direction or difficult angle.

WALL PASSES

Wall passes are also known as one-two passes. Just before an opponent tackles you, pass the ball quickly to a team-mate, then run around your opponent before he has time to recover. Your team-mate acts as a 'wall'. He passes the ball back to you quickly and you take it forward up the field.

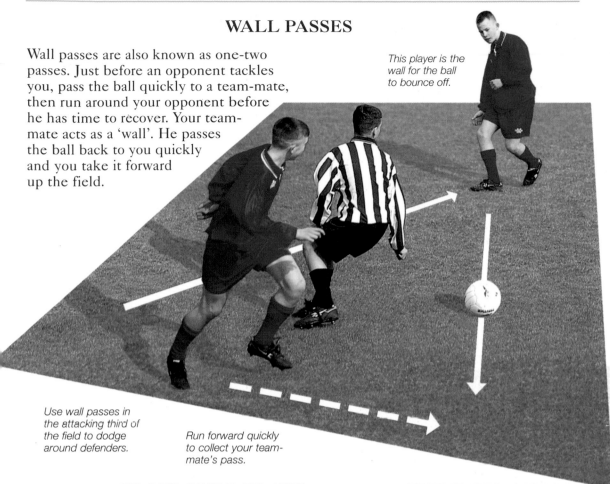

This player is the wall for the ball to bounce off.

Use wall passes in the attacking third of the field to dodge around defenders.

Run forward quickly to collect your team-mate's pass.

CROSS-OVER PLAYS

This tactic uses a short outside foot pass to do two things. You bring two opponents together, creating space for your own team. You also change the path of the ball before they realize what you have done.

A and B can now move out to the wings.

Player A and Player B are both being marked. Player A has the ball. A and B run towards each other, taking their markers with them.

As they cross each other, A quickly passes the ball to B with the outside of his foot. The markers are confused and get left behind.

THINKING AHEAD

In order to make your team's tactics effective, keep thinking ahead. Check the position of players around you to work out what they will do next. This will help you to decide what to do, too.

Here, Portugal's Luis Figo has escaped Neil Lennon of Northern Ireland, and is looking up to work out his next move.

SUPPORT PLAY

Supporting means helping your team-mates when you don't have the ball yourself. Each player only has the ball for a small part of each soccer match, so what he does for the rest of the time is very important for his team's success.

FINDING SPACE

Another term for finding space is 'running off the ball'. It means escaping opponents and getting into an open space so that team-mates can pass to you. Opponents may soon catch up, so you need to keep moving into different positions.

It can be tempting to run towards the ball even if a team-mate has it. Try not to do this. Think about where he could pass to, and run there instead.

DECOY RUNS

A 'decoy run' means running into a good position, but then not receiving a pass. It is a way of fooling opponents into running away from the ball.

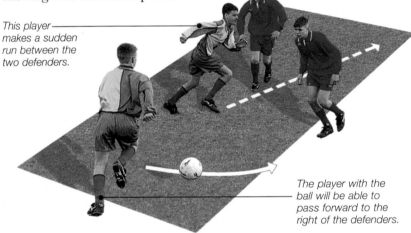

This player makes a sudden run between the two defenders.

The player with the ball will be able to pass forward to the right of the defenders.

One kind of decoy move is making your marker think you are about to receive the ball, then letting it run on to a team-mate.

CREATING GOOD ANGLES

'Creating a good angle' refers to how useful your supporting position is. A good angle is one where your team-mate can see you and where you are in a good position for him to pass to.

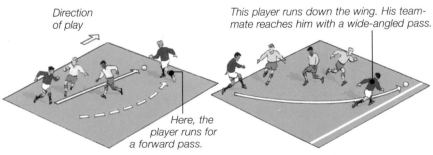

Direction of play

This player runs down the wing. His team-mate reaches him with a wide-angled pass.

Here, the player runs for a forward pass.

This defender is drawn away from the ball by a decoy run.

Always try to place yourself where your team-mate can pass forwards, not across.

A wide-angled pass is less easy to predict, and is more likely to split your opponents' defence.

Another decoy move is turning away from the ball, taking a defender with you, so that your team-mate can run forward.

'PASS AND MOVE'

It is always exciting when you have possession of the ball. However, as soon as you pass it on to another player, you need to start supporting again straight away. Always move to follow up your pass, or to find another good supporting position.

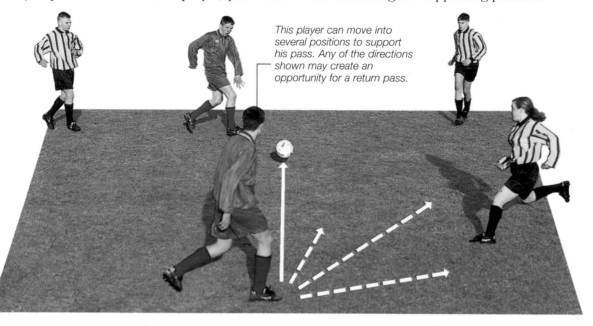

This player can move into several positions to support his pass. Any of the directions shown may create an opportunity for a return pass.

PASS AND MOVE EXERCISE

This exercise helps you to get into the habit of following up your passes. You need three or more players. Divide up into two opposite rows.

The first player in one row passes to the first in the other, then runs to the end of the opposite row.

The player at the front of that row passes back and follows the ball. Carry on like this.

SUPPORT GAME

This game is best played by seven players, two defenders (labelled D) and five attackers (A). As you play, use the support skills that you have learned. Run off the ball to find space, work out the best kick to use before passing and follow up your passes.

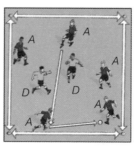

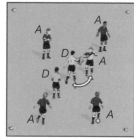

Mark out a pitch about 20m (66ft) square. You need one ball. The As have the ball and try to pass to each other without the Ds intercepting.

If a D manages to intercept, he swaps places with the A player who passed. If the As manage ten passes in a row, the Ds swap with two As anyway.

HEADING IN ATTACK

Using headers in attack or to go for goal is one of the most exciting elements of the game. It often means taking advantage of split-second opportunities, so you have to be courageous, take risks and really attack the ball.

DOWNWARD HEADERS

When heading for goal, you should try to keep the ball down to make it more difficult for goalkeepers to save. To make the ball go down when you head it, you need to get above it to hit the top part of it, then nod your head down firmly as you make contact.

1. To catch the top part of the ball with your forehead, you often have to jump.

2. As you would for any header, try to keep your eyes open all the time.

3. As you head the ball away, push forwards and down with your forehead.

DIVING HEADERS

Usually, you use a diving header to try for goal. This is a very dramatic way of scoring, but bear in mind that once you have committed yourself you will be on the ground and unable to play another move until you get up again.

This player watches where the ball has gone. He must now get up quickly in case he needs to follow it up.

Approach a diving header with plenty of speed. This will add to its power.

Keep your eyes on the ball and dive forwards, letting your legs leave the ground.

Direct the ball to the left or right by turning your head as you make contact.

As you hit the ground, try to relax your body so that you don't hurt yourself.

HEADING PRACTICE

This is a practice for three players. Mark out a goal 6m (20ft) across. Place a marker 15m (49ft) in front of it. One player is the goalkeeper.

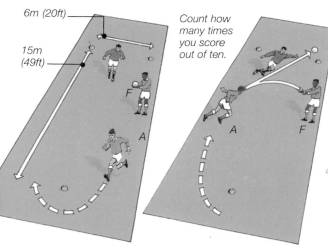

6m (20ft)

15m (49ft)

Count how many times you score out of ten.

One player (F) stands at the side of the goal. The other (A) stands between the goal and the marker. A runs around the marker as F throws the ball to him.

A has to dash for the ball and head at goal. F should vary the height of the ball for A to try different headers. Rotate players after ten goes.

THROW-HEAD-CATCH GAME

This game is for eight or more players. Divide into two teams. Each team has a goal and goalkeeper. Everyone else marks a player from the other team. To play, you must follow the sequence 'throw, head, catch', even when you intercept the ball. You can only score a goal with a header.

FLICK-ON HEADERS

There is one exception to the rule of using your forehead when heading, and that is when you let the ball glance off the top of your head. You usually do this to lift the ball out of the reach of a defender, to a team-mate who may be able to shoot.

As the ball passes over you, jump straight into the air and let it glance off your head. It carries on in basically the same direction, though you can direct it left or right slightly.

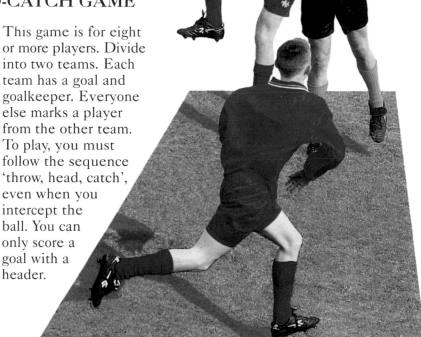

SHOOTING TO SCORE

Once you have mastered all the different kicking techniques and passing skills, you have all the basic skills that you need for shooting, too. However there are several things to bear in mind which can make a big difference to the number of goals you score.

WHAT WILL HELP YOU TO SCORE?

Try to keep the ball low. It is easier for a goalkeeper to stretch for a high ball than to reach down for a low one.

Aim at the far corners of the goal. The goalkeeper can more easily save shots which come straight at him.

Vary your approach to goal. If you always take the same approach, defenders will be likely to intercept you.

Shoot whenever you have the chance. Go for risky shots. It's better to have a go and miss than not to have a go at all.

Try not to look in the direction you are going to shoot. This makes your shot too easy to anticipate.

Practise shooting from an acute angle. Angled shots are difficult to anticipate and to save.

ACCURACY

You may think you need power to be shoot effectively. It is true that hard shots are difficult to save, but they are also difficult to control. There is no point in a hard shot if you miss, so it is better to work on your accuracy first.

REBOUND SHOTS

When you shoot, don't stop to see what happens. The ball may hit the post, or the goalkeeper may drop the ball.

If you keep moving and follow your shot in towards the goal, you can shoot again if the ball rebounds.

WHEN NOT TO SHOOT

Whenever you can see a clear path to goal you should try a shot. Sometimes, though, it's not so clear and a team-mate may have a better chance of scoring than you. Then, it is better to pass than to shoot.

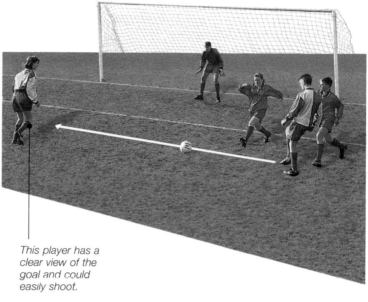

This player has a clear view of the goal and could easily shoot.

TARGET PRACTICE

The best way to improve your shooting is to practise aiming at a target. You can do this by marking a target on a wall to shoot at, but it is even better to practise against a goalkeeper. This exercise is for five players. It should improve your speed and accuracy.

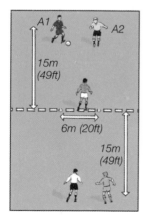

Keep the shots as low as possible.

Aim for the corners of the goal.

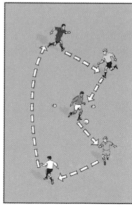

Mark out a goal 6m (20ft) wide. Stand in pairs, 15m (49ft) in front and behind the goalkeeper.

A1 passes to A2, who tries to shoot. A1 becomes a defender and tries to stop him.

The ball now goes across to the B players who follow the same pattern. B2 tries to score.

Next, swap around as shown and play until everyone has had ten shots. The best score out of ten wins.

APPROACHES TO GOAL

To improve their chances of scoring, attackers need different strategies to outwit the goalkeeper and defenders. These are some you can use, on your own or working with team-mates, to create good shooting opportunities as you reach the attacking third of the field.

CROSSING THE BALL

As a general rule you should try to pass the ball forward. Sometimes, however, it can be effective to pass the ball across, when you are on the wing in the attacking third – you can pass it to a team-mate so that he can shoot. This is called crossing the ball.

This player is in a good position to try a header.

By using a long, high cross, this player sends the ball across the goalmouth.

Use a variety of passes to get the ball into the penalty area, so that a team-mate can shoot as it crosses in front of the goal.

Once you have decided to cross the ball, cross it as soon as possible before defenders can take up good positions.

Make sure there is a team-mate to make use of your cross. There is no point in crossing the ball straight to a defender or the goalkeeper.

SHOOTING FROM CROSSES

Check the position of other team-mates. If you clash over the same cross a good chance may be lost.

If a defender is marking you, try to dodge him just as your team-mate crosses the ball.

Act really quickly when you see the opportunity to score and don't be put off by your opponents. Dash for the ball and have a go at a shot. Try to shoot down with a diving or downwards header, or a volley.

DRAWING THE GOALKEEPER OUT

Goalkeepers often come out of goal as you approach, because this narrows down the area you can shoot at.

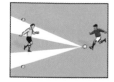

Here, it is difficult for the goalkeeper to cover the big areas that you can shoot at.

As he moves out the areas get smaller, but there is now a big space behind him.

If you can, use this opportunity to pass to a team-mate out to the side so that he can shoot.

Even if the goalkeeper jumps at the right time, he will not be able to reach this high chip over his head.

You could also try chipping the ball, lifting it over the goalkeeper's head as he approaches and down into the goal. Make sure you send the ball high enough.

TURN AND SHOOT

There are often times when your back is to the goal. By turning to shoot quickly, you may take defenders by surprise. This exercise helps you practise this. It is for four players – a goalkeeper, a defender and two attackers.

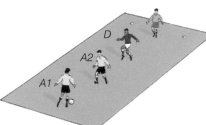

Mark out a goal. One attacker (A1) faces the goal. The other (A2) has his back to the goal and the defender (D) stands behind him.

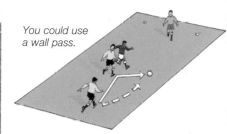

You could use a wall pass.

A1 passes to A2, who has to turn quickly. A1 is now a supporting player, so A2 can pass to him or shoot. D tries to stop him scoring.

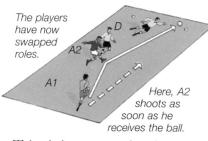

The players have now swapped roles.

Here, A2 shoots as soon as he receives the ball.

Take it in turns to be the attackers. You could play as two teams of two and see which side does best as the attacking team.

ATTACKING PLAY

When your team has the ball, you are in attack, whatever your position. To play a good attacking game, you combine all the skills you have learned with a positive attitude and the determination to win. These two pages should help you develop the competitive edge that you need to do this.

FOUR PASS DRILL

To play this game, you need to use quick and varied passing skills. You need a big group – fourteen is best, but you could play with a few less or a few more. Mark out a pitch 50m (164ft) long and 30m (98ft) wide. Divide it into three equal areas.

30m (98ft)

'A' zone

50m (164ft)

'D' zone

'A' zone

1. Get into two groups of five attackers (A) and one group of four defenders (D). The Ds go into the middle zone, the As into the end zones. One A group has the ball.

2. These As pass the ball to each other four times while two of the defenders try to stop them. If the As succeed, they pass the ball over the D area to the other A team.

3. The other two defenders go into the other A area as the As try for four passes. If a D intercepts the ball at any time, he takes the place of the A who passed.

PASSING REMINDER TIPS

★ Communicate with your team-mates so that they know where to pass to.

★ If you don't have the ball, support by running around to find space.

★ Choose passes that you know you can carry out accurately.

★ Make use of wall passes and cross-over plays to dodge defenders.

★ Hold your pass until a team-mate is in a position to receive it.

★ Unless you want to clear defenders, keep your passes as low as possible.

SMALL-PITCH SHOOTING GAME

The area that you have for this game is very confined, so you have to make quick decisions and try to shoot as much as possible.

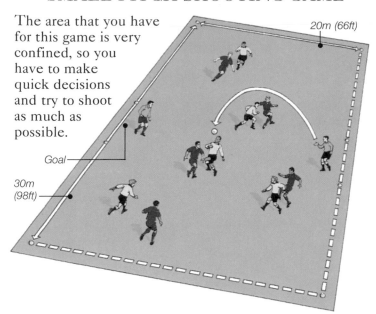

20m (66ft)

Goal

30m (98ft)

Mark out a pitch 20m (66ft) long and 30m (98ft) wide, and mark out two goals. You need at least ten players, in even numbers if possible.

Divide into two teams with a goalkeeper each. One goalkeeper starts the game each time by kicking the ball into the middle.

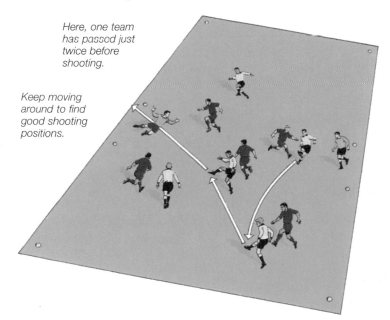

Here, one team has passed just twice before shooting.

Keep moving around to find good shooting positions.

Players from each team mark each other closely. Each team is only allowed up to three passes before trying a shot at goal.

If no one tries a shot after three consecutive passes, the ball goes over to the other team. Keep a record of the score.

STAR SHOT

Being an attacker or striker takes lots of determination and courage. If you watch star players, you will see that they do not hesitate to take opportunities to go for the ball and shoot.

This is Brazilian attacker Juninho playing at full stretch in a match against Sweden.

SHOOTING REMINDER TIPS

★ Always have a go if you see an opportunity. Don't worry that you might miss.

★ Vary your shots. Try shots from difficult angles, not just in front of the goal.

★ Keep alert when your team shoots. There may be a rebound opportunity.

★ Use crosses to make opportunities for diving headers and volleys.

★ Keep the ball down and aim for the bottom corners of the goal.

★ Make your shots accurate rather than powerful.

WORLD SOCCER QUIZ

16. Which of these national teams plays in orange shirts and white shorts?

a. Denmark
b. Holland
c. Germany

17. What is the claim to fame of the Centenario Stadium in Montevideo?

a. It is the world's largest
b. It was the first to have an artificial surface
c. It was the first to stage a World Cup match

18. Who captained England's World Cup winning squad of 1966?

a. Geoff Hurst
b. Bobby Moore
c. Bryan Robson

19. In 1994, Russia's Oleg Salenko set an individual record for goals scored in a World Cup match. How many times did he score?

a. 4
b. 5
c. 6

20. What was special about the World Cup match between Yugoslavia and France on June 16, 1954?

a. It was the first televised World Cup match
b. The scoreline was the highest ever
c. It was the first time substitutes were allowed

21. Which country hosted the 1995 Women's World Cup?

a. Sweden
b. Germany
c. Argentina

22. Which international team played in its first World Cup in 1994?

a. Nigeria
b. Chile
c. Egypt

23. In 1994, Cameroon striker Roger Milla became the oldest man to score in a World Cup match. How old was he?

a. 38
b. 42
c. 45

24. Which country won the 1995 Under 17 World Championship?

a. Ghana
b. Italy
c. Romania

25. What does the emblem on England's team kit show?

a. A unicorn
b. Three lions
c. A red cross

26. Which player was voted FIFA World Footballer of the Year in 1995?

a. Gianluca Vialli
b. Paolo Maldini
c. George Weah

27. What was Khalid Ismail Mubarak given as a reward for scoring the United Arab Emirates' first ever World Cup goal?

a. A Rolls Royce
b. A gold-plated soccer ball
c. $100,000

28. Which international team has played in the most World Cup Finals?

a. Italy
b. Brazil
c. West Germany

29. Until 1991, the leading goalscorer in Europe each year was given a special award. What was it called?

a. The EuroStriker Bowl
b. The UEFA Medal
c. The Golden Boot

30. Who of the following has not been a manager of the England national team?

a. Glen Hoddle
b. Graham Taylor
c. Bryan Robson

31. What does Chilean player Carlos Caszely hold the unfortunate record for being?

a. The first player to be given a red card in a World Cup match
b. The first player to score a World Cup own goal
c. The player who has missed the most World Cup penalties

SOCCER QUIZ ?

PART THREE
DEAD BALL SKILLS

CONTENTS

DEAD BALL BASICS

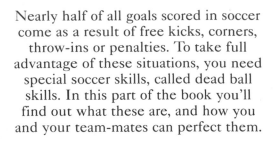

Nearly half of all goals scored in soccer come as a result of free kicks, corners, throw-ins or penalties. To take full advantage of these situations, you need special soccer skills, called dead ball skills. In this part of the book you'll find out what these are, and how you and your team-mates can perfect them.

This player is getting ready to take a penalty (see page 92).

WHAT IS A DEAD BALL?

Every so often in a soccer match, a player will hit the ball off the pitch, break one of the rules, score a goal, or suffer an injury. In each case the game stops temporarily. The ball is said to be 'out of play', or 'dead'. To restart the game, you have to use a particular kind of kick or throw to bring the dead ball back into play.

Because a dead ball is out of play, you can use your hands to place it before you take the restart kick.

RESTART KICKS AND THROWS

If the ball goes off the pitch, play is restarted with a goal kick, corner kick or throw-in, depending on where the ball left the pitch.

If the game stops because a player has broken a soccer rule, it is restarted with a free kick or, in certain cases, a penalty kick.

Whenever a player scores a goal, or after a break in play between periods of the match, the game is restarted with a centre kick.

If play is stopped for any other reason, such as injury, it is restarted with a drop ball. You'll find out more about each type of restart later on.

DEAD BALL ADVANTAGES

Here, the team in red is about to take a free kick. This typical dead ball situation shows three of the main advantages of playing the ball when it is dead, rather than when it is in normal, 'open' play.

★ You have plenty of time and space. The other team's players have to stand a set distance away, and cannot interfere by tackling or obstructing you.

Players on the yellow team have to be at least 9m (30ft) away from the red player taking the free kick.

★ The ball is stationary. This makes it easy to control, so you can kick it accurately and confidently.

★ Your team-mates can take up good positions. The break in play gives them a chance to move up into attack or drop back into defence.

USING SET PLAYS

The other major advantage of a dead ball is that it gives you a chance to use a carefully pre-planned team move, or 'set play'. You can rehearse various set plays in training, and use them to outwit your opponents during a match.

Throughout this part of the book you'll find pitch diagrams. These show specific set plays for you and your team-mates to try. On these diagrams, a dotted red arrow shows the path of a player and a solid blue arrow shows the path of the ball.

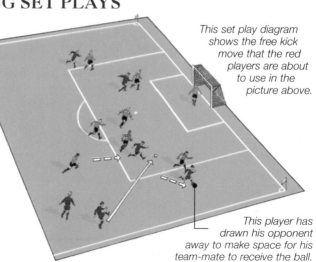

This set play diagram shows the free kick move that the red players are about to use in the picture above.

This player has drawn his opponent away to make space for his team-mate to receive the ball.

SOCCER WORDS

To explain the techniques and tactics involved in playing a dead ball, this part of the book uses a number of soccer words. These pages give you a reminder of the basic soccer terms, and introduce a few new ones that you'll come across as you read about dead ball skills.

FINDING YOUR WAY AROUND THE PITCH

If you kick the ball towards your opponents' goal, you are playing it **upfield**. Towards you own goal is **downfield**.

The **wings** are the edges of the pitch along either touchline. A ball played across from either wing to the middle of the pitch is a **cross**.

The third of the pitch nearest to your own goal is your team's **defending third**.

The middle third of the pitch is the **midfield**.

The third of the pitch nearest your opponents' goal is your team's **attacking third**.

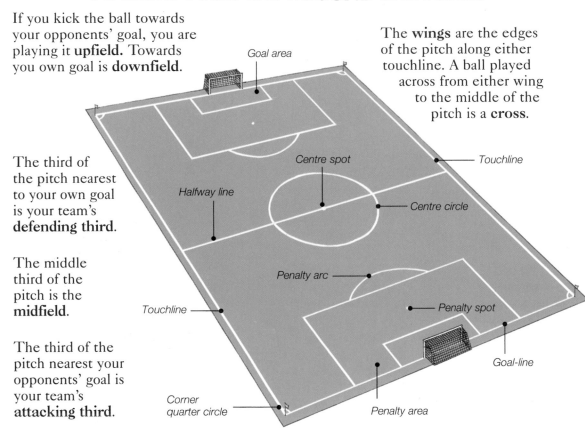

Goal area

Centre spot

Touchline

Halfway line

Centre circle

Penalty arc

Penalty spot

Touchline

Goal-line

Corner quarter circle

Penalty area

THE REFEREE

The **referee** is an official who controls a soccer match. It is his job to decide when to stop and restart play. He uses a whistle and special arm signals (which you'll read about later on) to show the players his decisions.

REFEREE'S ASSISTANTS

Two **referee's assistants** help the referee by watching the game from opposite sides of the pitch. Each assistant uses a flag to signal to the referee if the ball goes out of play or if he sees a player breaking the rules.

TYPES OF PLAYER

A soccer team is made up of a **goalkeeper**, who guards his team's goal, and ten **outfield** players. Each outfield player **marks** a particular member of the other team. This means keeping close to him to stop him from receiving or moving with the ball.

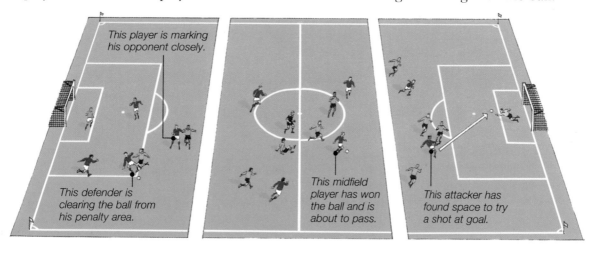

This player is marking his opponent closely.

This defender is clearing the ball from his penalty area.

This midfield player has won the ball and is about to pass.

This attacker has found space to try a shot at goal.

Defenders play mostly in their defending third. Their main job is to prevent the other team's players from having a chance to score.

Midfield players are the link between defence and attack. They move the ball upfield, and try to pass to a team-mate who can score.

Attackers push upfield into the attacking third, hoping to receive a pass which will give them a chance to shoot at goal.

WHAT DOES OFFSIDE MEAN?

You are not allowed to play the ball while you are in an **offside** position. You are offside if you are nearer to your opponents' goal-line than the ball at the moment it is passed to you, unless there are two or more opposition players at least as close to their goal-line. You can't be offside if you are within your own half of the pitch.

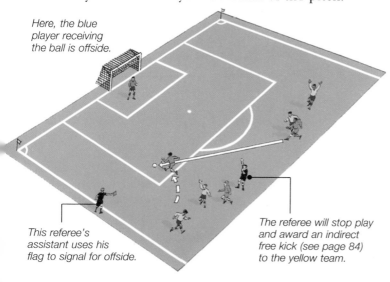

Here, the blue player receiving the ball is offside.

This referee's assistant uses his flag to signal for offside.

The referee will stop play and award an indirect free kick (see page 84) to the yellow team.

FOOT PARTS

Most dead ball skills involve using one of these three different parts of your foot.

The **inside** of your foot is the part from your big toe to your ankle.

The **outside** of your foot is the part from your little toe back to your ankle.

The **instep** is the area on the upper part of your foot covered by your bootlaces.

CENTRE KICKS

The referee tosses a coin to decide which team kicks off.

Every soccer match begins with a centre kick. This first dead ball opportunity, called the 'kick-off', gives you an early chance to take control. Centre kicks are also used to get the second half underway, to restart the game whenever a team scores a goal, and to begin any periods of extra time.

Wait for the referee to blow his whistle before you take the kick.

CENTRE KICK RULES

All centre kicks are taken from the centre spot. When you take the kick, every player must be in his own half. Once you've struck the ball, you mustn't kick it again until it has been touched by another player. You can't score straight from the centre spot.

Opposition players must be outside the centre circle when you take the kick.

You have to play the ball forwards from the spot, into the other team's half.

A SHORT, SAFE CENTRE KICK

A centre kick gives you possession of the ball in midfield. To keep possession, so that you can control play, use a short pass to a team-mate standing alongside you in the centre circle.

Use the inside of your foot to tap the ball forward gently into the path of your team-mate.

Make sure the ball crosses the halfway line completely.

Your team-mate can quickly pass the ball to one of your team's players who has space to receive it without being challenged.

PRESSURING THE OPPOSITION

STAR CENTRE

You can use a longer centre kick to move play upfield quickly and put pressure on the other team.

Kick the ball upfield into the attacking third. Aim for a space behind the other team's midfield players.

Your attacking players should sprint upfield from the halfway line to challenge for possession.

This tactic might well cause your team to lose the ball, but it can sometimes create an early scoring chance.

Here, the Croatian players Alen Boksic and Davor Suker talk tactics as they prepare to take a centre kick. Unless their team is trailing in the late stages of a match, they will probably opt for a short centre kick to make sure that their team keeps possession of the ball.

CREATING AN OVERLOAD

If you decide to try a long centre kick, your team will have a better chance of winning the ball if several of your players gather on one side of the pitch.

Angle your kick to the 'overloaded' side of the pitch, into the path of your attacking players.

The other team may realize what you are planning, and move across to the overloaded side of the pitch.

In this case, try switching your centre kick move at the last minute, playing the ball to the other side.

THROW-IN TECHNIQUE

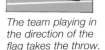

If an opposition player knocks the ball over either touchline, one of your team's players has to throw it back onto the pitch. This is known as taking a throw-in. It is the only type of restart which involves using your hands to bring a dead ball back into play.

A referee's assistant points his flag to signal a throw-in.

The team playing in the direction of the flag takes the throw.

THROW-IN RULES

To throw the ball back into play you have to bring it forwards from behind your head, using both hands. As you release the ball, part of both your feet must be touching the ground, on or behind the touchline.

You cannot score a goal by throwing the ball straight into the opposition's goal.

Feet on ground, on or behind touchline.

HOW TO HOLD THE BALL

Make sure that you hold the ball with your fingers spread around its back and sides. Your thumbs should nearly touch.

Holding the ball like this lets you control it more easily as you release your throw.

PRACTISING YOUR THROW-IN

You need to be able to throw accurately or you may give away the ball. To improve your throw, try this exercise with a partner.

Stand about 10m (33ft) apart. Use throw-ins to pass the ball back and forth. Throw the ball to your partner's feet so that he can control it easily.

As you get better at throwing the ball, your partner can give you a specific target area. Try throwing to your partner's head, chest and thigh.

TAKING A LONGER THROW-IN

Most professional soccer teams have at least one player who specializes in throwing the ball a long way. Practise the technique shown here to develop a long, accurate throw-in.

Arch your back to bring the ball as far back as possible.

Place your leading foot close behind the touchline.

At least part of your trailing foot must be touching the ground.

Use your hands and fingers to direct the ball's flight.

Leading leg

Hold the ball in front of your head and take a couple of quick steps towards the touchline.

Take a long final stride to reach the line, bringing the ball right back behind your head.

With the weight on your leading leg, whip the upper part of your body forwards to catapult the ball away.

THROWING AWAY POSSESSION

If you break one of the rules when you take a throw-in, the referee will ask the other team to retake the throw. Take care not to give away possession with a foul throw. The pictures below show the things you need to avoid to keep your throw-in legal.

FOUL THROW - The player's feet are too far over the touchline for a legal throw-in.

FOUL THROW - The thrower's right foot is off the ground as he releases the ball.

FOUL THROW - The player hasn't brought the ball far enough back over his head.

STAR THROW

Here, Gary Neville, playing for Manchester United, prepares to launch a long throw-in along the wing.

THROW-IN TACTICS

A throw-in is more than just a way of bringing the ball back onto the pitch. A good throw can start an attacking move, or ease the pressure on your defence. You and your team-mates can use the tactics introduced here to make the most of throw-in moves during a match.

THROW-IN TIPS

Always try to throw to a team-mate who can receive the ball without being challenged. Whenever possible, and especially in your own half, send the ball upfield.

Several of your players should move into throwing range to increase your choice of receiver.

As you prepare to throw, each of your players should try to find space by darting away from his marker.

A throw into space, for a team-mate to run onto, is often more effective than one aimed directly at him.

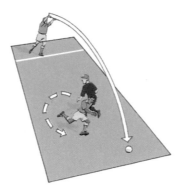

You can even throw over a team-mate into space behind him, so that he can turn and chase the ball.

You can often catch the other team off guard if the member of your team nearest to the ball when it goes out of play takes the throw-in quickly. However quickly you throw, make sure you bring the ball back over your head.

A DECOY MOVE

As you prepare to throw, your team-mates can use a decoy move like this to create space for a particular player to receive the ball.

1. Player A starts an angled run as though to receive the throw, drawing his marker away with him.

2. Player B, running in from the opposite angle, moves into the space created by Player A's 'decoy run'.

3. The thrower delivers his throw into the path of player B, who can receive the ball unchallenged and push upfield into attack.

USING A WALL PASS THROW-IN

Once you've taken a throw, get straight back into play. By using one of your team-mates as a 'wall' to knock your throw back to you, you can rejoin the action immediately. This wall pass move is particularly useful if all your players are closely marked.

Move forwards onto the pitch.

1. Throw to a nearby team-mate's feet, so that he can control the ball easily.

2. The receiver uses the inside of his foot to hit a first touch pass back to you.

3. You can build on this basic wall pass move by playing the ball upfield for the player who first received your throw to run onto.

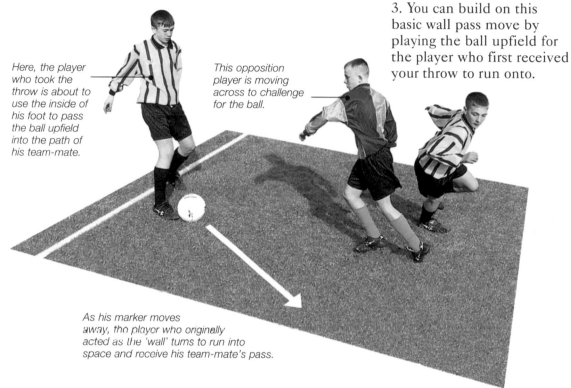

Here, the player who took the throw is about to use the inside of his foot to pass the ball upfield into the path of his team-mate.

This opposition player is moving across to challenge for the ball.

As his marker moves away, the player who originally acted as the 'wall' turns to run into space and receive his team-mate's pass.

THROWING INTO THE PENALTY AREA

If your team is awarded a throw-in within the attacking third, try using a long throw into the penalty area. Your team-mates can't be offside from a throw-in, so they can move upfield to threaten the opposition's goal.

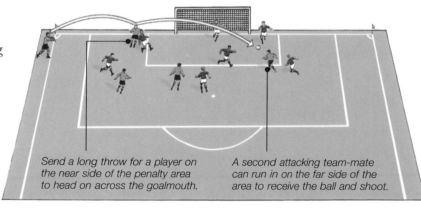

Send a long throw for a player on the near side of the penalty area to head on across the goalmouth.

A second attacking team-mate can run in on the far side of the area to receive the ball and shoot.

GOAL KICKS

If a player on the other team knocks the ball out of play over your goal-line, a member of your team has to restart the game with a goal kick. Like centre kicks, goal kicks give you a chance either to control possession of the ball or move play upfield quickly.

The referee will point at the goal area to signal a goal kick.

GOAL KICK RULES

To bring the ball back into play with a goal kick, you have to kick it from within your goal area, so that it leaves the penalty area. You can't kick the ball again until another player has touched it.

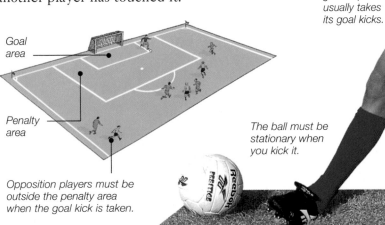

Goal area

Penalty area

Opposition players must be outside the penalty area when the goal kick is taken.

A team's goalkeeper usually takes its goal kicks.

The ball must be stationary when you kick it.

Notice how this player is leaning back to give his kick lift, and taking a high backswing for maximum power.

THE OUTFIELD KICKER OPTION

If your goalkeeper strikes a goal kick badly, an opposition player may intercept the ball and shoot while your keeper is out of position. You may prefer one of your outfield players to take the kick, so that your goalkeeper can stay in position.

There is a drawback to an outfield player taking a goal kick. It makes it harder for your defenders to catch opposition players offside (see page 69) after the kick. The kicker should rush forward to get level with his team-mates as quickly as he can.

TAKING A LONG GOAL KICK

You can use a long goal kick to move play out of your team's defending third. Use the kicking technique shown here to send the ball as far upfield as you can. By hitting the ball below its midline, you can make it rise and travel over players.

Lift your kicking foot in a high backswing.

Lean back slightly as you kick.

Use your arms for balance.

Take a short run up, from a slight angle, so that you can strike the ball with force.

With a long last stride, get your non-kicking foot slightly behind and to the side of the ball.

Swing your kicking foot forward to strike the lower half of the ball with your instep.

Follow through with your kicking leg to power the ball as far upfield as possible.

AIMING

Try to pick out a team-mate with your long goal kick, or at least aim it where there are enough of your players to stand a good chance of winning the ball. Here Dino Baggio (Italy) and John Sheridan (Republic of Ireland) challenge for a long goal kick ball.

USING A SHORTER GOAL KICK

You can make sure that your team keeps possession of the ball by sending a shorter goal kick to an unmarked team-mate near your own penalty area. Take care to deliver the ball so that it is easy to control. Some of your midfield players can drop back into your defending third so that at least one of your team-mates is free to receive the ball safely.

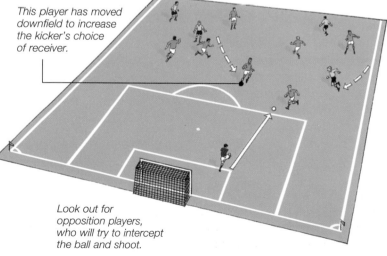

This player has moved downfield to increase the kicker's choice of receiver.

Look out for opposition players, who will try to intercept the ball and shoot.

CORNER KICKS

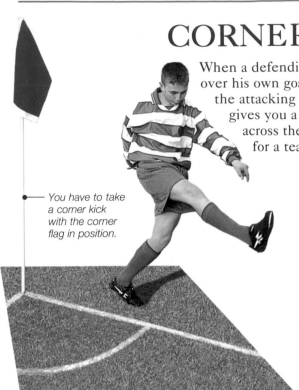

You have to take a corner kick with the corner flag in position.

When a defending player hits the ball over his own goal-line, the referee awards the attacking team a corner kick. This gives you a chance to play the ball across the opposition's goalmouth for a team-mate to strike at goal.

To signal a corner, the referee points to the corner flag.

CORNER KICK RULES

To take a corner, you kick the ball from within the corner quarter circle nearest to the point where it went out of play.

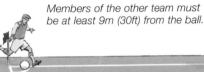

Members of the other team must be at least 9m (30ft) from the ball.

You're not allowed to play the ball again until another player has touched it.

PLACING THE BALL FOR A CORNER KICK

You need to place the ball in the corner circle in such a way that you can kick it without the flag blocking your run up or swing. The best place to put the ball will depend on whether you are left- or right-footed.

Here, the ball is placed correctly for a left-footed corner kicker.

Here, the ball is placed correctly for a right-footed corner kicker.

CROSSING FROM THE CORNER

If you hit a long, lofted corner kick to a team-mate just beyond the far side of the goal, he'll have a chance to shoot from behind the goalkeeper's view.

A player who receives a corner kick can't be offside, so your team-mates can move up towards the goalmouth to receive your corner cross.

INSWINGERS

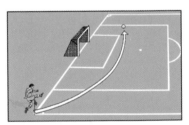

You can make your cross even more effective by bending it, so that the ball swings in towards the goal. A corner kick like this is known as an inswinger.

HOW DO YOU BEND A CORNER KICK?

The secret to bending a corner kick cross is to strike the ball off-centre so that it spins as it travels through the air. The easiest way to do this is to use the inside of your kicking foot to strike the outside edge of the ball. This right-footed player is about to hit an inswinger from the left corner in this way.

You also need to remember to hit the ball below its midline, so that your cross has plenty of lift.

Lean back as you kick.

Approach the ball from a slight angle.

Hit the ball with the part of your foot around your big toe.

Try to wrap your foot around the outside of the ball.

Get your non-kicking foot behind and to the side of the ball.

This view, from behind the ball, shows where you should strike it.

PRACTISING YOUR CROSS

As you get better at judging the distance, see how much you can bend each cross.

Try this practice with a partner to get used to the length and height of a good cross. Stand on the front corners of the penalty area – or about 40m (130ft) apart if you're not on a pitch. This is about the distance from the corner to the farthest post. Hit crosses to one another, trying to deliver the ball so that your partner can catch it just above his head.

WHO KICKS?

Bending a kick using the inside of your foot makes the ball swing away to the left if you're right-footed, or to the right if you're left-footed. Make sure that you pick the correct player to take an inswinger from a particular side of the pitch.

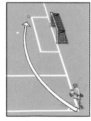

A right-footed player takes inswingers from left of the goal.

A left-footed player takes inswingers from right of the goal.

CORNER KICK MOVES

A cross from the corner is an example of a 'fifty-fifty' ball, as both teams have an equal chance of gaining possession. You can tip the balance in your team's favour by using a pre-planned corner move. These pages suggest several corner kick set plays for you to try.

FINDING SPACE TO RECEIVE A CROSS

For any corner kick move to be successful, one of your team-mates in the penalty area needs to be free to receive the ball and shoot. As you prepare to take a corner, your attacking players should try to move away from their markers to find space.

Here, the blue attacking players are getting ready to receive a cross from the right-hand corner.

The blue players in the far side of the penalty area can strike from a long cross or a flicked-on ball (see below).

This blue player is trying to find space to receive a shorter, driven cross (see page 82).

There is a good chance for a shot into this side of the goal, which the red team has left unguarded.

A FLICK-ON FROM THE NEAR POST

For this move, one of your team-mates needs to move into space around the goal-post nearest to the corner that you are kicking from. Send a short, inswinging cross to this player at the near post.

The player receiving the corner uses his head to flick the ball on across the goal. One of your other attacking team-mates runs in on the far side of the goal area to receive the flicked-on ball and shoot.

Judge your cross so that your team-mate can head the ball.

LAYING THE BALL BACK

This alternative near post move can be as effective as a flick-on across the goal. Send a cross to a team-mate at the near post. Instead of heading the ball across the goalmouth, the receiver 'lays it back'.

This means heading it down into the path of a team-mate running in from midfield.

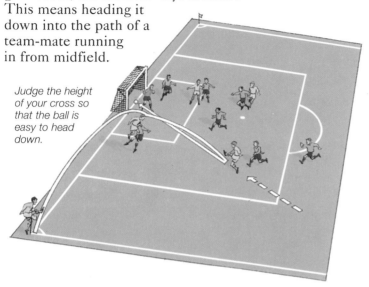

Judge the height of your cross so that the ball is easy to head down.

OUTSWINGING CORNERS

Another option is to bend your corner kick cross away from the goalmouth. This kind of corner is called an 'outswinger'. It makes it easier for your team-mates moving towards goal to head the ball well.

Play your cross so that the ball swings out towards the penalty spot.

Players can run onto your cross from the edge of the penalty area.

By moving out towards the corner, or over towards the far post, your team-mates can draw defenders away from the near side of the penalty area. This creates space for a player to run onto a shorter outswinging cross.

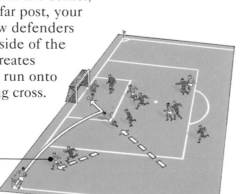

This player is drawing away his marker to create space.

CORNER ACTION

Try to spot different corner moves when you watch professional players in action. Here, the left-footed corner taker has hit an inswinging corner cross. His closely-marked team-mates will try to head the ball down into the goal.

WHO KICKS?

As with inswingers (see page 79), you need to pick the correct kicker to take an outswinging corner from a particular side of the pitch.

A right-footed player takes outswinging corners from the right-hand side of the goal.

A left-footed player takes outswinging corners from the left-hand side of the goal.

SHORT AND DRIVEN CORNERS

Because a swinging cross is the most popular corner kick option, it is also the most predictable. To keep the other team guessing, vary your corner kick tactics every now and then. You can use a driven corner for a faster-paced cross, or a short corner for an attack from a different angle.

TAKING A DRIVEN CORNER

When you hit a swinging, lofted cross, the ball takes a long time to reach the goal area because it follows a curved path through the air. By striking a low, straight, powerful cross, you can send the ball across the goalmouth more quickly.

As you run up, get your non-kicking foot right up alongside the ball. Don't lean back. Keep your body upright and over the ball.

With your knee over the ball, and your toes pointing down, strike the ball just below its centre with the instep of your foot.

Follow through with your kicking leg to power the ball across into the penalty area. It will travel in a straight line, rising slightly.

DRIVEN CORNER MOVES

Try to send a driven corner either to a player on the near side of the goal area, or one around the middle of the penalty area. A driven cross will stay low, so the receiver must be prepared to strike a waist-high volley, or even try a diving header. Your other team-mates can create space for him by moving as though to receive a longer cross (see page 78) or a short corner (see page 83).

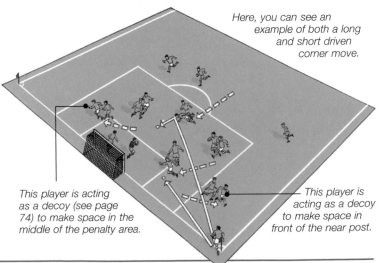

Here, you can see an example of both a long and short driven corner move.

This player is acting as a decoy (see page 74) to make space in the middle of the penalty area.

This player is acting as a decoy to make space in front of the near post.

PLAYING A SHORT CORNER

You can use this simple pass and return tactic, or 'short corner', to build up an attacking move from the corner of the pitch.

One of your team-mates moves within easy passing range of the corner. Send the ball along the ground to this nearby player.

As soon as you have taken the kick, run into space downfield from your team-mate, so that he can pass the ball back to you.

Use the inside of your foot to pass the ball to your team-mate.

Run on to collect the return pass.

A move like this lets you dribble the ball towards goal to hit a cross from closer in, or try a shot yourself.

SIGNALLING THE MOVE

When you've decided what kind of corner move to use, signal to your team-mates so that they know what you're planning to do. You need to agree on a system of corner kick signals during training. Keep them simple, but not so obvious that your opponents will know what to expect.

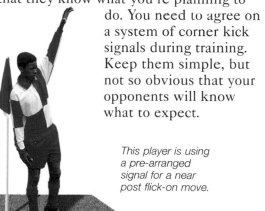

This player is using a pre-arranged signal for a near post flick-on move.

CORNER SKILLS GAME

Mark out a special pitch, 40m (130ft) wide but only about 15m (49ft) long. Play a game of five- or seven-a-side within this area. The short, wide pitch means that most of the action takes place around either goalmouth. This gives you lots of chances to try out different corner moves.

Restart play with a corner, wherever the ball goes off the pitch.

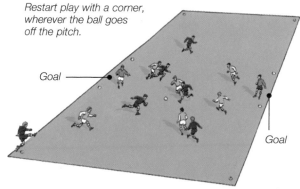

Goal

Goal

FREE KICK BASICS

The referee puts his arm out to signal a direct free kick.

If one of your opponents 'commits an offence' by breaking a soccer rule, the referee will stop the game and ask your team to restart play with a free kick. There are two types of free kick – direct, to punish serious offences, and indirect for less serious ones.

To signal an indirect free kick, the referee raises his arm.

SERIOUS OFFENCES

The referee will award a direct free kick if a player kicks, trips, charges, strikes, pushes, holds or jumps at an opponent; if an outfield player deliberately uses his hands to control the ball, or if a goalkeeper handles the ball outside his penalty area.

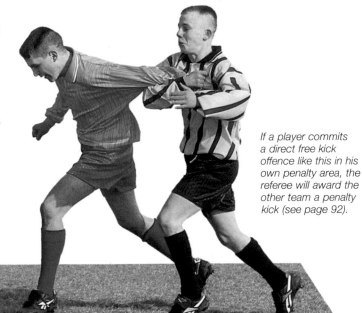

Here, the player in yellow is holding his opponent back, rather than playing the ball. An unfair challenge like this is known as a foul.

If a player commits a direct free kick offence like this in his own penalty area, the referee will award the other team a penalty kick (see page 92).

INDIRECT FREE KICK OFFENCES

These pictures show the various offences for which a referee will award an indirect free kick. The three types of offence illustrated on the top row are for goalkeepers only.

Time-wasting by holding the ball for a long time.

Using hands to receive a backpass from a team-mate.

Taking more than four steps while holding the ball.

Charging or obstructing the opposition's goalkeeper.

Playing dangerously (here, kicking a high ball).

Charging or obstructing a player who isn't on the ball.

Receiving the ball while in an offside position (see page 69).

FREE KICK RULES

To take a free kick, you kick the ball from the point on the pitch where the offence took place. The ball must be stationary when you kick it, and the other team's players have to be at least 9m (30ft) away. You can't play the ball again until it has been touched by another player.

If the free kick is direct, you are allowed to score straight from the kick.

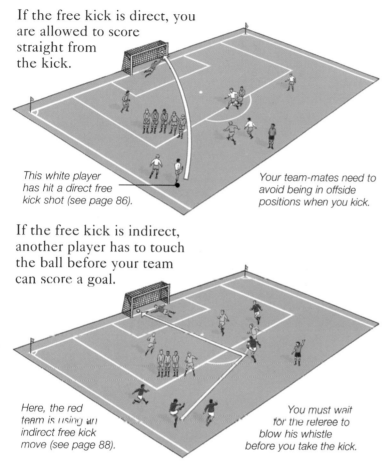

This white player has hit a direct free kick shot (see page 86).

Your team-mates need to avoid being in offside positions when you kick.

If the free kick is indirect, another player has to touch the ball before your team can score a goal.

Here, the red team is using an indirect free kick move (see page 88).

You must wait for the referee to blow his whistle before you take the kick.

SPECIAL CASES

If you are awarded a free kick in your own penalty area, you have to kick the ball out of the penalty area to bring it back into play.

Opposition players must be outside the penalty area when you kick.

If the kick is inside your goal area, you can take it from any part of that area.

If you are given an indirect free kick inside your opponent's goal area, you take the kick from the edge of the goal area.

Your opponents are allowed to stand on their goal-line, between the posts, despite being less than 9m (30ft) away.

TAKING A FREE KICK IN YOUR OWN HALF

The top priority when you take a free kick in your own half of the pitch is to make sure that your team keeps the ball. Use a simple pass to a player in space.

Aim your kick away from any nearby opponent hoping to steal the ball.

Send the ball upfield whenever possible.

DIRECT FREE KICKS

A free kick in the attacking third gives you a good chance to score a spectacular goal. You're most likely to score if you keep your free kick move simple. These pages look at the simplest of all attacking free kicks – a direct shot at goal from the edge of the penalty area.

THE DEFENSIVE WALL

When you take a free kick near the penalty area, your opponents will usually protect their goalmouth by forming a defensive wall. Several players will stand side by side to block your shooting line. To score, you need to get the ball past this wall of players.

The players in the wall will try to block one side of the goalmouth, while their goalkeeper guards the other.

BENDING YOUR SHOT AROUND THE WALL

By striking the outside edge of the ball with the inside of your foot, you can bend a free kick so that it swings away to your non-kicking side. Don't hit the ball too low down or it will rise over the goal.

To bend a kick in the other direction, so that it swings out to your kicking side, use the outside of your foot to strike the inside edge of the ball. Keep the toes of your kicking foot pointed down as you kick.

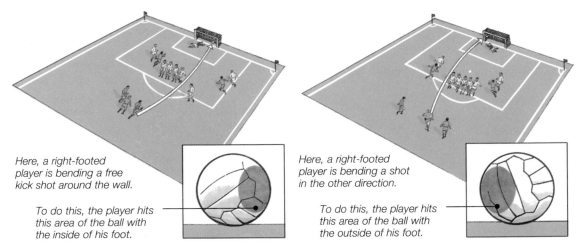

Here, a right-footed player is bending a free kick shot around the wall.

To do this, the player hits this area of the ball with the inside of his foot.

Here, a right-footed player is bending a shot in the other direction.

To do this, the player hits this area of the ball with the outside of his foot.

BENDING SHOT PRACTICE

To practise your swerving shot, put one corner flag in the centre of the goal, and another on the penalty spot. Place the ball on the penalty arc, in line with the flags. Try to bend a kick around one side of the nearest flag into the other side of the goalmouth.

Try bending shots in either direction.

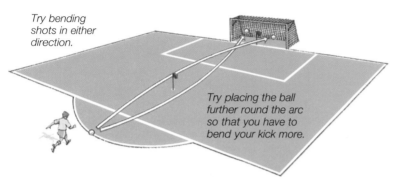

Try placing the ball further round the arc so that you have to bend your kick more.

SHOOTING STAR

Here, Roberto Baggio is powering a bending free kick shot at goal. One of his Juventus team-mates helps to shield the move until the last moment.

USING A DUMMY CROSS-OVER

You can use this tactic to disguise the direction of a direct free kick shot.

1. You and a team-mate (ideally a player who kicks with the opposite foot to you) both prepare as though to take the kick.

2. Your team-mate runs up to the ball, as though to shoot, but steps over it at the last minute.

Your team-mate's run will help to hide your shot.

3. Time your own run up so that just after your team-mate 'dummies' over the ball, you hit a powerful shot at goal. Your team-mate can continue his run to follow in your shot.

FREE KICK MOVES

Even if you can hit a hard, swerving shot, you are unlikely to score from a free kick unless you can create an element of surprise. You need to leave the opposition unsure which direction your attack will come from. Use one of the moves described here to baffle the defence.

STRETCHING THE WALL

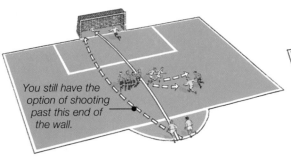

You still have the option of shooting past this end of the wall.

One or two of your team-mates join the end of the defensive wall, to block the goalkeeper's view of the free kick.

As you take the kick, your players in the wall break away to let your shot past, turning to follow it in.

MAKING YOUR OWN WALL

Two or three of your team-mates form a separate wall a few metres in front of the ball to hide the kick from view.

Your players move off as you kick. They need to hide the ball as long as possible, without getting in its way.

CREATING A GAP IN THE WALL

This move requires split second timing. One or two of your attacking team-mates try to squeeze right up in front of the middle of the defensive wall. By moving away from the wall as you shoot, they may be able to create a gap for your shot to pass through.

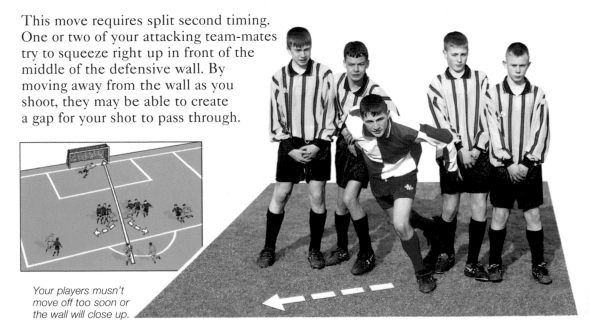

Your players musn't move off too soon or the wall will close up.

INDIRECT MOVES

From an indirect free kick you have to pass the ball before a player can shoot. A simple pass to one side lets you quickly change the angle of your attack so that one of your team-mates can have a clear shot at goal.

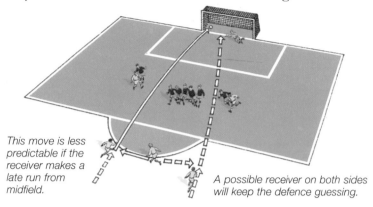

This move is less predictable if the receiver makes a late run from midfield.

A possible receiver on both sides will keep the defence guessing.

THE BACK PASS SWITCH

You can try this trick to switch the direction of an indirect free kick attack. Approach the ball as though to kick to a team-mate on one side. Instead, roll the ball backwards to a player on the other side to shoot.

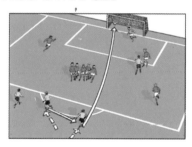

Use the underside of your foot to roll the ball to a team-mate behind you.

TWO PASS MOVES

Using two passes in a free kick move lets you move the ball to one side of the wall and closer to the goal, for a good shooting position. Try this basic two pass move.

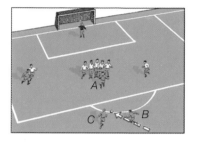

Player A takes up a position slightly downfield from the wall, facing back towards the ball. Left-footed player B and right-footed player C both prepare as though to take the free kick.

Player B dummies over the ball, running on diagonally to one side of the wall. As he does so, player C sends a pass along the ground to player A in front of the wall. He in turn passes the ball sideways for player B to run onto and shoot at goal.

MORE FREE KICK MOVES

You need to prepare suitable moves for free kicks from different positions in the attacking third. On these pages you can see some suggested moves for free kicks near either wing. You can also find out how you and your team-mates can perfect your own free kick moves.

FREE KICKS FROM THE WING

When your team is awarded a free kick at either side of the opposition's penalty area, the other team's players will usually move out to be level with their defensive wall. This stops your team-mates from taking up positions near the goal, where they would be offside.

In a free kick situation like this, you can attack by crossing the ball into space behind the defence, for your team-mates to run onto.

Here, the blue player taking the free kick has hit a long, outswinging cross from the wing.

Each attacker times his run so as to avoid being offside.

DISGUISING A FREE KICK CROSS

Try using this set play to disguise a free kick cross to the near post.

1. Player A, a left-footer, runs in as if to take the free kick. At the same time, players C and D move off as if to receive a long, outswinging cross to the far post.

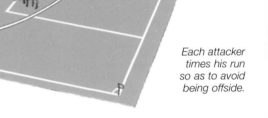

2. Player A dummies over the ball. His right-footed team-mate, player B, runs in to hit a short, inswinging cross into the space created by decoys C and D. Players E and F run onto the ball to shoot.

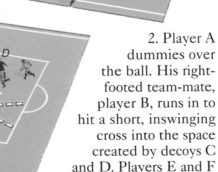

USING THE WING

A cross from a free kick at the side of the penalty area is fairly predictable. You may be able to surprise the opposition by using a move along the wing. Send the ball towards the touchline, into the path of a player making a run from midfield.

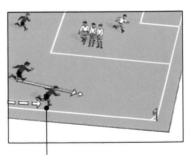

The receiver can dribble the ball upfield along the wing and send a cross into the goal area.

PRACTISING YOUR OWN FREE KICK MOVES

You can try out some of your own set plays for attacking free kicks by having a free kick competition. Split into two teams of seven or eight players. Each team takes one direct and one indirect free kick from each of five different positions outside the penalty area, while the other team defends the goal. The team which scores the most goals from their ten free kick attempts wins.

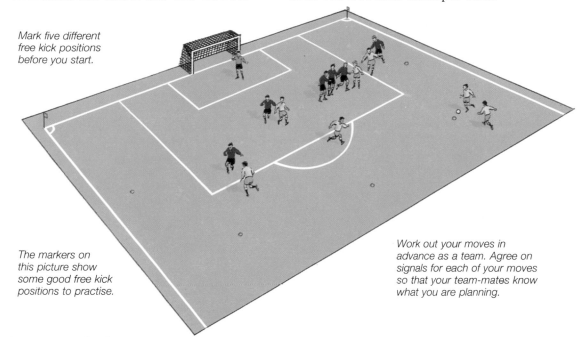

Mark five different free kick positions before you start.

The markers on this picture show some good free kick positions to practise.

Work out your moves in advance as a team. Agree on signals for each of your moves so that your team-mates know what you are planning.

★ Always take into consideration whether the kick is direct or indirect, and what position it is from.

★ Keep your free kick moves fairly simple. Ideally they should involve no more than three touches.

★ Remember that you cannot use any move that involves a team-mate being in an offside position.

VARYING YOUR CHOICE OF MOVE

Whichever attacking free kick move you use, it is unlikely to work if your opponents can tell what you're planning from the position of your players. Try to vary which move you use from each position. As an example, the pictures below show three very different moves involving a team-mate positioned at one end of the defensive wall.

By breaking away from the wall, the attacking player has here distracted attention from his team-mate's shot.

Here, the attacking player has moved out from the wall to take part in a two pass move (see page 89).

In this case, the player on the end of the wall has turned to run onto a ball chipped over the top of the wall.

PENALTIES

To signal a penalty, the referee points at the penalty spot.

When a player commits a serious offence inside his own penalty area, the referee awards the attacking team a penalty kick. A penalty is a high-pressure, 'one-on-one' situation in which you try to beat the opposition's goalkeeper with a direct shot at goal.

Place the ball yourself, so that you know it is on a sound surface.

PENALTY RULES

To take a penalty, you shoot at goal from the penalty spot. You can't play the ball again until it has been touched by another player.

The goalkeeper mustn't move until you play the ball.

All other players must be outside the penalty area, beyond the arc, and downfield from the spot.

STAYING COOL

When you take a penalty, don't be indecisive or hesitant. Pick your target area and concentrate on hitting a hard, low shot into that part of the goal.

A firmly hit shot just inside either post will be extremely hard to stop.

SHOOTING WITH POWER

1. The key to a low, hard shot is to keep your body over the ball as you kick, rather than leaning back.

2. Get your non-kicking foot alongside the ball so that the knee of your kicking leg is over the ball.

3. With your toes pointing down, use the instep of your kicking foot to drive the ball forward.

Use your arms for balance.

Follow through with your kicking leg for maximum power.

Strike the ball through its midline, so that it stays low.

SOFT OPTION

You may find it easier to place your shot accurately by hitting the ball with slightly less power, using the inside of your foot.

FOLLOWING UP THE PENALTY

Your team-mates should be ready to close in on the goalmouth as soon as you've taken your penalty kick.

If the goalkeeper blocks your shot, the ball may rebound to provide another chance.

THE PENALTY SHOOT-OUT

If the scores are level at the end of extra-time, the teams often have a penalty competition to decide which team wins the match. This is known as a penalty 'shoot-out'. If one team has scored more goals after both teams have had five penalty attempts, then that team wins the match. Otherwise, the shoot-out continues until one team's penalty score passes the other team's from the same number of attempts.

These players are using a practice penalty shoot-out in training to perfect their penalty skills.

In a shoot-out, each penalty has to be taken by a different player, so every member of your team needs to practise.

A practice shoot-out will also improve your goalkeeper's skills.

WINNING A DROP BALL

This page introduces the least common soccer restart, called a drop ball. This is a one-on-one challenge in which a member of each team competes for possession of the ball. To win a drop ball you'll need total concentration and sharp reactions.

DROP BALL BASICS

The referee uses a drop ball to restart play after any stoppage for which neither team is responsible, such as a break in play caused by injury. Unlike other restarts, a drop ball is meant to give both teams an equal chance of gaining possession of the ball.

Two players, one from each team, face one another at the point where the ball was last in play. The referee brings the ball back into play by dropping it onto the pitch between them. Neither player is allowed to play the ball before it hits the ground.

If your opponents had the ball when the game was interrupted by injury, it is good sportsmanship to let them win it back from the drop ball restart deliberately.

Concentrate on the ball. Try to get your foot to it as soon as it lands.

WINNING WAYS

The simplest approach to a drop ball is to use the inside of your foot to tap the ball to a team-mate on your non-kicking side.

If you think your opponent will block an inside foot pass, try using the outside of your foot to hook the ball away to the other side.

You can even try pushing the ball forwards through the gap between your opponent's legs. Dart past him to collect the ball.

CREATING CHANCES

Good dead ball skills will enable you and your team-mates to turn throw-ins, corners, free kicks and penalties into goals. To create as many opportunities as possible to use these skills during a match, you need to put pressure on your opponents so that they send the ball out of play.

PRESSURE PASSING

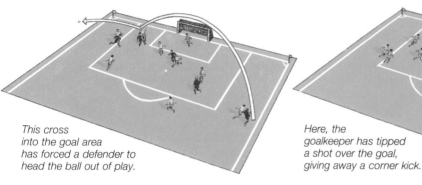

This cross into the goal area has forced a defender to head the ball out of play.

You can often win a throw-in or corner by passing the ball into space near the opposition's goal, for a team-mate to chase. Your opponents will be forced to clear the ball, rather than allow you a shot at goal.

SHOOTING

Here, the goalkeeper has tipped a shot over the goal, giving away a corner kick.

Even if you don't score, taking a shot at goal can create a second scoring chance. By blocking your shot, a defender or goalkeeper will often knock the ball out of play to give away a corner kick.

DRIBBLING INTO ATTACK

Here, the red player's attacking run gains his team a corner kick.

By dribbling into the other team's penalty area, or upfield along either wing, you will often force a defender to try a desperate tackle. In doing so, he may clear the ball for a throw-in or corner, or even give away a free kick or penalty.

CHALLENGING DEFENDERS

By closing in on a defender, you can force him to play the ball in a hurry.

If one of the other team's players has possession of the ball in his defensive third, move in to challenge him. Under pressure, he is likely to send the ball out of play. This would give your team possession in a good attacking position.

STAR PHOTO

Here, by attacking along the wing, Emmanuel Amunike (Nigeria) forces a defender to clear the ball for a throw-in.

WORLD SOCCER QUIZ

32. Which competition is the oldest international soccer tournament in the world?

a. The European Championship
b. The African Nations Cup
c. The Copa America (South American Championship)

33. Which England striker was the top scorer of the 1986 World Cup?

a. Gary Lineker
b. David Platt
c. Peter Beardsley

34. The first World Cup of the twenty-first century, in 2002, will be hosted by two countries. South Korea is one, what is the other?

a. Japan
b. Malaysia
c. Singapore

35. Which legendary World Cup player has both captained and coached World Cup winning teams?

a. Bobby Charlton
b. Franz Beckenbauer
c. Pele

36. Which World Cup had a stick figure called 'Ciao', with a soccer ball for a head, as its official mascot?

a. 1982, Spain
b. 1986, Mexico
c. 1990, Italy

37. What was special about Dutch player Robbie Rensenbrink's goal against Scotland in 1978?

a. It was fastest goal ever in a World Cup match
b. It was the first time a goalkeeper had scored
c. It was the 1000th World Cup goal

38. Which of these countries has only hosted the World Cup once?

a. Brazil
b. Mexico
c. Italy

39. Which West German striker has scored more World Cup goals than any other player?

a. Uwe Rahn
b. Gerd Müller
c. Karl-Heinz Rummenigge

40. In 1982, Hungary set a new record for the number of goals scored by one team in a World Cup match. How many times did they score?

a. 10
b. 8
c. 6

41. Which of these is the French stadium that was ruled too small to stage the 1998 World Cup Final?

a. Nou Camp
b. Parque Central
c. Parc des Princes

42. Which international team was the first to win the World Cup three times?

a. Argentina
b. Italy
c. Brazil

43. Which country won the 1996 African Nations Cup?

a. Nigeria
b. South Africa
c. Cameroon

44. Which of these international teams does not play in red and white?

a. Croatia
b. Colombia
c. Switzerland

45. Which international soccer confederation does Australia belong to?

a. UEFA
b. CONCACAF
c. Oceania

46. Enzo Francescoli was voted 1995 South American Footballer of the Year. What country does he play for?

a. Uruguay
b. Brazil
c. Colombia

47. Which of these teams did not make it through to the semi-final stages of the 1994 World Cup?

a. Bulgaria
b. Sweden
c. Germany

SOCCER QUIZ

PART FOUR
DEFENDING

CONTENTS

ABOUT DEFENDING

When your team loses the ball, you need to get it back as quickly as possible. This is what defending is all about. Defending is every player's responsibility – when the other team has the ball, you are defending, even if you play in an attacking position. A good team defence plays a big part in winning matches.

A LOOK AT THE PITCH

Here you can find out the names for different areas of the pitch mentioned in this part of the book. Although you can defend anywhere on the pitch, some areas are mentioned more than others because you need to defend more urgently when the other team gets close to your goal.

Good defending is a mixture of individual skills, team skills and tactics. This part of the book covers all of them. It also looks at the roles of players who are specifically defenders, such as centre halfs and full backs.

The 'far' post is the goal-post furthest from the ball.

The goal area is the box around the goal. The goalkeeper usually tells other players what to do in this area.

Goal-line

The penalty area

The 'near' post is the goal-post nearest the ball at any time.

Half-way line

THE DEFENSIVE STANCE

When you adopt the 'defensive stance', it is almost like being ready to pounce. You don't have the ball so you don't have to worry about controlling it – you can concentrate on your movements instead.

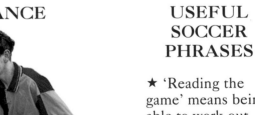

Use your arms for balance.

You should crouch as low as you can so that you are ready to spring.

Your weight should be over your toes so that you can move quickly into action.

USEFUL SOCCER PHRASES

★ 'Reading the game' means being able to work out how the game is going, anticipate attackers' moves, see what help your team-mates need and go to help them.
★ 'Winning the ball' means taking the ball off another player by tackling or intercepting it.

AN IMPORTANT RULE: STAYING GOAL-SIDE

One of the main rules for defending players is to get into a goal-side position and stay there. This means placing yourself between attackers and your goal, never between attackers and the ball. This is crucial for successful defending.

Direction of goal

This is the correct direction to take to reach a goal-side position.

If the defender runs to intercept and fails, he gives the attackers a very big advantage.

You may think it makes sense to get between the ball and your opponent, but then you can't see what he's doing.

If he does receive the ball, you have to chase him up the field and he is free to run straight towards your goal.

If you are in a goal-side position, you are able to watch and anticipate the attacker's moves from behind.

Although he is likely to receive the ball successfully, you are in a position to stop his attack and challenge him.

HOW TO MEASURE

For many of the games and exercises in this part of the book, you need to measure out an area to do them in. As before, measurements are given in metres (m) and feet (ft). 1m (3ft) is about one big stride, so you can measure by counting out your strides.

GOAL-SIDE GAME

This game is for two players, an attacker (A) and a defender (D). Mark out a pitch 20m (66ft) long and 10m (33ft) wide.

20m (66ft)   10m (33ft)

A tries to dribble down the pitch. D tries to stop him by staying goal-side, without tackling.

Whenever A gets goal-side of D, he gets a point. At the end, swap roles. See who scores the most.

PRIORITIES IN DEFENCE

The main purpose of a defender or defending team is to stop opponents from attacking. There are many ways to do this, depending on how urgent the situation is. Here, you can find out about the most important things you need to know. They are all covered in detail later in the book.

YOUR TOP PRIORITY

If your opponents reach the defending third, they are in a very strong position. You must stop them from scoring.

First, help your goalkeeper to block any shots at goal. Next, clear the ball out of the danger area – 'if in doubt, get the ball out.'

Here, a defender stops a shot and clears the ball.

CHALLENGING FOR THE BALL

Whatever the situation, someone must try to win the ball back. This responsibility passes from player to player, so everyone must be ready to take on the challenge if the ball comes his way.

Attacker — *Defender*

You can challenge by putting pressure on the player with the ball.

If your opponent makes a mistake, you or a team-mate can intercept the ball.

As a last resort, you can challenge your opponent directly with a tackle.

DELAYING YOUR OPPONENTS

A very important way of preventing an emergency situation from happening is to delay your opponents as long as possible.

Delay allows members of your own team to get into a stronger position, which may stop the attack from getting any further.

This player jockeys to give his team-mate time to get into position.

AWARENESS AND TEAM WORK

Even if one player's skills are very good, he will not stand a very big chance of challenging for the ball successfully if his team is not working with him.

Each player has a part to play in making it difficult for the other team to progress up the field. To do this you need to communicate well.

Everyone needs to be aware of where the ball is, but not everyone should crowd around it.

All players should be aware of what the attackers are doing, especially the players they are marking.

The defenders in this team are marking attackers very closely.

Each player needs to understand his team's formation and how his own position works within it.

DEFENCE INTO ATTACK

If you only think about stopping the other team from scoring, you are less likely to score yourself. A good defence makes the whole team strong, but it should always be used as a springboard for attack.

Think positively all the time so that you can turn defensive situations into an attack as soon as you get the chance.

This team gains possession in the defending third, then sends the ball quickly up the pitch.

STAR DEFENDER

German player Dieter Eilts is a good example of a defender who can read the game well, then act courageously to turn defence into attack.

JOCKEYING

Jockeying is one of the most important defending skills. It means delaying your opponent's attack by getting in his way. This allows your team-mates to get into a position where they can help you to challenge. If you do this effectively, you may also pressurize your opponent into making a mistake.

MOVING INTO POSITION

If your opponent is approaching your goal you need to close in on him quickly, but not too quickly. If you are going too fast he will be able to judge your run and dodge round you easily.

The defender watches the ball carefully.

Direction of goal

Once you are close to the attacker, hold off slightly. You should be close enough to touch him, but if you get much closer it will be easy for him to dash round you.

Adopt the 'defensive stance'. If your weight is over your knees, you are in a strong position to challenge.

Make sure you stay goal-side. If the attacker gets past you, he has beaten you. You will no longer be able to jockey.

MAINTAINING THE PRESSURE

As well as delaying your opponent, try to force him into a weaker position. First of all, try to work out which is his weaker side – if he usually uses his right foot to dribble or kick, he is weak on his left side.

This player jockeys on the left.

Cover your opponent to the front and to one side so that it is difficult for him to turn.

The attacker is forced into the side-lines.

If you jockey on his strong side, he will only be able use his weak side, so he may make a mistake.

Here, the attacker loses the initiative.

Once you have your opponent under pressure, watch for opportunities to win the ball.

PREVENTING A FULL TURN

If the attacker is still facing away from your goal when you reach a jockeying position, you have a big advantage. The best thing you can do is prevent him from turning.

1. Jockey on his stronger side, getting close up behind him. You must stay goal-side, so don't come round to his front.

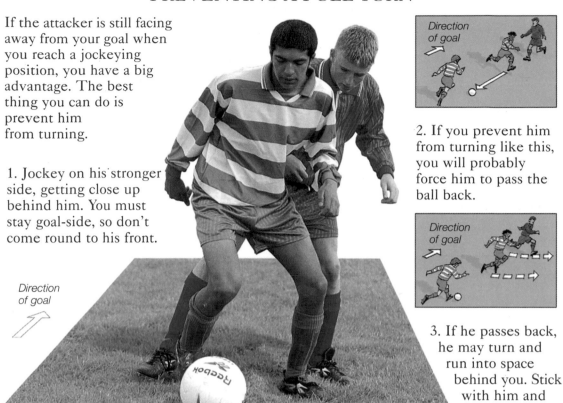

Direction of goal

2. If you prevent him from turning like this, you will probably force him to pass the ball back.

Direction of goal

Direction of goal

3. If he passes back, he may turn and run into space behind you. Stick with him and stay goal-side.

ZIGZAG JOCKEYING EXERCISE

This exercise helps you to work on speed and a good defensive stance. Any number can join in, as long as you work in pairs. Mark out a row of zigzags about 30m (98ft) long and 5m (16ft) wide. One end of the row is the defender's goal. In each pair, decide on an attacker and a defender.

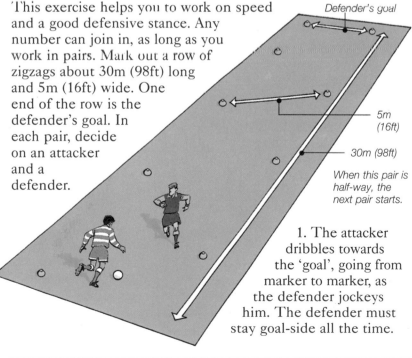

Defender's goal

5m (16ft)

30m (98ft)

When this pair is half-way, the next pair starts.

1. The attacker dribbles towards the 'goal', going from marker to marker, as the defender jockeys him. The defender must stay goal-side all the time.

2. The defender can't tackle, but he scores a point for intercepting the ball if the attacker loses control. The attacker scores if he dodges round the defender. At the end of the row, swap roles and start again.

CHALLENGING

When you challenge, you make a direct attempt to get the ball back from your opponents. The most direct way to challenge is to tackle, but it is not always the best. If you can intercept the ball instead, do so, because this will leave you with more control.

Defender

APPROACHING AN OPPONENT

You usually move in to challenge when your opponent is about to receive a pass. Always get into a goal-side position.

The defender should not run right to the back of his opponent in the direction of the curved arrow.

Approach your opponent at an angle. If you are directly behind him, he can easily run out to the side.

Don't get in too close to him, as he may be able to dodge round you.

Judge your speed carefully. If you come in too slowly he may run on. If you are too fast, you have less control.

This defender has come in too fast and too close. He is off balance.

If the defender approaches in this direction, he will be able to challenge the attacker.

Direction of goal

INTERCEPTING

Intercepting is the best way to win the ball back. Your opponents are usually moving in the wrong direction, and you are more balanced than if you tackle. This means that you have time and space to launch an attack.

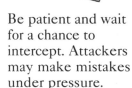

Be patient and wait for a chance to intercept. Attackers may make mistakes under pressure.

You must be on your toes and ready to dash around your opponent from your goal-side position.

Wait, then intercept later.

If you don't think you can intercept successfully, hold on to your goal-side position instead.

TIMING A DIRECT CHALLENGE

If you are close to your opponent, you will probably need to tackle in order to win the ball. In judging your tackle, the most important factor is timing.

One of the main rules of timing is to watch the ball, not the player. This way, you won't be fooled by his movements. Wait until he is off balance, for example when he is turning or half-turned, then move in quickly to steal the ball. You can find out more about tackling techniques on pages 106-107.

As this player turns with the ball, the defender dashes across the front of him and pushes the ball away.

INTERCEPTING EXERCISE

This exercise is to help you develop your agility and speed at intercepting. Play in threes (A, B and D). Mark out a 10m (33ft) square. A and D stand in the middle of it, B along one edge. The direction of play is towards A and D.

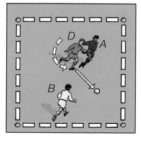

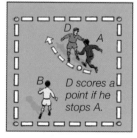

D scores a point if he stops A.

D stands goal-side of A. B passes towards them. D must judge whether to intercept or stay goal-side.

If D intercepts, he scores a point and passes the ball back to B before A can challenge him.

If A gets the ball, D tries to stop him reaching the far side of the square before B can count to ten.

A scores a point for turning and reaching the other side. After five goes, swap your roles around.

TACKLING SKILLS

To tackle well you need a combination of good technique and plenty of determination. You need to tackle cleanly to avoid giving away a foul, and whenever possible you need to keep possession of the ball, too. These are the main techniques that you need to learn.

FRONT BLOCK TACKLE

Watch the ball, not your opponent. With your weight forward, go into the tackle with your whole body.

Use the inside of your tackling foot to make contact with the middle of the ball.

If you watch your opponent instead of the ball, you may be tricked by a feinting move.

The impact of the tackle can often trap the ball between your foot and your opponent's foot. If this happens, drop your foot down and try to flick or roll the ball up over your opponent's foot.

TACKLING FROM OTHER ANGLES

You can use a block tackle to challenge from the side, but not from behind as this is a foul.

Turn your whole body towards your opponent so that all your strength is behind the tackle. Use the side of your tackling foot as you would if you were face on. Lean into your opponent, but don't push.

BLOCK TACKLE PRACTICE

In pairs, mark out a 10m (33ft) line. Start at either end. One player dribbles, the other challenges.

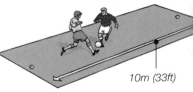

10m (33ft)

The dribbler tries to get to the end of the line, while the challenger tries to win the ball from him. Whoever succeeds scores a point.

SLIDING TACKLES

Sliding tackles are a last resort. You should only use them in a real emergency, for several reasons. You will probably not gain possession of the ball, you are out of the game until you get up again, and you may also give away a foul.

Approach from the side. Keep your eyes on the ball and slide your tackling leg forward to push the ball as far as possible.

If you kick the ball and not your opponent, you will not be penalised if he has to jump over you.

After tackling, get up quickly. This is easier if you tackle with the leg furthest from your opponent.

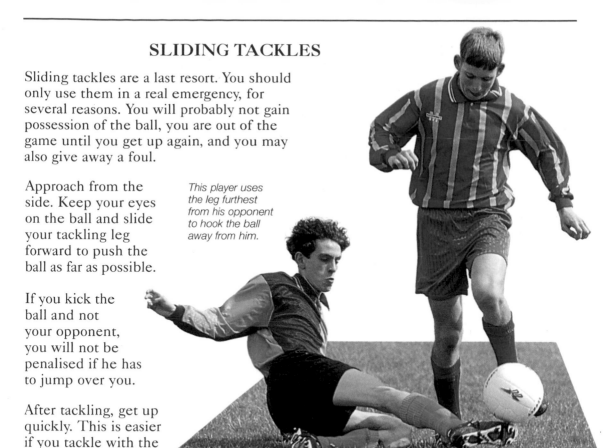

This player uses the leg furthest from his opponent to hook the ball away from him.

LEARNING TO SLIDE TACKLE

Until you are sure of your technique, it is best to practise sliding tackles without an opponent, as you are less likely to hurt someone. Try this practice with a friend.

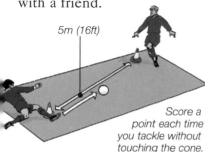

5m (16ft)

Score a point each time you tackle without touching the cone.

Place two obstacles 5m (16ft) apart (they needn't be cones) and put the ball close to one of them. These are your 'opponents'. Each of you starts next to an obstacle.

One of you runs up and slides the ball away, trying not to touch the obstacle. The other collects the ball and puts it next to his own obstacle. He slides it back.

KEEPING IT CLEAN

Tackling your opponent from behind, kicking him or tripping him are fouls which lead to a direct free kick, or a penalty if you are in the penalty area. To avoid fouling, remember these tips:
★ Keep your eyes on the ball, not on your opponent.
★ Be patient. If you wait for the right moment to tackle, you are more likely to do so cleanly.
★ Never tackle half-heartedly. If your weight is not behind the tackle, you may be unbalanced, and you could hurt yourself as well as your opponent.

PLAYING SAFE

Usually, you are defending whenever your team loses the ball. However, when the ball is in your defending third, you may need to play defensively even when your team has possession.

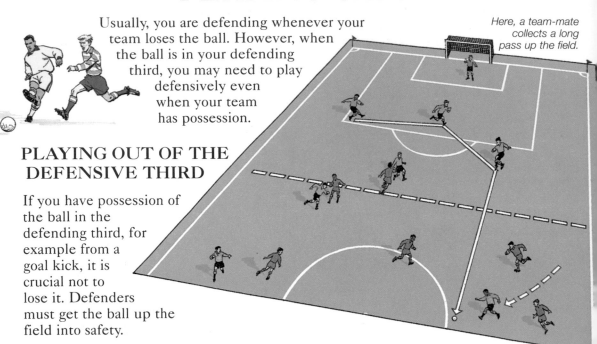

Here, a team-mate collects a long pass up the field.

PLAYING OUT OF THE DEFENSIVE THIRD

If you have possession of the ball in the defending third, for example from a goal kick, it is crucial not to lose it. Defenders must get the ball up the field into safety.

Never dribble out of the defending third. Any attacker who wins the ball may be able to shoot.

This attacker wins the ball and can now go for goal.

You can pass between yourselves at the back until you get a good opportunity to pass up the field.

When you pass up the field, send the ball as far as you can, to a team-mate if possible.

BACK-PASSES

A 'back-pass' usually means passing the ball back to the goalkeeper. If you want to pass up the field but find yourself surrounded, this is sometimes your only option.

1. Never pass across your goalmouth, as this may give your opponents a chance to run in and shoot.

2. Don't pass back to the goalkeeper if he is under pressure. It is better to kick the ball out of play.

3. Play the ball low, to the goalkeeper's kicking foot. This makes it easier for him to control.

BACK-PASS RULES

There are particular rules for back-passes to bear in mind.
★ If you kick the ball to him, the goalkeeper can't pick it up. He has to kick it instead.
★ The goalkeeper can pick up any back-pass that you make with your head, chest or thighs.
★ The goalkeeper can pick up any accidental back-pass.

GOING FOR TOUCH

'Going for touch' means sending the ball off the pitch on purpose as an emergency move. The other team still has the initiative because they get the corner or throw-in, but it can stop them from scoring while your team uses the time to strengthen its position.

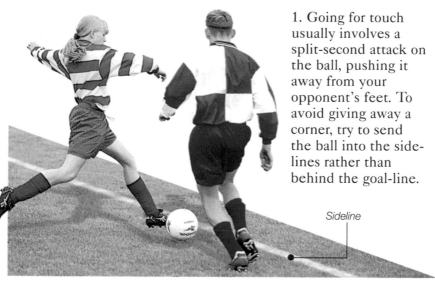

1. Going for touch usually involves a split-second attack on the ball, pushing it away from your opponent's feet. To avoid giving away a corner, try to send the ball into the side-lines rather than behind the goal-line.

Here, a throw-in gives defenders time.

Sideline

2. If you have played for touch, your whole team must make use of the time you have gained to run into a stronger position.

THE PENALTY AREA: GETTING INTO POSITION

In your penalty area, you should do everything you can to prevent a goal, but don't take any risks.

Keep a close guard on other attackers close to the penalty area.

Help your goalkeeper by listening to him carefully.

This player jockeys while other defenders get into position.

Position yourself to stop any shots, as this player is doing.

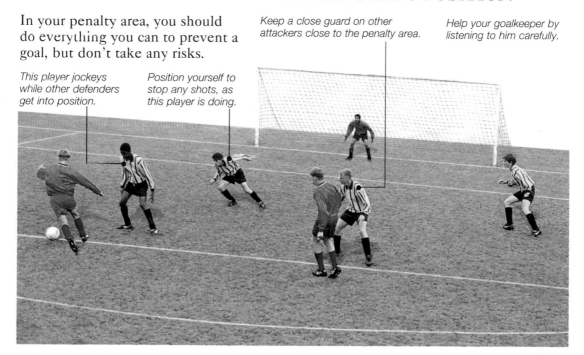

You should still try to delay your opponent for as long as possible.

Don't try to tackle the player with the ball unless you are sure of success.

Help the goalkeeper by getting into a position to block any shots at goal.

If you get a touch of the ball, use it to clear the ball out of danger (see page 110).

CLEARING THE BALL

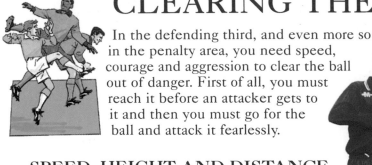

In the defending third, and even more so in the penalty area, you need speed, courage and aggression to clear the ball out of danger. First of all, you must reach it before an attacker gets to it and then you must go for the ball and attack it fearlessly.

SPEED, HEIGHT AND DISTANCE

Volleys are good for sending the ball high.

You must get to the ball quickly. When you get to it, aim for the wings. Attackers are more likely to come up the centre of the field.

Send the ball as high as you can. This gives your team time to get into position, even if it doesn't go very far.

It is even better to send the ball high and a long way. Use a powerful kick such as a lofted drive to get height and distance.

DEFENSIVE HEADERS

As for any header, keep your mouth shut and your eyes open.

Take the ball as early as possible. This will automatically send your header higher and further.

Brace your legs and take off on one leg, springing at the ball and arching your back in the air.

Aim to hit the ball from underneath so that your forehead sends it high over attackers' heads.

If you need to, turn your head as you make contact to send the ball away from the penalty area.

CLASHES IN THE AIR

The penalty area is often crowded, so clashes with attackers in the air are bound to happen. Success in this situation requires courage and dominance, so take the initiative. Attacking the ball aggressively actually gives you greater control.

Communicate with your goalkeeper and team-mates to avoid clashing with them as well as with attackers.

Timing is crucial. Try to jump before the attacker. He may then push you up further from underneath.

Be careful not to give away a free kick. Don't push the attacker with your arms.

CLEARANCE PRACTICE

This practice is best for seven players in the positions shown, but you can vary it. The two Ws stand on either side of the penalty area and everyone else in the goalmouth.

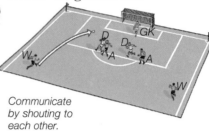

Communicate by shouting to each other.

One of the Ws sends a high pass into the goalmouth. The GK and Ds have to communicate quickly and decide who will go for it.

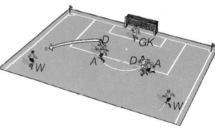

If a D gets to the ball, he should try to direct it out to a W with a header, lofted drive or volley. If an A gets to the ball, he tries to shoot.

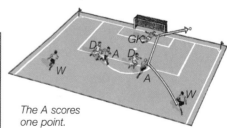

The A scores one point.

Whoever gets the ball first scores a point. Ds score two for getting the ball out of the penalty area, As two for scoring. Swap roles after five passes.

STAR HEADER

When you watch professional players, see how they approach the ball in the penalty area. You will see that they are never afraid to leap into the air and go for the ball, and they are not afraid of making physical contact with other players.

Here, Spanish midfielder 'Felipe' Minambres leaps for the ball in a match against Korea.

SUPPORT PLAY

Individual defending skills are very important, but in order to win matches you must also work well as a team. While one player challenges for the ball, everyone else should try to stop other attackers from getting into a strong position.

Here, one player challenges while the others close down on opponents.

CLOSING DOWN SPACE

Your opponents will try to spread the game out and make holes in your defence by running into space. 'Closing down space' means moving to cover attackers who are free, while one or two players move in to cover the player with the ball.

Direction of goal

Everyone should run into a goal-side position. Make sure you cover all the players who are likely to receive a pass.

Try to move up the field together. Working well with each other makes it much harder for attackers to find space in between you.

The result should be that the attackers' route is blocked, and that they have nowhere to pass the ball.

COVERING A CHALLENGE

If you are close to a player challenging for the ball, you must give him all the help you can to stop the attack. If the attacker gets past him, you should be ready to take up the challenge. Here, you can see a two-on-two situation where two defenders mark two attackers.

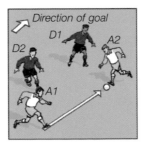

As one attacker (A1) passes to the other (A2), one defender (D1) moves in to challenge him.

The other defender (D2) moves back at an angle so that he can still keep an eye on A1.

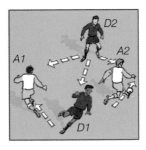

D1 now has cover behind him if he loses the challenge, but A1 is still being marked by D2.

MARKING

Good marking is one of the keys to a solid defence. When and who you mark may depend on your marking system (see pages 114-115) but the basic principles stay the same.

This player is in a position to see the ball and his opponent.

Direction of goal

You need to be goal-side and at the correct angle from your opponent so that you can watch him and the game at the same time.

This player cannot see the ball.

If you mark directly behind your opponent, you may block your own view of the game. It is also difficult to intercept any passes to him.

This attacker manages to get around the defence.

If you turn to watch the ball without keeping an eye on the player you are marking, he may be able to sneak around you.

JUDGING YOUR DISTANCE

To judge the right distance to keep, work out how fast your opponent is. Do this by watching him carefully at the start of the game. If he is slower than you, stay quite close to him. You may be able to intercept passes coming his way.

By marking tightly, this defender can dash round the attacker.

If your opponent is faster than you, stay at about arm's length from him. If you get too close, he may be able to dodge around you when he receives the ball.

This defender is ready to challenge.

MARKING SYSTEMS

A marking system is a way of organising your team so that everyone knows who should be covering which attacker. These are the systems used most often, which can be adapted to fit the strengths and weaknesses of your team.

MAN-TO-MAN MARKING

When your team marks man-to-man, a specific defender marks each of the attackers from the other team. They watch this attacker throughout the game and stay goal-side of him whenever necessary.

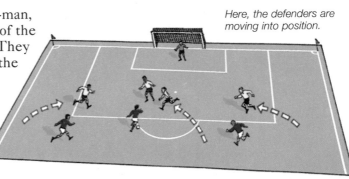

Here, the defenders are moving into position.

Playing man-to-man works well in the defending third, as long as you have some spare defenders to put the attackers under pressure. Never let just one player mark the opponent who has the ball.

As the play moves across the pitch towards the penalty area, the marking defenders stay with the same player, keeping goal-side and marking tightly. This makes it difficult for the attackers to shoot.

ZONAL MARKING

In zonal marking, you are responsible for an area or zone instead of one player. This area depends on the position you are playing, but not too strictly. As you move up and down the pitch, your area moves with

you. Usually, you mark anyone who comes within 5-10m (16-33ft) of you.

In this example of how the zonal system works, an attacker (A) moves across the defence.

D1 covers the player until he moves out of his area, when D2 covers him instead.

The advantage of this is that D1 has not left a big space behind him for attackers to fill.

MIXING SYSTEMS

Many professional teams don't work with just one system. Often, they mix different systems to make the most of their skills. This takes a lot of discipline and organization to put into practice effectively.

When one player in the other team is very skilful, one defender might mark him man-to-man while the others mark zonally, as this picture shows.

One defender marks this fast winger closely, while the other defenders mark zonally.

Some teams play zonally in the attacking third and midfield, then use a man-to-man system in defence.

You can also mark different players at different times as a looser man-to-man system.

USING A SWEEPER

Whichever system you use, it is too risky to allow a one-on-one situation to develop in the defending third. To stop this from happening, you can use a 'sweeper', who doesn't mark anyone (see pages 116-117). He stays at the back and 'sweeps up' attackers who get past the main defence.

FINDING THE BEST SYSTEM

There is no 'best system' which works for every team in every situation. These are the factors which are important.

★ Whatever system you use, the whole team must fully understand it. Each player must know exactly what he is supposed to do.

★ Try to find out about your opponents and about their strengths and weaknesses. If they have some good players, make sure they are well marked.

★ Think about the skills of your own team – for example, you might put a row of strong players to mark zonally at the back, and you wouldn't place a weak player man-to-man against a strong opponent.

This sweeper gets into a good position to challenge an attacker who has broken through the defence.

Direction of goal

TEAM FORMATIONS

Along with a marking system, each professional team has a formation. A formation is almost like a map of the positions that the players stick to during the game. It can be different each time a team plays, though teams often use the one they feel most confident with.

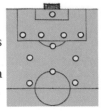

HOW IS A FORMATION BUILT?

A strong formation always has a strong defence. A team is usually built up solidly with a strong group of defenders at the back for the attackers to rely upon. The idea is that if the other team can't score, they can't win. This way of thinking, however, can lead to play that is too defensive and to games which end in a draw. To win, teams also need to give the midfield and attackers support and freedom to push forward and score, so modern formations are designed for this as well.

FOUR-FOUR-TWO

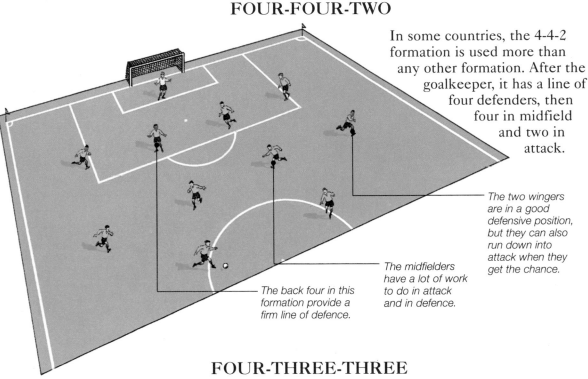

In some countries, the 4-4-2 formation is used more than any other formation. After the goalkeeper, it has a line of four defenders, then four in midfield and two in attack.

The two wingers are in a good defensive position, but they can also run down into attack when they get the chance.

The midfielders have a lot of work to do in attack and in defence.

The back four in this formation provide a firm line of defence.

FOUR-THREE-THREE

This formation is similar to the 4-4-2 formation. It has a goalkeeper, four defenders, three midfielders and three attackers. The advantage of this is that there is more emphasis on attack, but the problem can be that the midfield is not strong enough to push the ball forward in the first place.

Having less midfielders makes the defence weaker.

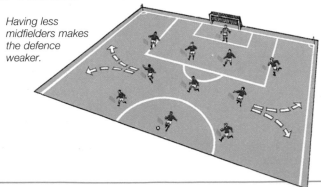

THE SWEEPER FORMATION

Using a sweeper changes a formation at the back. Traditionally, the system is based on a five-man defence. The usual line of four is backed up by a 'spare' man or sweeper.

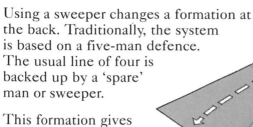

This formation gives a very secure defence. However, with so many players at the back, a team using it may find it difficult to attack.

Another version has more players in attack. It uses the usual back four, but one player drops back when necessary to play sweeper.

Direction of goal

There are rarely more than three attackers in an opposing team, so the sweeper is still a 'spare' player.

OTHER FORMATIONS

There are many other combinations which teams can try. This is an example. It is based on the 4-4-2 formation, but it is a lot more flexible.

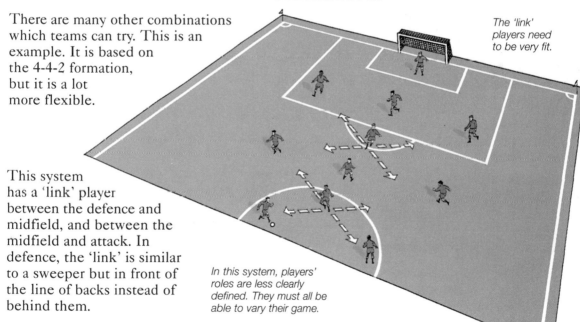

The 'link' players need to be very fit.

This system has a 'link' player between the defence and midfield, and between the midfield and attack. In defence, the 'link' is similar to a sweeper but in front of the line of backs instead of behind them.

In this system, players' roles are less clearly defined. They must all be able to vary their game.

WHICH IS BEST?

Each formation has its advantages and teams tend to get used to playing in one way. Many European teams, for example, use a sweeper. The following factors make a difference when you are deciding which to use.

★ Don't try to fit players to a formation which doesn't suit them. Choose one which suits their skills.
★ If you use a very traditional formation, your game may be too easy for your opponents to read.

★ If you use a new, flexible formation, you must all be able to read the game well, and you must also be very fit.
★ Make sure you have a strong defence. If it is weak, you may lose even if your attackers are good.

THE OFFSIDE RULE

The offside rule can sometimes be very useful for defenders, as attackers who are caught in this position have an indirect free kick awarded against them. Here you can find out about how the rule works and the best way for defenders to use it.

OFFSIDE

To be penalized for offside, an attacker must be in your half of the pitch and there must be fewer than two defenders between him and the goal-line. One of these defenders can be the goalkeeper. It is not always illegal to be offside, but it is in any of these cases:

1. A player can only be called offside when the ball is played, not when it is received.

2. Offside should be called if a player's offside position gives him an advantage, for example a chance to shoot.

3. If a player is offside and obstructs a defender to stop him from reaching the ball, he should be penalized.

LEGAL POSITIONS

An attacker will not be penalized for offside in any of these situations:

1. If one of the last defenders is level with him when the ball is passed. To be offside he must be closer to the goal-line.

2. If he receives the ball directly from a goal-kick, corner or throw-in. If he receives it indirectly, he is offside.

3. If he runs into an offside position after the ball has been played, or if he dribbles into an offside position.

4. If he is offside, but not interfering with play at all – for example, if he is on the other side of the pitch or if he is lying injured.

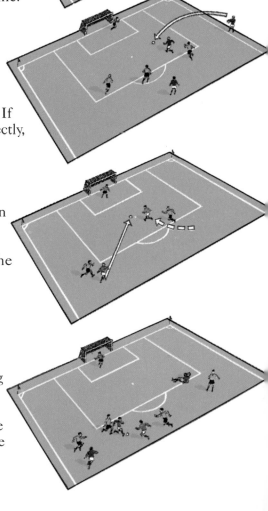

USING OFFSIDE IN DEFENCE

You may see professional defenders trying to place an attacker offside by moving up the pitch together, just at the point when another attacker passes to him. Here you can see how this 'trap' works.

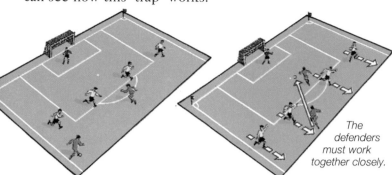

The defenders must work together closely.

The back line of defenders see that an attacker is about to receive a pass.

They all move up the pitch just before or just as the pass is made.

DISADVANTAGES OF USING OFFSIDE

A big problem with using offside is that you depend upon the referee. If he does not call offside, you leave your defence in a very weak position. Also, the trap may not work. If an attacker manages to dribble past you instead of passing, he can go straight for goal.

OFFSIDE QUIZ

Which of these situations show a player in an offside position? Think carefully before you decide. The answers are on page 258.

1.

2.

3.

4.

This attacker fools the defence by dribbling past them instead of passing.

The defenders expect the ball to be passed to this player.

The defenders have all moved up, so it will be difficult for them to help the goalkeeper defend against the attacker.

DEFENSIVE POSITIONS

Some particular positions, such as centre half and
full back, are more defensive than others, and
require special skills. Here you can find out
about the skills needed by players in the
midfield and at the back.

PLAYING CENTRE HALF

The centre half's number
one job is to stop the
other team from scoring.
★ You mustn't be afraid
to challenge for the ball
and tackle. It helps if you
are strong.
★ You need to be able to
head the ball well.
★ You need to read the
game from the back and
communicate well with
your team-mates.
★ If you move forward
when your team attacks,
you must be able to
move goal-side
quickly if your
opponents
counter-
attack.

*Main area of
responsibility:*

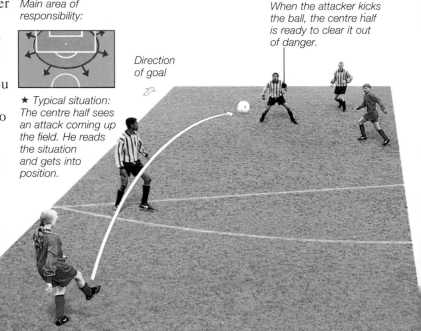

*Direction
of goal*

★ *Typical situation:
The centre half sees
an attack coming up
the field. He reads
the situation
and gets into
position.*

*When the attacker kicks
the ball, the centre half
is ready to clear it out
of danger.*

PLAYING SWEEPER

In some formations, a
centre half drops back to
play sweeper (see page
117), so the skills needed
are similar. These are
the main differences:
★ You have to cover the
whole of the area behind
the back four, so you
must be quick and agile.
★ You must be an even
better judge of the
game, as you are further
back than a centre half
and in a position to spot
any danger.

*Main area of
responsibility:*

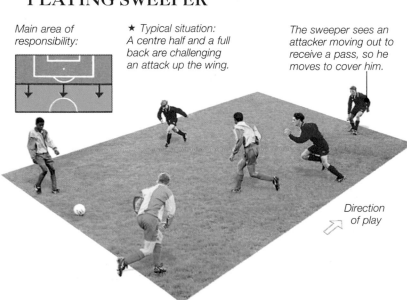

★ *Typical situation:
A centre half and a full
back are challenging
an attack up the wing.*

*The sweeper sees an
attacker moving out to
receive a pass, so he
moves to cover him.*

*Direction
of play*

PLAYING FULL BACK

A full back plays in defence, but on the wing. This is a varied role. You need lots of different skills to play it well.

★ Like a centre half, you need to be aggressive and strong to clear the ball out of danger.

★ Because you are on the wing, you need to be fast, fit and able to make runs up and down the pitch to support the attack as well as the defence.

★ You need to be good at jockeying attackers on the wing to give other defenders time to get into position.

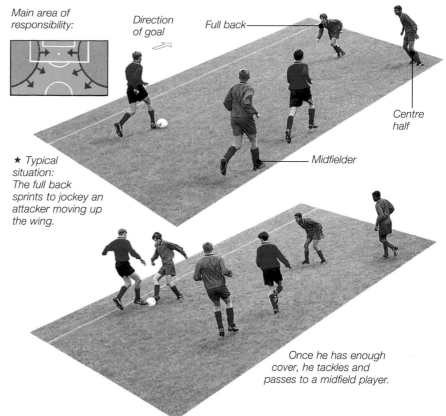

Main area of responsibility:

Direction of goal

Full back

Centre half

Midfielder

★ *Typical situation: The full back sprints to jockey an attacker moving up the wing.*

Once he has enough cover, he tackles and passes to a midfield player.

PLAYING IN MIDFIELD

Midfield players need to be all-rounders. They have to support the defence when needed, but they must also be good in attack. 'Anchors' and 'wing backs' are two kinds of midfielder with particular roles in defence.

Main area of responsibility for wing backs:

★ *Typical situation: The wing back works with a full back in the early stages of an attack.*

Together they close down space around the attacker.

Main area of responsibility for anchor:

★ *Typical situation: the anchor takes on a midfield challenge while the defenders run back into position.*

The 'anchor' links the backs and midfield players.
★ You must be able to jockey, challenge and attack.

★ You must be able to read the game in front and behind you and give support wherever it is needed.

Wing backs help challenge attacks on the wing.
★ You must be good at covering for defenders and giving support.
★ You must be fit and fast and be a good dribbler.

DEFENDING AT CORNERS

Corners are one of the most dangerous situations for a defending team. Your opponents have quite a high chance of scoring, so you need to be clear about what each player is going to do and be very disciplined in carrying out your tactics.

KEY POSITIONS

Think about what your opponents might try. Some moves are often used. One is swinging the ball in close to the near post, and another is swinging it out for a key attacker to head at goal. Prepare by placing your best players in the danger areas.

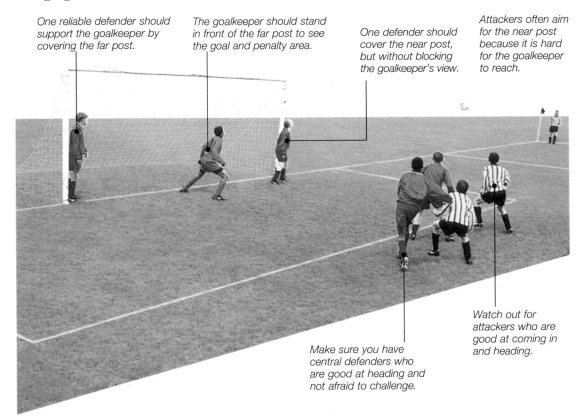

One reliable defender should support the goalkeeper by covering the far post.

The goalkeeper should stand in front of the far post to see the goal and penalty area.

One defender should cover the near post, but without blocking the goalkeeper's view.

Attackers often aim for the near post because it is hard for the goalkeeper to reach.

Make sure you have central defenders who are good at heading and not afraid to challenge.

Watch out for attackers who are good at coming in and heading.

CORNER RULES

There are two main rules which make a difference to defending at corners:
★ Remember that an attacker cannot be offside from a direct corner kick.
★ All defenders have to keep a distance of 9m (30ft) from the player taking the corner.

HELPING THE GOALKEEPER

The goalkeeper is usually in charge of the goal area at corners, so listen out for his instructions and don't block his view. This is very important around the near post and goal area.

Here, Belgian goalkeeper Michel Preud'homme reaches for the ball in a match against Morocco.

COVERING SHORT CORNERS

If you see an attacker moving out towards the player taking the corner, your opponents may try a short corner. By making a short pass to another attacker they get a different angle of approach to goal, and they also hope to take your team by surprise.

Two of you can stop this attack by moving forward. Remember the 9m (30ft) rule. You need two players because the player taking the corner will move out as soon as he has done so.

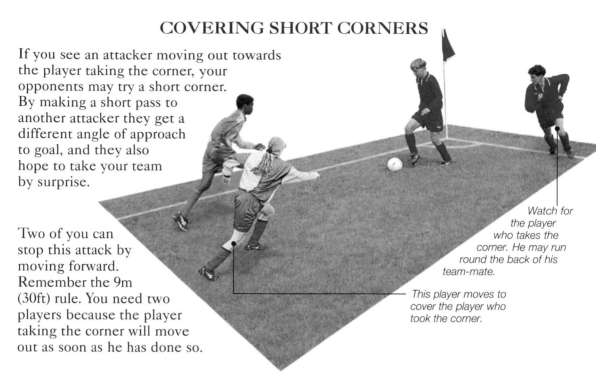

Watch for the player who takes the corner. He may run round the back of his team-mate.

This player moves to cover the player who took the corner.

FILLING IN THE GAPS

Once the key positions are covered, the rest of you must make sure there are no other holes. How you do this will depend on which marking system you use.

If you are marking zonally, the team spreads out evenly over the penalty area. Each player should cover the area in front of him.

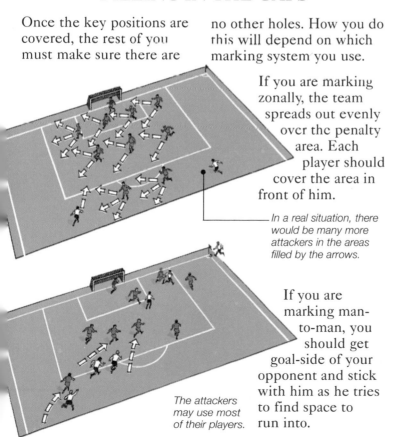

In a real situation, there would be many more attackers in the areas filled by the arrows.

If you are marking man-to-man, you should get goal-side of your opponent and stick with him as he tries to find space to run into.

The attackers may use most of their players.

ATTACKING THE BALL

When you are all in place and the corner is taken, you must all stay alert and make sure you are first to the ball to get it out of danger. As long as you challenge fairly, you don't need to worry about bumping into other players.

Here, Gareth Southgate and Paul Ince, playing in the England team, challenge for the ball together in a match against Switzerland.

FREE KICKS AND THROW-INS

Any dead ball situation that is awarded against you gives your opponents an advantage. Having gained possession, they will try to create good shooting opportunities, especially in your defending third. You need to keep alert and disciplined.

As the throw is taken, defenders move into goal-side positions.

DEFENDING AT THROW-INS

This player is not offside. A player cannot be offside from a direct throw-in.

Your opponents will take the throw-in as quickly as they can, so don't lose concentration and don't stop moving. Use the time to move into a stronger goal-side position.

Mark any player who is likely to receive the throw. Someone should mark the thrower so that he can't run into space after the throw.

Beware of long throws in the defending third. Treat them like corners (see page 122).

INDIRECT FREE KICKS

When an indirect free kick is awarded against you, you must go back 9m (30ft) from the ball. Your opponents cannot shoot directly at goal - another player has to touch the ball first. This means that as soon as the kick is taken, you can move in to close down the gap before an opponent shoots.

In or near the penalty area you can form a wall (see opposite). Be ready to move very quickly.

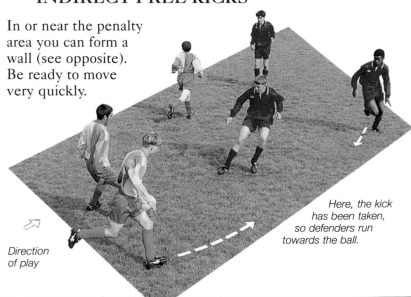

Direction of play

Here, the kick has been taken, so defenders run towards the ball.

DIRECT FREE KICKS

A direct free kick allows opponents a direct shot at goal. In your defensive third, you need a defensive wall to block the shot. This should cover as much of the goal as possible without blocking the goalkeeper's view, and must be 9m (30ft) from the kick. You should also move plenty of other players into the penalty area.

BUILDING A WALL

Watch the ball by lifting your eyes, not your head.

You must form the wall quickly.

Line up in order of height. The tallest player stands in front of the post furthest from the goalkeeper.

Everyone in the wall should stand very close to the player next to him so that there aren't any gaps.

Protect your head by tucking it down on your chest, and place your hands over your genitals.

CENTRAL KICKS

If the kick is in front of the goal, you will need up to five players in the wall. Line up so that the goalkeeper has a view of the ball.

Other players should mark attackers man-to-man, but also keep a good view of the ball.

The wall must hold firm as the kick is taken, then move quickly to follow up any rebounds.

KICKS FROM THE SIDE

If the kick is to the side of the goal, it is more likely that the kicker will try to cross the ball to another attacker.

Here, you only need two or three players in the wall. The rest of you should spread out.

As soon as the kick is taken, everyone must move towards the ball quickly to clear it out of danger.

DEFENCE INTO ATTACK

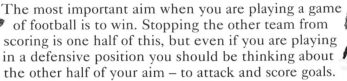

The most important aim when you are playing a game of football is to win. Stopping the other team from scoring is one half of this, but even if you are playing in a defensive position you should be thinking about the other half of your aim – to attack and score goals.

GETTING AN OVERVIEW

Your overall attitude when you are in defence is essential for your success. If your team falls apart as soon as you lose possession, the other team will probably win. Always believe that you can win the ball back, and be ready to attack again.

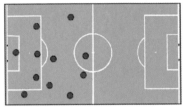
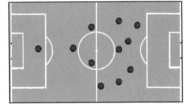

1. This team is in a weak position. It is spread out, leaving lots of holes. This makes it difficult to work together and push forward.

2. This team is in a much stronger position. Although it is in its defending third, the team can communicate and send the ball forward.

3. This team is in a strong position, too. Although there is a lot of space behind the defence, the attackers will find it hard to move into it.

DEFENDING FROM THE BACK

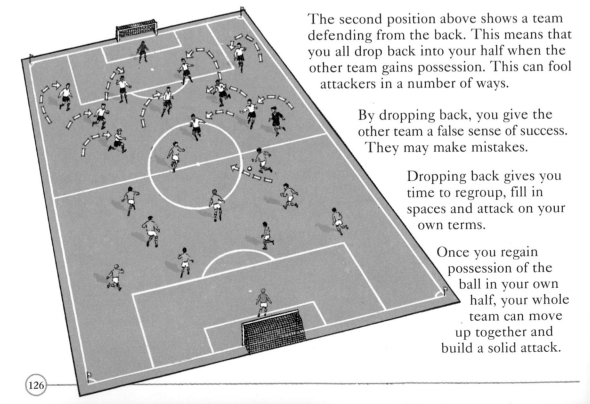

The second position above shows a team defending from the back. This means that you all drop back into your half when the other team gains possession. This can fool attackers in a number of ways.

By dropping back, you give the other team a false sense of success. They may make mistakes.

Dropping back gives you time to regroup, fill in spaces and attack on your own terms.

Once you regain possession of the ball in your own half, your whole team can move up together and build a solid attack.

DEFENDING FROM THE FRONT

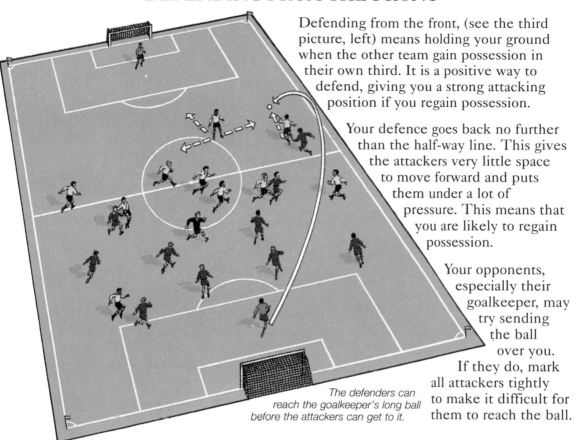

Defending from the front, (see the third picture, left) means holding your ground when the other team gain possession in their own third. It is a positive way to defend, giving you a strong attacking position if you regain possession.

Your defence goes back no further than the half-way line. This gives the attackers very little space to move forward and puts them under a lot of pressure. This means that you are likely to regain possession.

Your opponents, especially their goalkeeper, may try sending the ball over you. If they do, mark all attackers tightly to make it difficult for them to reach the ball.

The defenders can reach the goalkeeper's long ball before the attackers can get to it.

SUMMARY AND REMINDER TIPS

★ Always stay in a goal-side position from your opponent.

★ Delay your opponents as much as you can by jockeying.

★ Watch your man when you are marking. Don't let yourself be distracted.

★ When challenging for the ball, put your whole body into it.

★ Learn to clear the ball with strong headers and lofted drives.

★ Play wisely in your defending third. Don't take silly risks.

★ Concentrate when the ball goes out of play. Use the time to get into position.

★ As a team, close down the space and options open to opponents.

★ Make sure you understand your team formation and your position in it.

★ Above all, think positively and keep working as a team, so that when you gain possession you are in a strong position to launch an attack.

WORLD SOCCER QUIZ

48. Which country was successful in its bid to host the 1998 World Cup?

a. Russia
b. Brazil
c. France

49. In 1958, Brazilian legend Pele became the youngest player ever to play in a World Cup Final. How old was he?

a. 16
b. 17
c. 19

50. Why was Argentinian star Diego Maradona banned from the 1994 World Cup?

a. He used his hands to score a goal
b. He hit a referee
c. He failed a dope test

51. What colour kit do the Brazilian national team usually play in?

a. Yellow shirts, blue shorts
b. White shirts, blue shorts
c. Yellow shirts, yellow shorts

52. In 1958, French striker Just Fontaine set a new record for the most goals in a World Cup tournament. How many did he score?

a. 6
b. 13
c. 10

53. Which English player scored the only ever hat trick in a World Cup Final?

a. Geoff Hurst
b. Bobby Charlton
c. Nobby Stiles

54. Which World Cup had a smiling green chilli pepper called 'Pique' as its official mascot?

a. 1982, Spain
b. 1986, Mexico
c. 1990, Italy

55. Who beat Brazil in the 1996 Olympics to win the gold medal?

a. Nigeria
b. France
c. Argentina

56. Which of these countries won the 1996 European Championship?

a. Czech Republic
b. Germany
c. France

57. Who captained the winning team in the 1994 World Cup tournament?

a. Romario
b. Dunga
c. Bebeto

58. How often is the Copa America (South American Championship) held?

a. Every two years
b. Every four years
c. Every five years

59. In what way did the Pontiac Silverdome, a stadium used in the USA 1994 World Cup, make World Cup history?

a. It was the first World Cup venue with a capacity of over 100,000
b. It was the first World Cup venue with an artificial pitch surface
c. It was the first stadium to stage a World Cup match indoors

60. Which country won Gold in the first ever Women's Olympic Soccer Tournament in 1996?

a. Germany
b. Japan
c. USA

61. From which year were both the host nation and the World Cup holders allowed to qualify automatically for the World Cup Finals?

a. 1934
b. 1938
c. 1958

62. In a 1982 first round match, France scored a goal when the Kuwaiti team had stopped playing. Why had they stopped?

a. They thought they heard the referee's whistle
b. One of their team had broken his leg
c. They were protesting at one of the referee's decisions

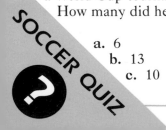

SOCCER QUIZ

PART FIVE
ATTACKING

CONTENTS

INTO ATTACK

To win a soccer match, you need to score goals – and to score goals, you need to attack. Whenever your team has the ball, your team should be looking for ways to attack your opponents' goal, set up a chance to shoot, and score. This part of the book looks at the individual and team skills you will need to do this successfully.

WHAT MAKES A GOOD ATTACKER?

Intelligence
An attacker's top priority is to spot any defensive weaknesses, and make intelligent choices to exploit them.

Fitness and confidence
A player with stamina, pace and a real belief in himself can put the defence under constant pressure.

Control
To make sure his team keeps possession in an attack, a player needs to move confidently with the ball, and pass accurately.

Team spirit
Solo skills alone won't win matches. A good attacker is always thinking of how he can work well with his team-mates.

Cunning
A predictable attack is easy to defend against. An attacker must disguise his intentions, and vary his approach.

Determination
The 'will to win' is crucial for good attacking play. The best attackers play fairly, but are very competitive.

FIT FOR ATTACK

Professional soccer players train regularly so that they have the skills and fitness they need to play well throughout the 90 minutes of a match. They combine this with a healthy diet, as both diet and exercise are important for staying fit.

Here, the players in blue tracksuits are using long track runs in training to build up their stamina.

The red players are using special sprinting routines, called 'shuttle runs', to improve their pace.

STAGES OF ATTACK

An attack begins when your team wins possession. This part of the book looks at the stages of attack which follow.

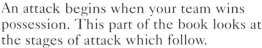

1. You need to move the ball upfield into the 'attacking third' (the final third of the pitch). Pages 132-141 cover this first stage, known as the 'build-up'.

The final pass is often known as the 'assist'.

2. For your team to score, you need to get the ball to a player who is in a good position to shoot. Pages 142-149 look at the skills involved in this second stage of an attack.

3. The picture below shows the final stage of attack – the shot at goal, or 'finish'. Pages 150-155 cover shooting techniques and tactics.

'SMALL-SIDED' TEAM PRACTICE

Understanding theories about how to attack is important, but only if you back up what you have learned with regular team practice.

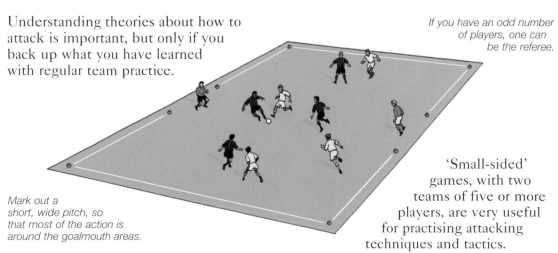

If you have an odd number of players, one can be the referee.

Mark out a short, wide pitch, so that most of the action is around the goalmouth areas.

'Small-sided' games, with two teams of five or more players, are very useful for practising attacking techniques and tactics.

RUNNING OFF THE BALL

Each player has only a few minutes of possession during the course of a match. You spend the rest of the time playing without, or 'off' the ball. Success in attack therefore depends on how good you and your team-mates are at running off the ball to find good positions on the pitch.

FINDING SPACE IN A GOOD POSITION

When your team is attacking, try to move into a position on the pitch where you can receive a pass, and where you will pose a threat to the other team's defence once you have the ball.

Try to find space upfield, so that by receiving a pass you move play towards goal.

If your team-mate can't pass straight upfield, move so he can reach you with an angled pass.

LOSING YOUR MARKER

As you move off the ball, one of your opponents will try to stay close to you to prevent you from receiving the ball. He is your 'marker'. Finding a good position is pointless if he is close enough to intercept a pass, so use a sudden change of direction to get away from him.

Draw your marker away from the area you want to run into, by moving off in the opposite direction first.

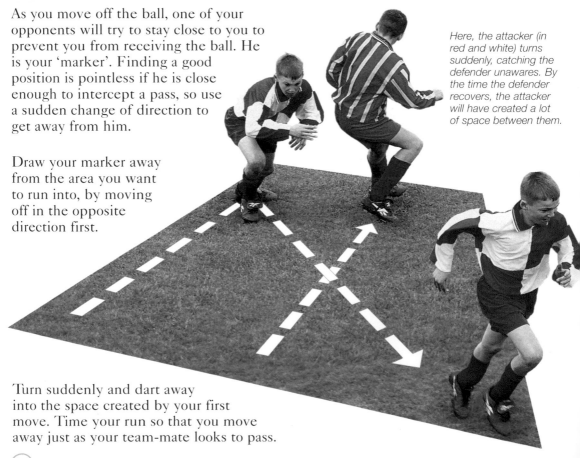

Here, the attacker (in red and white) turns suddenly, catching the defender unawares. By the time the defender recovers, the attacker will have created a lot of space between them.

Turn suddenly and dart away into the space created by your first move. Time your run so that you move away just as your team-mate looks to pass.

'PASS AND RUN' PLAY

Here, this defender begins to follow the pass.

If you've just passed the ball, don't stop and relax. Your marker will often follow your pass, giving you an immediate chance to dart away from him.

Free of his marker, the attacker who passed can move into space.

Move into space as soon as you've released the ball. This 'pass and run' play, also known as 'give and go' play, is one key to successful attack.

DIAGONAL RUNS

Even if you don't receive the ball yourself, running off the ball can draw your marker away to create space for a team-mate. A diagonal run upfield is especially good for pulling defenders out of position.

Above, player A makes a diagonal run. His marker follows him, leaving space for B to collect the ball (below).

STAYING ONSIDE

You can't receive a pass if you are 'offside'. You are offside if you are nearer your opponent's goal-line than the ball when it is passed to you, unless two or more of your opponents are at least as close to their goal-line. You can't be offside in your own half of the pitch.

If you're caught offside, the referee will give the other team a free kick.

When you're running off the ball in attack, make sure you don't take up an offside position. You'll find out more about how to stay onside on page 142.

BASIC MOVES

To move play into the attacking third, you need to combine intelligent running off the ball with controlled, accurate passing. These pages introduce some simple passing moves that you can use to push play upfield past your opponents.

MAKING A BLINDSIDE RUN

One good way of finding space upfield is to make a run behind an opponent's back, outside his field of view. This is known as making a blindside run.

Here, the blue player is concentrating on watching the red player on the ball.

This red player makes a blindside run behind the defender to receive a pass.

Above, a blindside run forms the second part of a 'pass and run' attacking move. Player A passes to player B. As the yellow player moves in to challenge B, A makes a run around his blindside. Player B hits a return pass upfield into A's path.

BEATING BALL-WATCHERS

Try to catch defenders 'ball-watching'. This means paying too much attention to play elsewhere on the pitch, instead of to their own positions. Grab your chance to make a blindside run into a good position.

Here, the green player takes advantage of his marker's lapse of concentration, making a blindside run behind him.

OVERLAPPING

Doing an 'overlap run' means running past a team-mate on the ball and into space upfield, so that he can pass the ball back up to you. A simple overlap move, like the one shown here, is a particularly good way of pushing the attack upfield along one of the wings.

Here, player A passes to his team-mate and follows his pass, overlapping to receive a return ball.

WALL PASSES

A wall pass, or 'one-two', is a great way of getting past a player. To do this, dribble straight at your opponent. Just before he challenges you, send a sideways pass to a team-mate. Your opponent will turn to follow the play, giving you a chance to sprint past him. Your team-mate acts as the wall, knocking the ball back into your path.

★ Don't pass the ball too soon or your opponent will be able to drop back and block the move.

★ The wall player needs to move into position at the very last moment, so that he loses his marker.

★ Make sure both passes are fast enough to beat the defender, but not too difficult for the receiver to control.

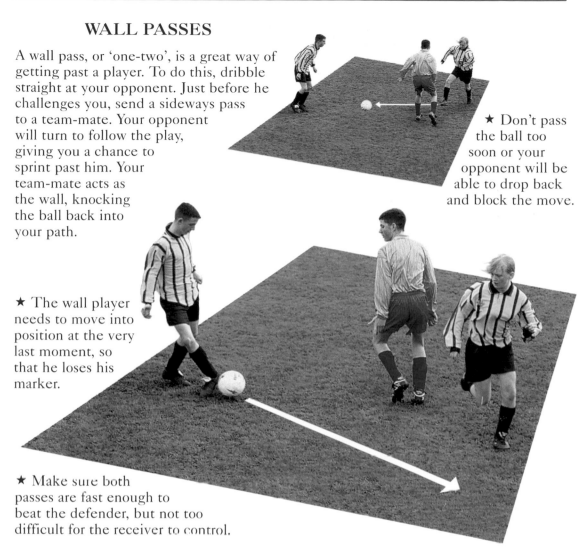

WALL PASS GAME

Mark out an area 24 x 6m (80 x 20ft) and divide it into four equal 'zones'. Five attackers and four defenders take up starting positions as shown.

The player with the ball tries to take it from one end to the other. He can dribble past a defender, or use a wall pass. He scores a point for each zone he crosses.

Change around so that each player has a go at being the dribbler and a wall player.

Use sports markers, bags or sweaters to mark out the game area.

BUILDING AN ATTACK

Good attacking play needs team co-ordination and co-operation, as well as individual running and passing skills. To build an attack, you and your team-mates need to work together to make the most of the space available on the pitch, and to keep the defence guessing.

GIVING AN ATTACK WIDTH

If all your attacking players gather around the player on the ball, so that they are clustered together in one area of the pitch, your attack will be easy to defend against.

Spread out across the pitch, so that your opponents are forced to defend across its whole width. By passing across the pitch, you can quickly change the path of attack.

WING ATTACKS

Your opponents will try to protect the central area of their defensive third, in front of their goal. You can often push upfield into attack more easily by passing the ball to a team-mate on the wing, where there is more space.

Here, Steve McManaman (Liverpool) beats his opponent on the wing.

GIVING AN ATTACK DEPTH

If your players form a flat line across the pitch, they have few passing options, and very little chance of breaking past the defence. Try to stagger your players, so you can use diagonal passing up and downfield to give your attack depth and flexibility.

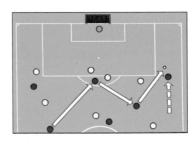

Below, the zigzag spacing of the blue attackers gives their attack depth.

Make sure you stay onside as you push upfield.

USING A CROSS-OVER MOVE

A cross-over move is when you and a team-mate run past each other to confuse your opponents.

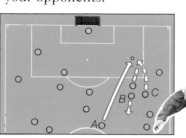

Above, player A looks to pass. B drops back as though to receive the ball, taking his marker with him. Player C 'crosses over' with B, and runs past him to receive the pass from A.

A cross-over move can be played with or without the ball. To play one with the ball, dribble across the pitch towards a team-mate who is running in the opposite direction.

As your paths cross, flick the ball across into your team-mate's path. He can take advantage of the defenders' confusion, and the space behind them, to push upfield into attack.

A cross-over move like this is a great way to change the direction of attack suddenly.

As with a cross-over off the ball, the aim is to draw two defenders together to create space elsewhere on the pitch.

COMBINING SKILLS FOR TEAM ATTACK

This is an example of how a team can combine good positioning, intelligent runs off the ball and accurate passing to build an attack and create a chance to score. The move starts with player A on the ball, moving up from midfield.

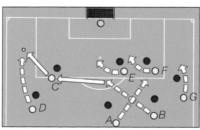

A and B use a cross-over move to switch the attack to C. Player D makes an overlapping run onto a pass from C. E and F draw their markers left.

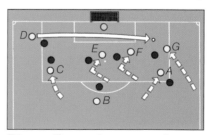

Player G runs into a good striking position, blindside of the defenders, to receive a long cross from D. The other players move up in support.

MOVING WITH THE BALL

If you have the ball and there is open space directly ahead, you can dribble upfield into attack rather than passing to a team-mate. For a solo run, you need good technique and confidence so that you can move quickly with the ball, changing pace and direction without losing control.

DRIBBLING TECHNIQUE

To keep the ball under close control as you move, use small, regular taps to push it gently forwards. Use different parts of your foot to steer the ball in the right direction. To improve your technique, mark out a slalom (a zigzag course) and dribble through it.

If you look down at the ball all the time as you dribble, you won't know where to direct your attack. If you and your team practise dribbling in a small area such as the centre circle, you can get used to looking up regularly to see where other players are.

Here, several players practise their dribbling within the centre circle.

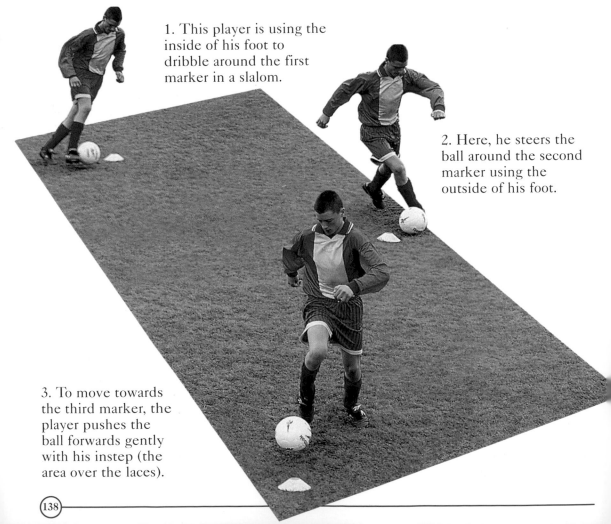

1. This player is using the inside of his foot to dribble around the first marker in a slalom.

2. Here, he steers the ball around the second marker using the outside of his foot.

3. To move towards the third marker, the player pushes the ball forwards gently with his instep (the area over the laces).

RUNNING WITH THE BALL

To attack at a fast pace, you need to move more quickly than a close dribbling technique allows. To run with the ball, use fewer touches, knocking it quite far ahead with each one, so that you can lengthen your stride and move faster.

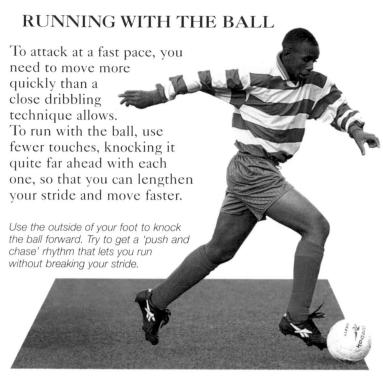

Use the outside of your foot to knock the ball forward. Try to get a 'push and chase' rhythm that lets you run without breaking your stride.

SOLO ATTACK

1. If a defender closes in on you, but you can see that there is a lot of space upfield behind him, knock the ball firmly past him.

2. Quickly sprint past your opponent to collect the ball, before he can turn to follow you. This is known as 'taking on' a defender.

Once you're past the defender, push upfield into space.

If you win the ball when your opponents are on the attack, try to counter-attack before they can drop back to defend. You can use a solo run, at full stretch, to move upfield as quickly as possible.

DRIBBLE AND SPRINT RELAY

This game will improve your skills on the ball. You need two teams, with a ball for each team. Lay out two identical slaloms, about 20m (66ft) apart. The teams start by forming two rows between the slaloms, facing in opposite directions.

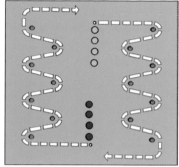

At the shout of 'Go!' the first player in each team starts a clockwise circuit with the ball, sprinting to the slalom on his right. He dribbles through the first slalom, and then sprints across towards the second.

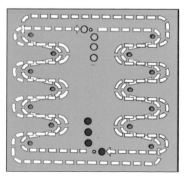

Next, he dribbles through the second slalom, and sprints back to his starting position. The next player takes the ball and begins his circuit. When one of the running players catches the other, his team wins.

POSITIONAL PLAY

To make the best use of the space on the pitch, professional teams play in a 'team formation'. This means that each of the ten outfield players takes up a particular position. These pages look at a typical '4-4-2' formation – four players in defence, four in midfield, and two in attack. You can also find out about how the roles of players in different positions contribute to the attack.

DEFENCE INTO ATTACK

The goalkeeper, centre backs and full backs are mainly responsible for defence. When they win the ball, though, they play an important attacking role by 'distributing' it upfield. This means making careful choices about where to pass the ball. Good distribution by defenders is vital if your team is to seize opportunities to counter-attack.

As a back, you can help to move the ball into attack by overlapping with midfield team-mates. Here, the red full back overlaps with the outside right.

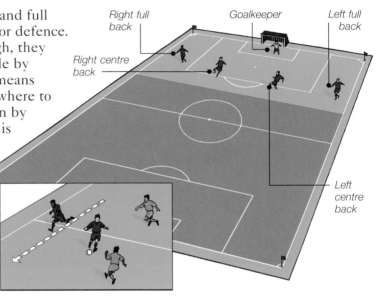

Right full back

Goalkeeper

Left full back

Right centre back

Left centre back

SKILLS IN MIDFIELD

Playing as a midfielder is all about moving the ball into a scoring position. You need to be able to create gaps in the defence by running off the ball, using intelligent and accurate passing to give an attack width and depth, and dribbling past defenders to threaten goal. You also need to shoot confidently whenever you get a chance.

The outside left and outside right, or 'wingers', need to perfect the skills of running with the ball and crossing it (see pages 144-147), so that they can attack along the wing.

Outside right (right winger)

Right midfield

Outside left (left winger)

Left midfield

PLAYING CENTRE FORWARD

The main role of a centre forward, or 'striker', is to score goals. To be a successful striker you need excellent shooting and heading techniques so that you can score in a variety of situations. These may be when you receive a through ball (see page 142), a cross (see page 144), or when you are on the run. You also need to work on finding space, and staying onside (see page 142).

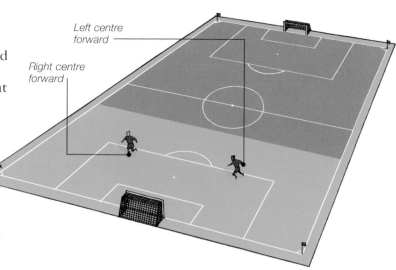

Left centre forward

Right centre forward

TARGET MAN

As centre forward, you play an important role as a 'target man'. This means that when one of your team-mates hits a long pass upfield to you, you are able to keep possession of the ball, 'holding it up' until your team-mates have moved up to support you.

Here, Gabriel Batistuta (Fiorentina) shields the ball, giving his team-mates time to move upfield.

TEAM TALK

Good positional play is only part of making the most of the pitch area. The other vital factor is good communication with your team-mates.

'Up the wing!'

If you're in a good position to receive a pass, call for the ball, or signal for it by raising your arm.

'Over!'

Shout if you think a team-mate should let the ball run on to you instead of playing it himself (see page 143).

'Man on!'

Warn your team-mate if you can see an opponent running in on his blindside to challenge him.

'And back!'

Talk your team-mates through a move. Here, the player calls for a return ball to complete a wall pass.

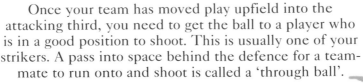

THE THROUGH BALL

Once your team has moved play upfield into the attacking third, you need to get the ball to a player who is in a good position to shoot. This is usually one of your strikers. A pass into space behind the defence for a team-mate to run onto and shoot is called a 'through ball'.

PLAYING A THROUGH BALL

A through ball requires good co-ordination between the passer and the receiver. If you pass the ball too late, the receiver will be caught offside. You also need to judge the weight of the pass. If it's too hard or too soft, a defender or the goalkeeper will be able to get to the ball first, and block your attack.

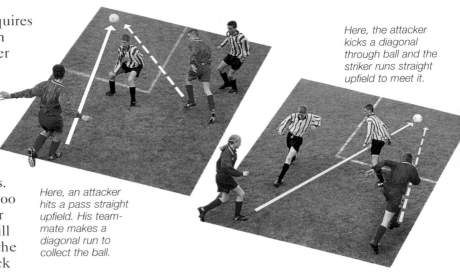

Here, an attacker hits a pass straight upfield. His team-mate makes a diagonal run to collect the ball.

Here, the attacker kicks a diagonal through ball and the striker runs straight upfield to meet it.

THE OFFSIDE TRAP

The other team may try to use a defensive tactic called the 'offside trap' to prevent your attack.

As an attacker prepares to play a through ball, the row of defenders rush forward together.

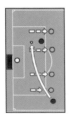

If they time the trap well, the defenders are likely to catch at least one of your players offside.

STAYING ONSIDE

If you're about to run onto a through ball, be alert in case the defence use the offside trap. Use these tactics to avoid being caught offside.

'Flatten' your run, and move across the pitch in line with the defenders until the moment your team-mate passes.

Make your run from midfield. Your team-mate then times his pass for when you draw level with the line of defenders.

If you play a through ball to yourself, you can't be offside. Knock the ball past defenders into space behind them, and sprint through to collect it (see page 139).

ONE TOUCH PLAY

When you receive the ball, you may see
a chance to play it through to a team-
mate. If so, try to use your first
touch to play your pass, rather
than taking time to control the
ball. This gives your attack
extra pace and surprise.

A wall pass (see page 135) on the
edge of the penalty area, like the one
shown here, is a great example of how you can
use 'one touch play' in attack to break past defenders.

USING YOUR IMAGINATION

The more varied your passing, the harder
it is for the other team to anticipate and
block your attack. Look out for inventive
ways to play the ball past the defence.

*Your team-mate shouts
'Over!' to tell you to let
the ball through.*

For a
'dummy', or
'over', make as though to
play the ball as it comes to you, but
then let it run on to a team-mate beyond you.

If a defender has his legs wide apart as he
jockeys, play a through ball between
them. This is known as nutmegging him.

To play a through ball in an unexpected
direction, use your heel to 'backheel' the
ball to a team-mate behind you.

CROSSING TECHNIQUE

If you've built an attack down the wing, you need to get the ball back across the front of the opposition goal to give a team-mate the chance to shoot. Sending a long pass from the wing to a player in the centre is known as crossing the ball. More than half of all the goals scored in open play come from crosses.

TARGET AREAS

The idea of a cross is to move the ball from the wing, where it is difficult to shoot or score from, into the 'danger area' behind the defence and in front of the goal.

You can use different lengths of cross to create different attacking moves. The three main areas to aim for, shown below, are called the near post, mid-goal and far post areas.

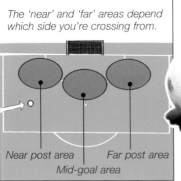

The 'near' and 'far' areas depend which side you're crossing from.

Near post area
Far post area
Mid-goal area

CROSSING TECHNIQUE

To hit a cross, you use the inside of your foot to strike through the lower half of the ball. Strike the ball slightly off-centre. This makes it spin, so that your cross swings into the target area.

Take a good backswing.

Get your non-kicking foot slightly behind and to the side of the ball.

Kick the lower half of the ball to make it rise.

Wrap your foot around the outside of the ball as you kick, to make it spin.

Swing your kicking leg across your body as you follow through.

GETTING IN YOUR CROSS

You need to be able to cross even if you are being jockeyed by an opponent.

Push the ball upfield along the wing, past the jockeying defender.

You don't need to beat the defender – just create enough space to hit a cross.

Quickly get your cross in before the defender has time to block the ball.

'CHECK-BACK' CROSS MOVE

A 'check-back' is when you stop the ball suddenly. Sprint down the wing as though you mean to cross with the foot nearest the touchline. Stop the ball, and drag it back downfield.

Your check-back will throw your marker. Hit a cross with your other foot, while he is off balance.

CROSSING DRILL

Place two markers as shown. Player A passes to player B, who dribbles along the wing. At the second marker, he crosses the ball to player C.

The players all move round one position, as shown, with player C taking the ball back to the first marker. The sequence then begins again.

★ Vary the position of player C to practise different lengths of cross.

★ Move the second marker for crosses nearer to, or further from, the goal-line.

★ Add a defender whose job is to prevent player B getting in his cross.

CROSSING MOVES

Scoring regularly from crosses takes more than just good technique on the part of the player crossing the ball. At least one team-mate in the penalty area has to find space to receive the ball and shoot. You can improve your chances of success by practising specific crossing moves.

RUNNING ONTO A CROSS

As you run in to receive a cross, make sure you stay onside. Don't get upfield of your team-mate with the ball, unless there are defenders between you and the goal.

As your team-mate crosses the ball, try to lose your marker (see page 132). Here, the striker runs as though to receive a long cross, then darts back to the near post area.

NEAR POST CROSSES

A cross to a player in the near post area gives him a good opportunity to head the ball down into the near side of the goal. If the goalkeeper is guarding the near post, the receiver can try glancing a header across into the far side of the goal.

To angle his header, the player flicks his head to the side as he makes contact with the ball.

USING A FLICK-ON HEADER

If you can't get a clear header at goal yourself, you may be able to flick the ball on to a team-mate who is in a better position to shoot.

For a flick-on header, use the top of your head, rather than your forehead, to make contact with the ball.

MID-GOAL MOVES

By varying the speed and height at which you deliver the ball, you can make crosses to the mid-goal area harder to defend against. In the example on the right, a low, hard cross into the mid-goal area allows a striker to use a side-on volley (see page 151).

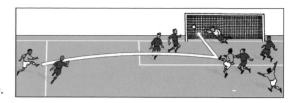

FAR POST MOVES

A goalkeeper will usually move over to cover crosses to the far post area. You may be able to wrong-foot him by heading the ball back across and into the other side of the goal, as shown in the picture below.

Because the goalkeeper is covering the far post, the striker coming in down the centre has a clear chance to score.

If you can see a team-mate running into a shooting position, you can head the ball down into his path, as shown on the right, rather than head it at goal yourself. This is known as laying the ball back.

USING AN INSWINGING CROSS

Here, the player on the left wing uses a check-back move (see page 145) to lose his marker. He then hits a cross with his right foot, making the ball swing in towards the goal.

Make sure that as your team-mate checks back, you stay onside.

CROSSING LATE

One of the most effective cross moves is a cross hit almost on the goal-line. Swinging a late cross into the goalmouth gives your team-mates a chance to close right in on goal without being offside.

SOLO ATTACK

You don't always have to receive a through ball or a cross to find a chance to shoot. You may be able to try a solo attack on your opponents' goal, taking the ball past defenders yourself. A weaving run into the penalty area is a great way to put pressure on the other team's defence.

BASIC FEINTING

If you're dribbling towards goal with a defender straight in front of you, try to get past him by using a feint.

Feinting means fooling an opponent into thinking you are going to move one way, and then going the other.

The idea is to make the defender take his eye off the ball and watch your body instead, so you need to exaggerate your movements as much as possible.

Decide which side you're going to aim for. Pretend to go the other way, dropping your shoulder so that you look like you're about to swerve off in that direction.

As the defender moves across to cover you, quickly dodge past him in the opposite direction to your feint.

THE SCISSOR TRICK

Work on variations of the basic feint, so that you can use a range of feinting tricks to throw defenders off balance. Try using a check-back move, like the one on page 145, or use the 'scissor' feinting move shown here.

Here, the attacker makes as though to go left, but swings his foot over the ball.

He then uses his right foot to push the ball away quickly in the other direction.

As the defender follows the feint to the left, the attacker sprints past him.

TURNING ON THE EDGE OF THE PENALTY AREA

If you've received a pass on the edge of the penalty area from a team-mate downfield, you will have your back to the goal. To shoot, you need to turn to face the goal without losing the ball. As you receive it keep your body between the ball and your marker to 'shield' it. Then use one of the two turns below.

To turn to your non-kicking side, hook the inside of your foot around the ball. Lean across into your turn.

Drag the ball across your body and around to your side, turning as you do so on your non-kicking leg.

You can accelerate away past the defender, or hit an immediate shot past him to surprise the goalkeeper.

To turn to your kicking side, hook the outside of your foot around the ball. Lean into your turn.

Sweep the ball away to the side in an arc, turning your body to follow it so that you're facing the goal.

From an 'outside hook' like this, use your other foot to hit a fierce instep drive as you complete your turn.

TURN AND SHOOT DRILL

Try this drill with four players. Player A passes to B, who has to turn and shoot past defender C. B scores one point for getting in a shot, and two for scoring. Have five goes, then change places.

STAR TURN

Being able to turn and shoot is a vital attacking skill. Here, George Weah (Milan) prepares to turn the ball away from defender Winston Bogarde (Ajax).

SHOOTING TECHNIQUES

You can use any of the basic kicking techniques to shoot, but the most effective choice will depend on whether the ball is rolling, bouncing, or in the air. You need to be able to strike the ball accurately and confidently, regardless of how you receive it.

THE INSTEP DRIVE SHOT

If you've dribbled into a shooting position, or received the ball along the ground, use your instep to drive a low, hard shot at goal.

Use your arms for balance.

Keep your head down, and your eye on the ball.

You need to get your non-kicking foot right up alongside the ball.

Get your knee over the ball and point your toes down as you kick.

Strike through the middle of the ball with your instep, keeping your head down. Follow through to power the ball away.

THE FRONT, OR FACE-ON VOLLEY

If you take the time to control the ball when it comes through the air, you may miss a chance to score. By hitting a shot 'on the volley' instead, you can often turn a half-chance into a spectacular goal. This is easiest when you are facing the ball.

Get yourself into position so that the ball will drop in front of you.

As the ball comes near, bring up your knee and point your toes.

Keep your head down and over your knee, so that your volley will stay low.

Strike the ball with your instep, stretching out your ankle as you kick.

THE SIDE-ON VOLLEY

To volley from the side, use this 'side-on' technique, also known as volleying on the half-turn. It is more difficult than a face-on volley, so watch the ball closely as it comes towards you in order to time it properly. Use your arms for balance.

Lean away from the ball, and swing your kicking leg up and around to your side.

Strike the ball with your instep. Hit it just above centre to keep your shot low.

Follow through by swinging your kicking leg right across your body.

SHOOTING ON THE HALF-VOLLEY

To half-volley, you kick the ball a split second after it bounces. It is quite hard to keep a half-volley shot down, as the ball is already starting to rise when you strike it.

USING YOUR HEAD

From a high ball, such as a corner or cross, use a header to shoot. You have a better chance of scoring if you can direct the ball downwards. To do this, make contact with the top half of the ball. You may need to jump – if so, take off from one foot to gain maximum height.

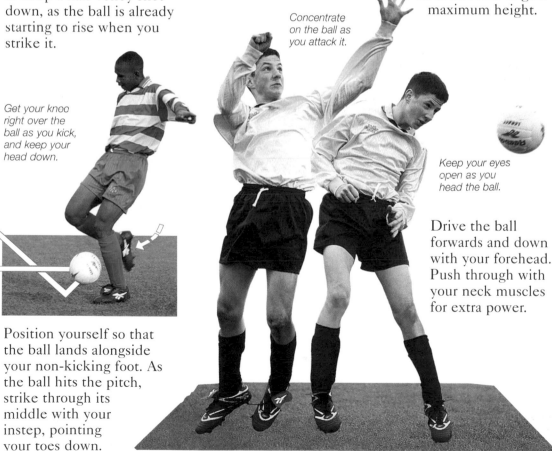

Get your knee right over the ball as you kick, and keep your head down.

Concentrate on the ball as you attack it.

Keep your eyes open as you head the ball.

Position yourself so that the ball lands alongside your non-kicking foot. As the ball hits the pitch, strike through its middle with your instep, pointing your toes down.

Drive the ball forwards and down with your forehead. Push through with your neck muscles for extra power.

SHOOTING TACTICS

Shooting is about tactics as well as technique. Even a powerful shot won't go in if you hit the ball straight at the goalkeeper. To maximise your chance of scoring, you need to pick the most vulnerable part of the goal, and the best approach to beat the goalkeeper.

PICKING YOUR TARGET

Always try to keep your shot low. It's far harder for a goalkeeper to reach down from a standing position to cover a low shot than it is for him to stretch to reach a high one.

The further your shot is from the goalkeeper, the harder it will be for him to reach the ball. Aim just inside whichever post is furthest away from the goalkeeper.

Follow your shot in. If it rebounds from the goalkeeper, post or crossbar, you may get another chance to score.

Accuracy is more important than power – carefully pushing the ball past the goalkeeper is better than blasting it wildly at goal.

LONG RANGE SHOTS

Don't hesitate to shoot from a long way out because you're worried that your team-mates will blame you if you miss. The more shots you try, the more likely your team is to score. Bear in mind that players between you and the goal may block the goalkeeper's view, or even deflect your shot, making it harder to save.

A good striker shoots whenever he gets the chance. It's better to try for a goal and miss than not to try at all.

BEATING THE KEEPER

A goalkeeper will often try to reduce the area you can aim at by moving out towards you as you approach goal.

Here there are large areas on either side of the keeper to aim at.

By moving off his goal-line, the goalkeeper reduces the target areas.

If the goalkeeper 'narrows the angle' like this, and you think he is likely to block a shot to either side, try dribbling the ball past him instead.

1. You need to make the goalkeeper commit himself. Make as though to shoot past him so that he 'spreads' to block the ball.

2. Once he is on the ground, take the ball past him, or chip it over him. Run on and aim the ball carefully into the goal.

WHEN NOT TO SHOOT

However good your shooting skills are, you will sometimes find that your angle of approach and the defenders in your path mean that you've little chance of scoring. If you can see that one of your team-mates is in a better position, pass the ball to him.

ADVANCED SHOOTING

The mark of a good striker is the ability to create goals from half-chances. You need to be able to think quickly and have the determination to beat others to the ball. You also need to be inventive and go for unexpected shots.

Try to hit the top of the ball to aim your shot down.

OVERHEAD KICK

This acrobatic technique means you can shoot from a cross even if you have your back to goal. Don't try an overhead kick if other players are close to the ball, as you are likely to kick one of them.

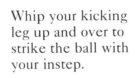

Watch the ball as it approaches. Lift your non-kicking leg and lean back.

To reach the ball, take off from your kicking leg, lying back as you jump.

Whip your kicking leg up and over to strike the ball with your instep.

Put out your arms to break your fall. As you land, roll onto your shoulder.

DIVING HEADERS

To reach a low ball passing slightly ahead of you, a diving header may be your only shooting option. This is a shot that you must approach with courage and commitment.

Direct the ball by turning your head as you hit it.

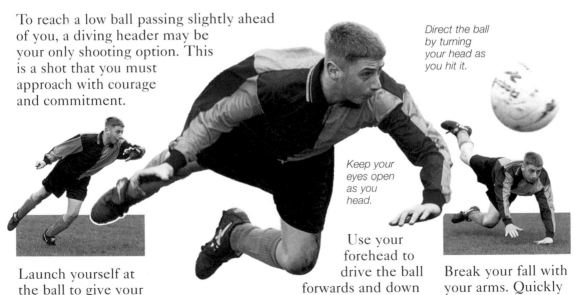

Keep your eyes open as you head.

Launch yourself at the ball to give your header power.

Use your forehead to drive the ball forwards and down into the goalmouth.

Break your fall with your arms. Quickly get back into play.

SWERVE SHOTS

If your direct shooting line is blocked, you may be able to score by bending your shot. The secret of a 'swerve shot' is to strike the ball off-centre, making it spin.

If you hit the outside of the ball (the right-hand side if you use your right foot) with the inner part of your instep, your shot will swing away to your non-kicking side.

By hitting the inside of the ball (the left-hand side if you use your right foot) with the outside of your foot, you can make your shot swerve in the other direction.

ACUTE ANGLES

Don't be afraid to try a shot from an acute angle. It's harder to hit the target, but you may take the goalkeeper by surprise.

Here, the attacking player, approaching from an acute angle, drives a hard, low shot just inside the near post.

In this case, the attacker uses a bending shot to swing the ball around the keeper, so that it curls just inside the far post.

CHIPPING THE KEEPER

If the goalkeeper comes out as you approach the goal (see page 153), he leaves a space behind him. Try chipping the ball over his head, so that it drops down into the goal.

For a chip, kick the bottom of the ball with a sharp, stabbing action.

GETTING A TOUCH

You don't always need a clear shooting chance to score. You can often knock the ball into the goal simply by reacting quickly enough to get a touch on a cross or a deflection on a team-mate's shot.

Here, striker Hristo Stoichkov (Bulgaria) tries to get in a vital touch against Spanish goalkeeper Andoni Zubizarreta.

THROW-INS AND CORNERS

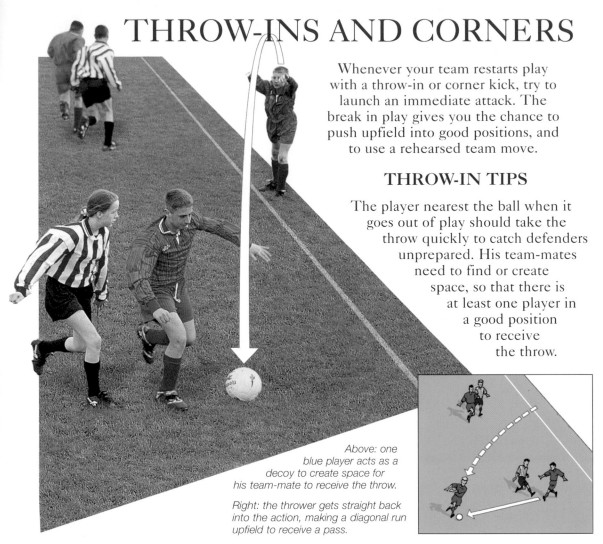

Whenever your team restarts play with a throw-in or corner kick, try to launch an immediate attack. The break in play gives you the chance to push upfield into good positions, and to use a rehearsed team move.

THROW-IN TIPS

The player nearest the ball when it goes out of play should take the throw quickly to catch defenders unprepared. His team-mates need to find or create space, so that there is at least one player in a good position to receive the throw.

Above: one blue player acts as a decoy to create space for his team-mate to receive the throw.

Right: the thrower gets straight back into the action, making a diagonal run upfield to receive a pass.

★ The thrower needs to deliver the ball so that the receiver can control it quickly and easily.

★ Whenever possible, the thrower should send the ball upfield, preferably to an unmarked team-mate.

★ Don't rush an attacking throw-in, or you're likely to do a foul throw, giving away possession of the ball.

USING A LONG THROW-IN

You can use a throw-in in the attacking third rather like a cross (see pages 144-147), with the added advantage that the player receiving the ball cannot be called offside. At least one player should perfect his long throw-in technique, so that he can reach the near side of the penalty area.

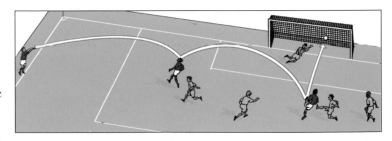

Because you can't be offside from a throw-in, you can all move right up, but usual offside rules apply once

the throw has been received. Here, the receiver uses a flick-on header to an onside team-mate.

ATTACKING FROM CORNER KICKS

The most direct way to attack from a corner kick is to cross the ball into the goal area, so that team-mates in front of the goalmouth can head or volley at goal. An inswinging cross to the near post area is the most popular option. The receiver can shoot, flick the ball on, or lay it back to a team-mate (see page 147).

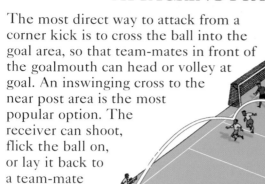

Here, the yellow player at the near post flicks on a corner kick cross to a team-mate running in to shoot.

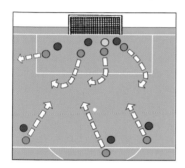

Attacking players in the centre have a number of options, as shown on the left. They can move out from the goal-line to find space as the cross comes in, or run in late from outside the penalty area.

You can vary your corner kick tactics by using different kinds of crosses (see page 147). Whichever kind of cross you choose, your attacking players must work together to find or create space.

SHORT CORNER MOVES

By moving the ball out from the corner, you can create a different angle of attack. Instead of hitting a cross, the corner taker passes along the ground to a team-mate within easy range of goal. Three possible 'short corner' moves are shown below.

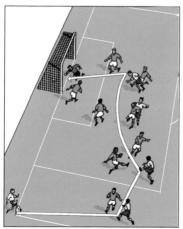

Here, two short passes move the ball from the corner to a player in a good position to hit a cross.

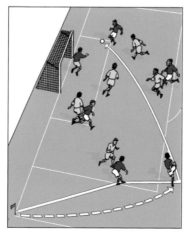

In this case, the corner kicker passes to a team-mate downfield, then overlaps him to receive a return ball.

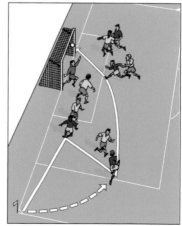

Here, the attacker at the near post moves out along the goal-line to play a one-two with the corner taker.

FREE KICK ATTACKS

A free kick in the attacking third gives your team a great opportunity to attack. Because of the break in play, though, the other team has time to drop back and organize its defence. You need a well-thought-out, well-rehearsed move to find a weakness and score.

When a free kick is within range of your opponents' goal, some of their players will form a human wall to block your shot.

BEATING THE WALL

If the kick is direct, try swerving a shot around either side of the wall (see page 155), or chipping a shot over the top.

To take an indirect kick, you have to pass the ball. Try to create a good angle for a team-mate to shoot past the wall.

TIPS FOR TAKING FREE KICKS

A free kick shot is much more likely to go in if you can create an element of surprise to confuse the goalkeeper and defenders. Try using some of these free kick tips to fool your opponents.

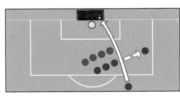

Try using a wall of your own players to hide your kick from the goalkeeper, so that he sees the ball as late as possible.

  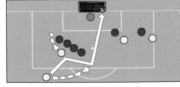

Use a dummy cross-over to disguise the direction of a free kick. Two attackers run in as though to kick, one from either side.

The first player to the ball dummies over it, leaving his team-mate to kick it in a different direction a split second later.

Use a more complicated indirect move to change the angle of attack. Don't be too ambitious – no more than three touches is best.

FREE KICKS FROM THE WING

If you get a free kick to one side of the penalty area, you probably won't be able to score with a direct shot because of the narrow angle. Use a cross instead.

In this picture, the kicker has hit an inswinging cross around the defensive wall to players running in down the centre.

Attacking players need to time their run onto a cross to make sure they stay onside.

Instead of crossing directly from the kick, you can use a pass along the wing to move the ball further upfield first.

TAKING PENALTY KICKS

Of all restarts, a penalty offers the best chance of scoring a goal. If you can hit a low, hard, accurate instep drive, you're almost sure to beat the goalkeeper. As with all shots, you and your team-mates should follow in your penalty strike in case it rebounds.

Important matches are sometimes decided by a penalty shoot-out between the teams, so don't neglect your penalty kick practice.

Roberto Baggio's penalty shoot-out miss put Italy out of the 1994 World Cup Final.

Don't be hesitant – pick a target to aim for, and stick with your decision.

Try to look away from where you mean to kick, as this will help to fool the goalkeeper.

WORLD SOCCER QUIZ

63. Which of these teams did not enter the first ever World Cup, in Uruguay?

a. United States
b. England
c. Belgium

64. Why did India withdraw from the World Cup in 1950?

a. FIFA had banned the team from playing barefoot
b. Too many of the Indian squad were injured
c. Their manager resigned at the last minute

65. Brazil beat the host nation in the final to win the 1997 Copa America. Which nation was this?

a. Chile
b. Colombia
c. Bolivia

66. Which two nations have hosted the World Cup after suffering a terrible earthquake?

a. Brazil and Argentina
b. Mexico and Chile
c. Italy and Mexico

67. In the 1990 World Cup, England and Germany met in the semi-finals. After 90 minutes the score was 1-1. Who scored the English goal?

a. Paul Gascoigne
b. David Platt
c. Gary Lineker

68. Which of these qualifying teams for the 1998 World Cup in France had never qualified before?

a. Jamaica
b. Iran
c. Tunisia

69. In 1978, Argentina won the World Cup as the host nation. Which team did they beat in the Final?

a. Holland
b. Germany
c. Uruguay

70. When the European Championship first began in 1960, it had a different name. What was it?

a. European Winners Cup
b. European Nations Cup
c. European Trophy Competition

71. What nationality was Escobar, the player tragically shot by a fan for scoring an own goal in the 1994 World Cup?

a. Spanish
b. Moroccan
c. Colombian

72. Laszlo Kiss scored a hat trick in a record 10-1 victory against El Salvador in the first round of the 1982 World Cup Finals. Who was he playing for?

a. Hungary
b. Poland
c. Austria

73. How did a black and white dog named Pickles become famous in 1966?

a. He was the English team's mascot
b. He stole the ball during one of the 1966 World Cup matches
c. He found the World Cup Jules Rimet Trophy when it had been stolen

74. In 1962, Brazil won the World Cup. Who were the runners-up?

a. Yugoslavia
b. Czechoslovakia
c. Soviet Union

75. Which country won the World Cup twice in a row, in 1934 and 1938?

a. Brazil
b. Argentina
c. Italy

76. When Mexico and Bulgaria met in the second round of the 1994 World Cup, the game was stopped for fifteen minutes. Why?

a. Fans ran onto the pitch
b. One of the crossbars broke and had to be replaced
c. The referee collapsed from the heat

77. Which team didn't score any goals at all at Euro '96?

a. Turkey
b. Portugal
c. Switzerland

PART SIX

TACTICS

CONTENTS

WHAT ARE TACTICS?

In soccer, fitness and good ball skills are essential to success. But the way your team plays together is just as important. Tactics are the way a team is organized and how the players work with each other. Tactics can make all the difference between two closely-matched sides. When a less skilful side beats a better team, it can be luck, but is often more to do with team tactics.

PLAYING AS A TEAM

Any player, no matter how brilliant, is still one out of eleven. You cannot just turn up and play your own game of soccer. You are part of a team. This is the single most important principle of soccer tactics.

The whole team must play according to the same plan to ensure its success. When learning about tactics, it is helpful to know the correct terms. The most commonly used terms are shown below.

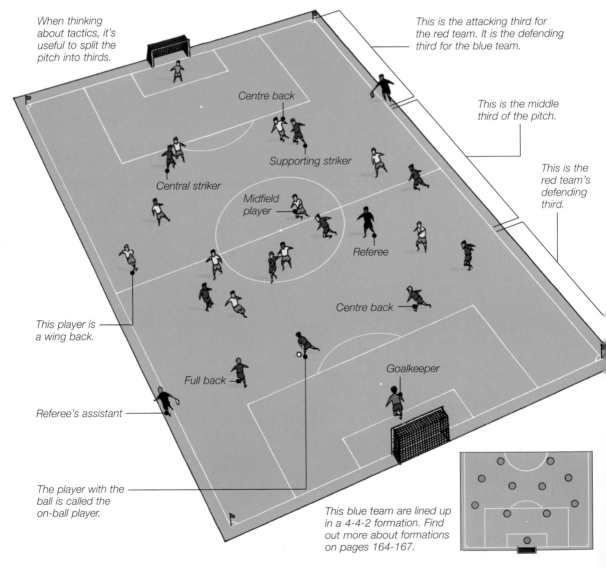

When thinking about tactics, it's useful to split the pitch into thirds.

This is the attacking third for the red team. It is the defending third for the blue team.

This is the middle third of the pitch.

This is the red team's defending third.

Centre back

Supporting striker

Central striker

Midfield player

Referee

This player is a wing back.

Centre back

Goalkeeper

Full back

Referee's assistant

The player with the ball is called the on-ball player.

This blue team are lined up in a 4-4-2 formation. Find out more about formations on pages 164-167.

PITCH MARKINGS AND MOVEMENT

Soccer pitches may vary slightly in size, but they all have the same pitch markings.

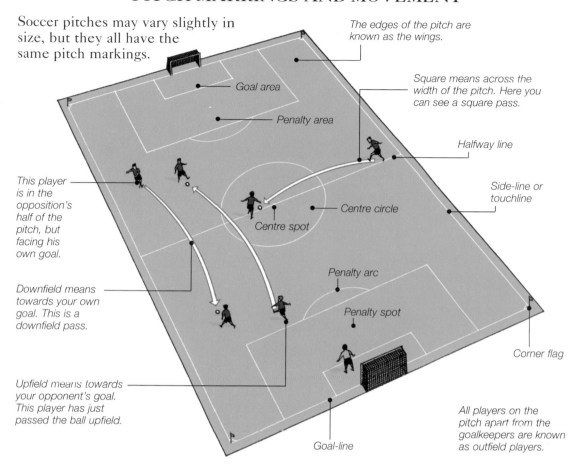

The edges of the pitch are known as the wings.

Goal area

Penalty area

Square means across the width of the pitch. Here you can see a square pass.

Halfway line

This player is in the opposition's half of the pitch, but facing his own goal.

Side-line or touchline

Centre circle

Centre spot

Downfield means towards your own goal. This is a downfield pass.

Penalty arc

Penalty spot

Corner flag

Upfield means towards your opponent's goal. This player has just passed the ball upfield.

Goal-line

All players on the pitch apart from the goalkeepers are known as outfield players.

IN POSITION

Why don't teams with the best players win all of their games? Because it's a question of how these players are used. A team must use its players in the best way possible. For example, a right-footed player may find it very difficult to play on the left. The right-footed player in the picture has made a good run down the left wing. But he has to cut back to deliver a cross with his right foot, wasting time and losing his advantage.

See how as the winger cuts back, the defence can now cover him.

BE POSITIVE

Whatever tactics your team decides to use, you as an individual player must be positive about yourself and also your team-mates and the match officials. Never give up. Your team can be outplayed for almost the whole game, but still get to score a late goal and win. That's what makes soccer such an exciting game.

Paul Ince, playing here for England against Italy, still attacks with only moments left to play.

FORMATIONS

A formation is the basic shape of a soccer team. Most formations are described in numbers of outfield players from the defence forwards. So 4-2-4, means four defenders, two midfield players and four attackers. To be successful, a team must have some shape so that players know where they should play and where their team-mates will be. Successful formations balance attack and defence and make the best use of the players in a team.

FOUR-FOUR-TWO

The midfield area is an important area of the pitch. Teams often pack their midfield with players. 4-4-2 is a common, defence-minded formation. It relies on the forwards covering much ground.

A line of four defenders and four midfield players feed two forward players.

The two wide midfield players can act as wingers when their team attacks.

The forwards will both chase back for defence and search for space in attack.

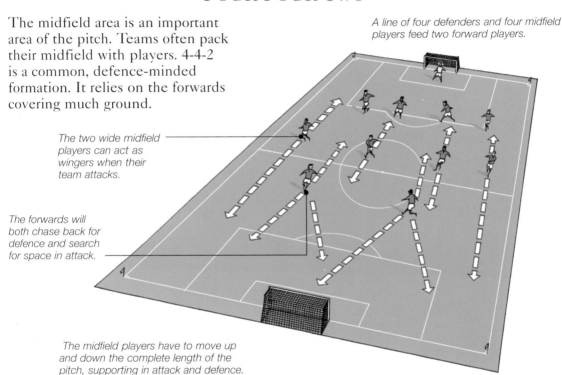

The midfield players have to move up and down the complete length of the pitch, supporting in attack and defence.

FOUR-TWO-FOUR

In 4-2-4, two midfield players act as a link between the four men in attack and the four in defence. They must cover a huge amount of ground for the formation to work. Because of the huge strain put on the two midfield players, 4-2-4 is today played rarely by teams.

FOUR-THREE-THREE

4-2-4 is sometimes altered by dropping an attacking player back into the midfield to make a 4-3-3 formation. This yellow side have adopted a 4-3-3 formation with two central strikers and one winger. The winger may switch wings during the game, searching for openings.

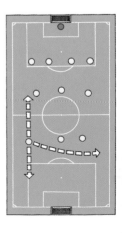

THREE-TWO-TWO-THREE

This system uses three centre backs and two wing backs out wide. In defence, one of the centre backs may be given the task of man-marking a particularly dangerous opposing forward. You can learn more about man-marking and defensive tactics on pages 170-171.

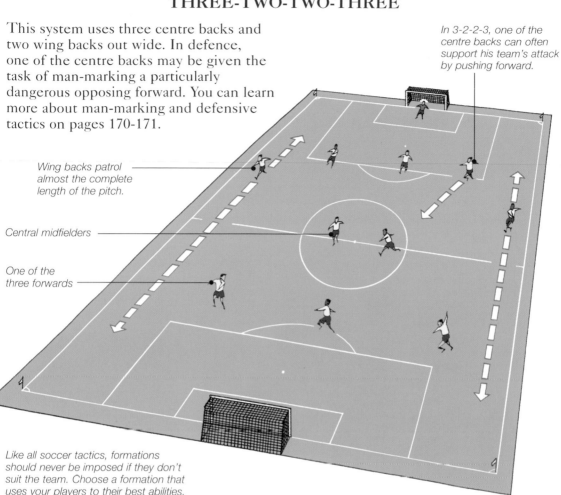

In 3-2-2-3, one of the centre backs can often support his team's attack by pushing forward.

Wing backs patrol almost the complete length of the pitch.

Central midfielders

One of the three forwards

Like all soccer tactics, formations should never be imposed if they don't suit the team. Choose a formation that uses your players to their best abilities.

DEFLECTIONS AND LUCKY LONGSHOTS

No formations or tactics are foolproof. Sometimes, a bizarre event or piece of luck loses a team a match. You can't defend against a deflection off a player or an incredible long-range shot. Remember, just because your team has lost by a single goal does not necessarily mean that the formation and tactics you used were wrong.

No tactics can ever stop an overhead kick such as this spectacular effort by German striker, Jürgen Klinsmann.

FORMATIONS AND SYSTEMS

Systems are the way a group of players work within a complete team formation. In recent times, coaches and managers have worked on new formations and systems to give their sides an advantage.

CHRISTMAS TREE

This formation has four defenders, three midfield players, two attacking support players and a lone central striker, who is the furthest forward.

The formation provides good links between the midfield and the attackers. It relies on the two supporting attackers being flexible and working hard.

TOTAL FOOTBALL

Total football abandons a fixed formation in favour of more flexibility. Those in the best positions make forward runs, with their team-mates providing cover and support. This system is hard to defend against, but requires excellent ability, fitness and understanding between players.

This supporting attacker must join the central striker at the right moment or roam wider and act as a winger.

This formation gets its name from the fir tree shape that the 4-3-2-1 arrangement makes.

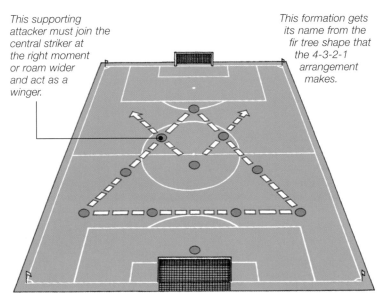

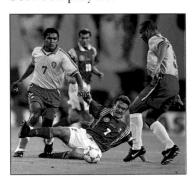

Total football was first played by Holland in the 1970s and adopted by national sides like Brazil, shown here.

VERSATILITY

Even if your team doesn't intend playing total football, you should still try to improve all of your soccer skills. Don't specialize in one position too soon. You can learn a lot from playing in different positions, and it can be fun as well.

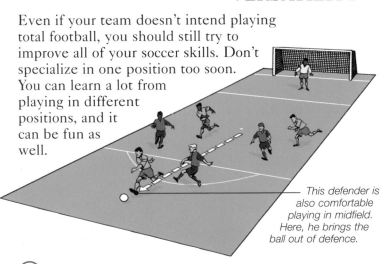

This defender is also comfortable playing in midfield. Here, he brings the ball out of defence.

Irish international, Roy Keane, plays in midfield and in defence, depending on what tactics his team is using.

SYSTEMS IN FORMATIONS

Within the framework of a formation, teams can play in different ways. For example, one team can play 4-4-2 defensively by pulling their forwards back behind the ball.

4-4-2

This team is playing an attacking 4-4-2. The midfield players push up to support the two strikers.

Within a formation, some players may play as part of an additional system. For example, the forwards and central midfielders in a team playing 4-2-4 may play the diamond system (see below).

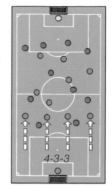

4-3-3

The defenders in a 4-3-3 formation can use the offside trap (see page 173).

THE DIAMOND SYSTEM

The diamond system requires great discipline from the attacking players, but it is very hard to defend against. Ideally, the players will be able to play in all the different positions, rotating the diamond shape.

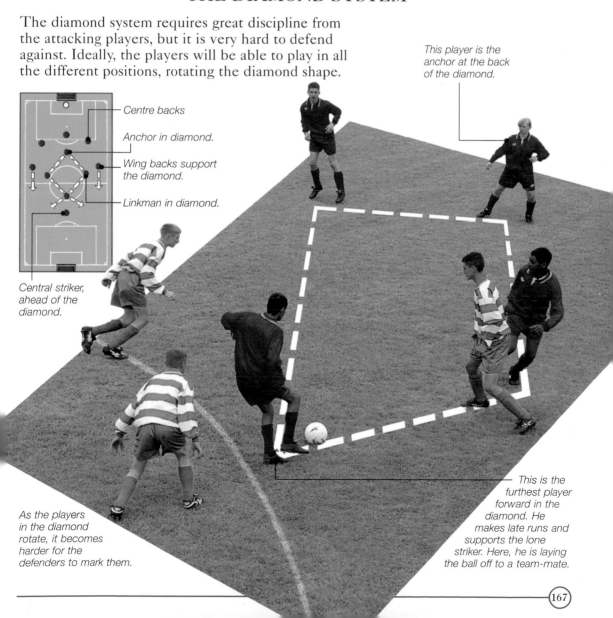

This player is the anchor at the back of the diamond.

Centre backs

Anchor in diamond.

Wing backs support the diamond.

Linkman in diamond.

Central striker, ahead of the diamond.

As the players in the diamond rotate, it becomes harder for the defenders to mark them.

This is the furthest player forward in the diamond. He makes late runs and supports the lone striker. Here, he is laying the ball off to a team-mate.

DEFENSIVE TACTICS

All successful teams, no matter how good their attack, always have a strong defence too. A good defence mixes individual skills and effective tactics. Defending is not just for defenders. The whole team is responsible for defence. This means, for example, that in man-to-man marking systems, midfield players mark opposing midfielders.

PRIORITIES IN DEFENCE

Defending is all about stopping the opposition scoring goals. But as a defender you shouldn't just launch into a tackle.

This defender has closed up on the attacker. He's slowing the attacker down without giving him the space to go past.

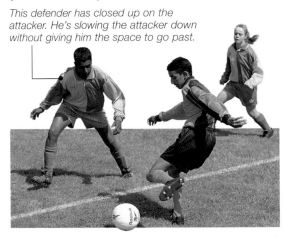

1. **Delay** the opponent to allow the rest of your defence to get into stronger positions. Jockey him and get in his way to try to slow down the momentum of the attack.

Here, the defender has waited until he has cover before he commits himself to winning the ball cleanly.

3. **Destroy** the attack by challenging your opponent for the ball. You can do this either by tackling him directly or by intercepting a pass.

When faced with an on-ball attacker, this is what you should try to do: **delay, deny, destroy** and **develop**.

This defender is forcing the attacker out wide. Notice that he isn't so close that the attacker can just burst past.

2. **Deny** the opponent the space and position he wants. This means stopping him from turning to face goal or shooting and forcing him away from danger areas.

This defender has made a short pass upfield to a team-mate in midfield.

4. **Develop** play. Once you have the ball, you need to get it away from your goal and develop an attack for your team. You may be able to pass or continue a run yourself.

PROVIDING COVER AND SUPPORT

It's essential for defenders to communicate with and support their team-mate who's facing the on-ball attacker. Defenders should try to provide direct cover in case the attacker gets past the on-ball defender.

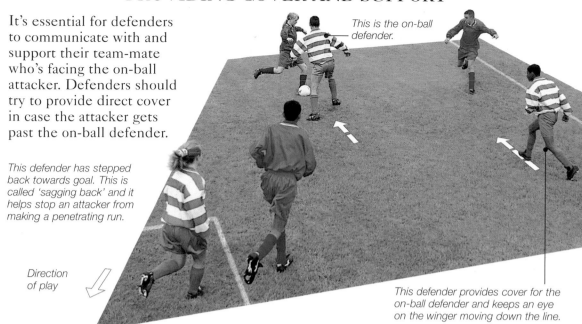

This is the on-ball defender.

This defender has stepped back towards goal. This is called 'sagging back' and it helps stop an attacker from making a penetrating run.

Direction of play

This defender provides cover for the on-ball defender and keeps an eye on the winger moving down the line.

WORKING AS A TWO-MAN UNIT

With two defenders in position, you can do more than just delay an attacker. Once you have cover, you can think about a direct challenge, or two players can work together to squeeze the ball away from the attacker.

The on-ball defender can position himself slightly to one side of the attacker, forcing the attacker towards a second defender. Here, the second defender has 'sagged back' both to provide cover and watch the second attacker.

If the on-ball attacker passes the ball, the defenders can slide around to continue the same move on the new on-ball attacker. The two defenders must communicate with each other for the move to be successful.

This defender is providing cover, so that the on-ball defender can make his tackle.

The off-ball defender can move in and tackle the attacker in a move sometimes known as double-teaming. This move should be timed to surprise the attacker, giving the defenders a good chance of gaining the ball.

MARKING SYSTEMS

Defending as an individual is important, but so is the type of marking system you use. Your team has to decide whether to go for man-to-man, zonal or combination marking (see page 187).

MAN-TO-MAN MARKING

In man-to-man marking, your defenders and some or all of your midfield players, are each assigned an attacker to mark throughout the game. These players watch their attacker and stick close to him when the other team has the ball. Man-to-man marking works well in your defending third with spare players, such as your attackers, putting pressure on the opposing player with the ball. Each defender can be matched up against an opponent's specific skills. As the game progresses, you can identify any weaknesses of the player that you are marking.

Scottish international defender, Colin Hendry, is particularly good in the air. He usually man-marks the opposing side's most dangerous aerial attacker.

MARKING GAME

Play five-a-side for 20 minutes. You each mark a player when his team has the ball. When your team has it, the object is to get away from your marker.

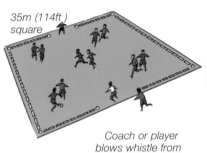

35m (114ft) square

Coach or player blows whistle from time to time.

Players should stop as soon as the whistle is blown. Each defender should be within touching distance of the player he is marking. If not, he should go in goal or take over the whistle from the player on the sideline.

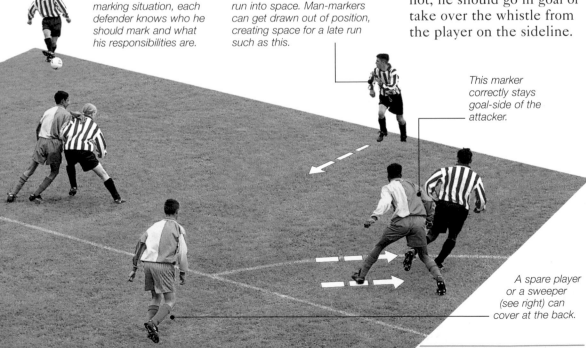

In this man-to-man marking situation, each defender knows who he should mark and what his responsibilities are.

This attacker is making a late run into space. Man-markers can get drawn out of position, creating space for a late run such as this.

This marker correctly stays goal-side of the attacker.

A spare player or a sweeper (see right) can cover at the back.

ZONAL MARKING

Zonal marking means you defend an area of the pitch. Each defender is assigned a zone which overlaps with neighbouring defenders' zones. Unlike man-to-man marking where defenders can be dragged around the pitch, zonal marking helps keep the defence together in a compact shape.

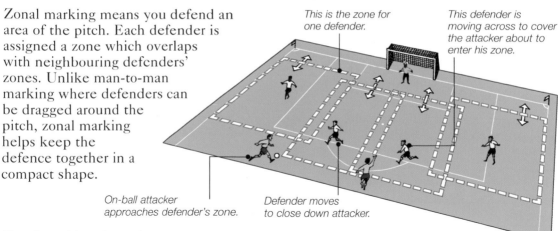

This is the zone for one defender.

This defender is moving across to cover the attacker about to enter his zone.

On-ball attacker approaches defender's zone.

Defender moves to close down attacker.

Zonal marking does give attackers more time and space. It requires good awareness of the area you're defending. Communication between defenders must be good, especially when handing over a moving attacker from one zone to another.

Although defenders must know where the ball is, they should not ball watch. Instead, they must be aware of the play as it develops and particularly, any attackers straying into their own zone or neighbouring ones.

Zonal marking can create an overload in defence (more defenders than attackers) in areas near its goal. This makes it much harder for the attacking side to score. Both defenders and attackers seek to obtain overloads whenever possible.

This defender has no attacker in his zone. He provides cover for the on-ball defender and can join him in his zone to put more pressure on the attacker.

This defender decides whether to delay the attacker, force him one way or tackle him.

The defender furthest from the action should be in a good position to see how play develops.

This on-ball attacker is entering a defender's zone.

ADVANCED DEFENSIVE TACTICS

There are various other defensive tactics your team can employ. Amongst the most common are using sweepers, offside traps and the catenaccio defence.

THE ROLE OF THE SWEEPER

The sweeper is so called because he usually plays behind the defence, sweeping up any loose balls or attacks that get past the main defence. A sweeper has to be very agile and good at 'reading' the game. Along with the goalkeeper, he should organize the defence, directing the other defenders and making sure they are in the correct place.

Sweepers provide cover when another defender has the ball. This sweeper has passed to his full back, and is providing cover in case the full back loses the ball.

Sweepers don't man-mark, but there are times when an unmarked attacker appears in the defence. This sweeper is picking up the unmarked attacker.

Another role of the sweeper is to cut out through balls. Here, this sweeper reacted early to intercept a potentially dangerous pass.

Sweepers can also start an attack. The sweeper above has taken the ball and is moving forward to link with midfield. Because sweepers are rarely marked, they can add surprise and variety to the attack.

The sweeper can now move upfield with the ball.

CATENACCIO (CHAIN) DEFENCE

Mattheas Sammer, the German sweeper, covers for his team-mates, mopping up any loose balls and quickly closing gaps.

Catenaccio (*cat-an-nacho*) is Italian for 'big chain'. It is when three or four defenders line up across the pitch with a defensive sweeper behind them. Catenaccio is a very defensive measure used to restrict goal-scoring chances. Midfielders and even attackers fill much of the remaining space between their goal and the attacking team. With so many players behind the ball, it makes it hard for the team playing catennacio to launch an attack. Teams playing catenaccio rely on fast breaks by small numbers of fast-moving attackers to score.

PLAYING AN OFFSIDE TRAP

A player is offside, if, when the ball is played, he is in the other team's half and there are fewer than two defenders closer than him to the goal-line. An offside trap is where a defence pushes up in a line square to the pitch. By doing this quickly, the defence can catch opposing forwards offside. It's a risky tactic, though, especially if the referee's assistants are not experienced. If your team intends playing the offside trap, make sure every player knows how to do it.

The red team are defending.

Here is an offside trap played at a corner. A1 has received a short corner pass. The defence push up, keeping goal-side of the ball.

D1 is nearest the ball. He closes down A1. D2 has moved from the goalpost to provide cover.

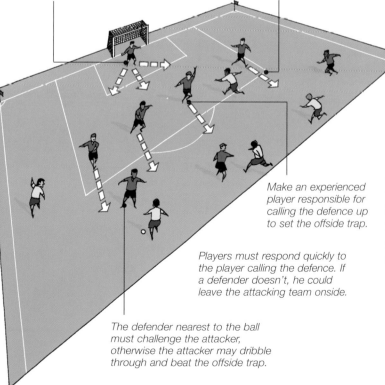

The goalkeeper should be prepared to cover his defence in the role of a sweeper if necessary.

Use pitch markers, such as the edge of the penalty box, to get your defensive line straight.

Make an experienced player responsible for calling the defence up to set the offside trap.

Players must respond quickly to the player calling the defence. If a defender doesn't, he could leave the attacking team onside.

The defender nearest to the ball must challenge the attacker, otherwise the attacker may dribble through and beat the offside trap.

D2 must be level with his defending team-mates to catch the blue attackers offside. He must move away from his goal before A2 receives the ball.

MIDFIELD AND DEPTH

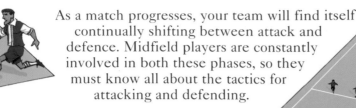

As a match progresses, your team will find itself continually shifting between attack and defence. Midfield players are constantly involved in both these phases, so they must know all about the tactics for attacking and defending.

The midfield is where the ball is most often won and lost. Midfield players have to be strong tacklers, incredibly fit and read the game well. When their team is defending, they must get back goal-side of the ball as quickly as possible. In attack, midfield players should provide support to their attackers.

The red team's midfield use the ball to launch an attack.

ATTACKING WITH DEPTH

Midfield players can help stagger an attack, giving it depth up and down the pitch. Depth gives the on-ball attacker a safe pass behind him if he runs into trouble. There is nothing wrong with passing the ball back to keep possession until your team finds a good attacking opening.

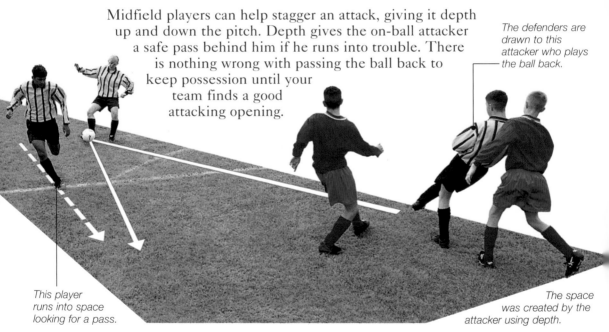

The defenders are drawn to this attacker who plays the ball back.

This player runs into space looking for a pass.

The space was created by the attacker using depth.

By giving an attack depth, a team gives itself more options. This team has attacked with depth. They have created valuable space for a penetrating pass.

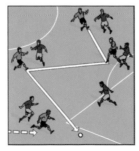

An attack without depth often breaks down. This team has attacked in a flat line. As a result, an attempted pass has been intercepted by the opposing defence.

CHANGING TACTICS

Top sides have coaches and managers who signal switches in tactics from the side-line or make changes at half time. Top players are well-coached and can slip into a new playing pattern easily. When you are losing heavily, reduced to ten men or suffering from injuries, a switch in tactics may be the answer. Otherwise, try to avoid unnecessary changes during a game.

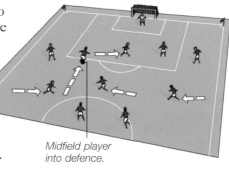

Midfield player into defence.

This team is changing from 4-4-2 to 5-3-2. They are adding an extra defender.

SUBSTITUTES

Substitutes aren't just for injuries, they can be used as a tactical tool as well. You can replace struggling players with fresh ones. These may have different skills which will create new problems for the opposing team. You can also protect a lead by replacing a striker with a more defensive player.

DOWN TO TEN MEN

If a player gets sent off, or injuries reduce your team to ten players, changes have to be made. Ten-men teams can make the mistake of becoming very defensive. This means that with no forward players, clearances just go straight back to the other team. Try to keep players forward if you can.

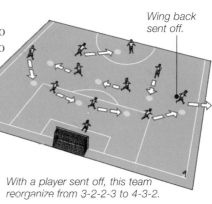

Wing back sent off.

With a player sent off, this team reorganize from 3-2-2-3 to 4-3-2.

KEEP WINNING

Any team can score a lucky goal, but to get two or more ahead is not just luck. It usually means your team has a definite advantage over the other team. Don't relax just because you're winning. Keep trying to use that advantage as best as you can.

These two players in yellow and green are defending hard even though their team is winning 3-0.

Even top stars such as Dutch winger, Marc Overmars, sometimes find themselves being substituted.

This defender is forcing the attacker to the right, where the second defender is placed.

POSSESSION

Much training concentrates on gaining possession of the ball, but just as important is learning how to keep it. You need to train with other players to learn this skill. Good awareness and passing is important, but you must have someone to pass the ball to safely. Team-mates must support the player on the ball in order to keep possession.

KEEPING POSSESSION

Playing mini-games in small areas is an excellent way of learning to keep possession. In this 3 v 1 game, the team of three try to keep hold of the ball for as long as possible. The game stops when they lose possession or the ball leaves the box.

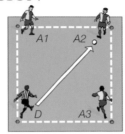

TEMPO

Tempo means the pace of the game. The tempo of soccer in some leagues is very high. This means that the game moves fast and pressure is applied to the players in possession of the ball in all areas of the field.

D has passed to A2. After A2 has touched the ball, D has started to close A2 down.

A1

A2

D

A1 and A3 are in good supporting positions. A2 can see them and pass to them as D approaches.

The markers show an 8m (26ft) square.

A3

Top club sides such as Barcelona play a more defensive formation and look to slow the game's tempo down when playing away from home.

The tempo of the game can also be slowed by getting players back behind the ball and keeping possession for long periods. Good sides can vary the tempo, slowing the game down when defending, and then attacking at speed when pushing forward. Great teams can control the tempo of the game effectively.

LONG BALL TACTICS

A long ball cuts out the midfield and lands in the attacking third of the pitch. Playing the long ball is risky. There's a chance your team may lose possession, but there's also the chance that you will gain a great attacking position. If your attacker collects the ball, team-mates can race upfield to join and support him.

The long ball depends on accurate passing skills from defence. The long ball is aimed at an attacker who is strong in the air and must come to meet the ball. Even the best attackers only win and control some long balls.

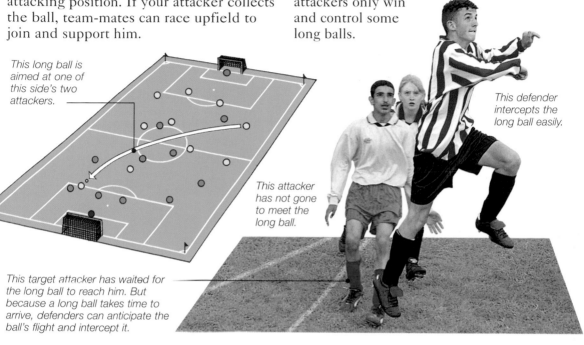

This long ball is aimed at one of this side's two attackers.

This defender intercepts the long ball easily.

This attacker has not gone to meet the long ball.

This target attacker has waited for the long ball to reach him. But because a long ball takes time to arrive, defenders can anticipate the ball's flight and intercept it.

WORKING ON THE LONG BALL GAME

If ever you spot your attacking third containing only one or two of your attackers with an equal number of defenders, consider playing the long ball.

Work on playing the long ball with the game shown in the picture to the right. Play 4 v 4 in the middle area of the pitch and 1 v 1 in both attacking end zones. Players in the 4 v 4 area can only pass into their end zone when they are inside their half of the pitch.

Players in this middle area are not allowed in the attacking area.

This attacker has waited for support. He's laid off the ball into the middle zone for a midfielder to have a shot.

20m (66ft) end zone

40m (132ft) middle zone

A defender may be able to counter-attack by sending a long ball to his own attacker.

Zones shown by markers.

20m (66ft) end zone

Goalkeeper

ATTACKING TACTICS

To score goals you've got to create attacking chances. Your team must strive to get the ball to team-mates in clear goal-scoring positions.

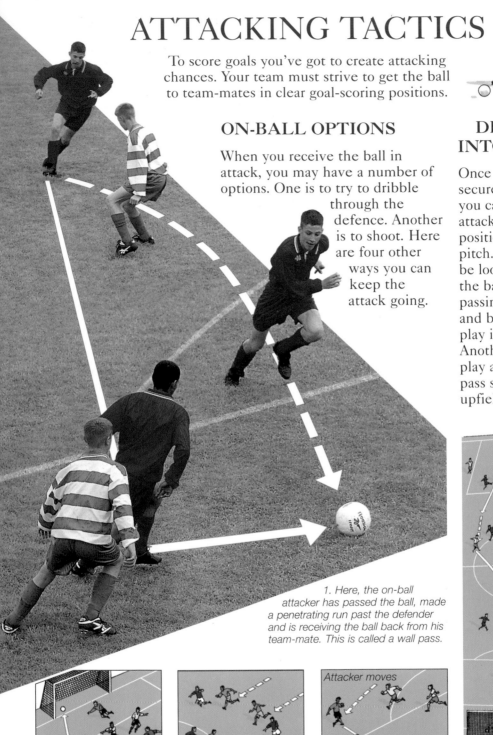

ON-BALL OPTIONS

When you receive the ball in attack, you may have a number of options. One is to try to dribble through the defence. Another is to shoot. Here are four other ways you can keep the attack going.

DEFENCE INTO ATTACK

Once your team has secure possession, you can launch an attack from any position on the pitch. You should be looking to move the ball forward by passing, running and building the play in midfield. Another option is to play an early long pass straight upfield.

1. Here, the on-ball attacker has passed the ball, made a penetrating run past the defender and is receiving the ball back from his team-mate. This is called a wall pass.

Attacker moves

The picture above shows a fast counter-move. Starting in defence, the ball is passed into midfield before a long direct pass is made to a forward player.

2. The on-ball attacker could pass to a player in a better shooting position.

3. The attacker could hold possession and wait for support from team-mates.

4. He could move into a better position to shoot, or make an attacking pass.

KEEPER'S DISTRIBUTION

The goalkeeper can start an attack in several ways. He can guarantee his side possession by passing or throwing the ball to one of his defenders. If he has intercepted a cross or through ball, he can also kick a long ball upfield quickly. Since the other team was moving forward on attack, a well-placed kick may find their defence out of position.

SUPPORT IN ATTACK

No attacker with the ball should ever be isolated. He should receive support from his team-mates. There are four principles behind how a team can and should support the on-ball attacker. These are depth (see page 174), width, mobility and penetration (see page 180-181).

A player with the ball, but no support will most likely lose possession. In this picture, the player's team-mates are working hard to provide him with a number of options.

Attackers making runs

GIVING AN ATTACK WIDTH

Using the full width of the pitch stretches a defence and creates more space for an attack. Defenders are either unable to mark players on the wings, or they move wide, leaving space in central areas. This space can be filled by other attackers.

You don't have to play wingers to use width in attack. Full backs or wing backs can come up and support, providing an extra option.

Ryan Giggs often drifts wide away from the defence to receive the ball. He then uses his pace and skilful ball control to set up an attack.

This full back is unmarked and is making an overlapping run on the outside.

MOBILITY AND PENETRATION

Mobility in soccer often means making runs to support the attack. Runs help the on-ball attacker by providing him with more options. Runs can also create more space for the on-ball attacker by drawing defenders away from him and to the player making the run.

MAKING DIAGONAL RUNS IN ATTACK

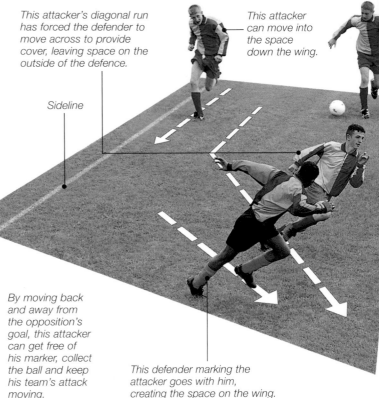

Defenders find it easiest playing against attackers who make moves straight up and down the pitch. These allow defenders to mark and cover. If you make diagonal runs, however, you can create confusion in the defence. Defenders are unsure whether to go with you or to mark the space. Defenders are most worried about the space between them and their goal. So, a move away from their goal can free you of your marker.

This attacker's diagonal run has forced the defender to move across to provide cover, leaving space on the outside of the defence.

This attacker can move into the space down the wing.

Sideline

Attacker moving back.

By moving back and away from the opposition's goal, this attacker can get free of his marker, collect the ball and keep his team's attack moving.

This defender marking the attacker goes with him, creating the space on the wing.

BLINDSIDE RUNS BEHIND A DEFENDER

Blindside running is when a run is made behind a defender. The attacker can see both the defender and the ball while he makes his run. The defender, on the other hand, can only watch the ball coming from one direction and the opposing player from another. This can make the defender indecisive which gives attackers an advantage.

This attacker passes the ball to his winger and starts his run behind the defender.

The defender has to worry about the ball, the attacker and the space.

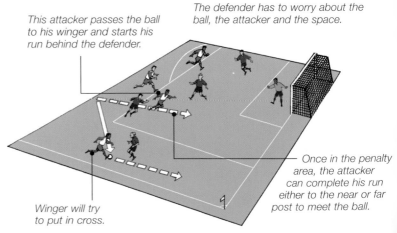

Once in the penalty area, the attacker can complete his run either to the near or far post to meet the ball.

Winger will try to put in cross.

PENETRATION

Penetration is all about getting into the attacking third of the pitch and behind the defence, while staying onside. Without penetration, attackers can only resort to long distance shots. To support the on-ball attacker, other players try to penetrate the opposition's defence. These players try to time their runs carefully to receive the ball in a shooting position or to act as decoys. Decoy runs help move defenders away from certain areas, creating space for other attackers. It is when players are trying to penetrate an opposition's defence that they are most likely to be called offside.

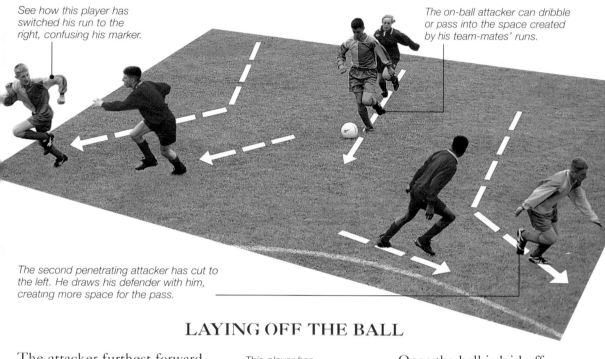

See how this player has switched his run to the right, confusing his marker.

The on-ball attacker can dribble or pass into the space created by his team-mates' runs.

The second penetrating attacker has cut to the left. He draws his defender with him, creating more space for the pass.

LAYING OFF THE BALL

The attacker furthest forward will try to penetrate the defence before he receives the ball. After controlling it, this player may pass the ball a short distance back or sideways to a supporting attacker, a move called 'laying off'. Laying off helps bring other players into the attack.

This player has controlled the ball before laying it off to a supporting team-mate.

Once the ball is laid off, attackers should start runs. Defenders often watch the ball as it is laid off, giving attackers a split second to get free.

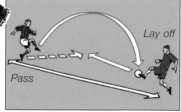

Pass

Lay off

You could work on laying off with a friend. One player delivers a long pass and moves forward to collect the lay off. The other player controls the ball and lays it off. Repeat the move, switching the roles around.

SHOOTING TACTICS

Soccer is all about scoring goals. Goals and nothing else win games. Some goals come from headers which require good, accurate crosses. Most goals, though, come from shots.

SHOOT OR PASS?

Every player should work on his shooting. In modern soccer, especially now that the forwards are so heavily marked, goals are expected from other sources, including central defenders and full backs.

Don't be afraid to shoot. It only takes one well-hit shot to win a game. That said, it's always worth checking to see if a teammate is in a better position to shoot than you.

This player has more space and time to shoot.

This attacker had time on the ball, but two defenders were blocking his shot at goal.

A quick square pass sets the far player up with a good shooting chance.

SHOOTING SIMULATION

Try to simulate shooting in match conditions by placing attackers and defenders between you and the goal. Don't just shoot from a static position. In a real match, you are far more likely to be kicking a moving and bouncing ball. To simulate this, get someone to throw, pass or bounce the ball to you before you shoot.

Defenders can only move in this game once the ball has been thrown out to the shooting player.

STAR SHOT

Midfield player David Beckham is in a good position as he shoots. He has his non-shooting foot beside the ball and his body over the ball.

FIVE AGAINST FIVE SHOOTING GAME

Much shooting training consists of hitting shots past a lone goalkeeper. Unfortunately, shooting chances like these are rare. Usually, your shot will have to beat defenders as well as the keeper. The picture on your right shows a fun game where you play a 5 v 5 mini match, but on an unusually-shaped pitch, 35m (114ft) long.

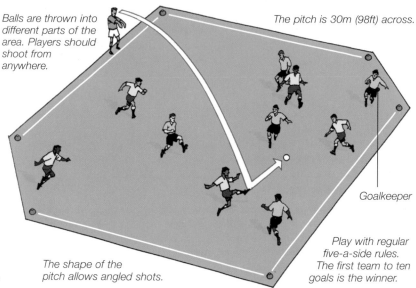

Balls are thrown into different parts of the area. Players should shoot from anywhere.

The pitch is 30m (98ft) across.

Goalkeeper

Play with regular five-a-side rules. The first team to ten goals is the winner.

The shape of the pitch allows angled shots.

SNAP SHOOTING GAME

Divide a goal into four imaginary boxes. Label them A, B, C and D. One player passes the ball and calls out a box name. The other player must turn and shoot immediately. Concentrate first on quick shots on the whole goal with few or no touches. Then work on hitting the correct box.

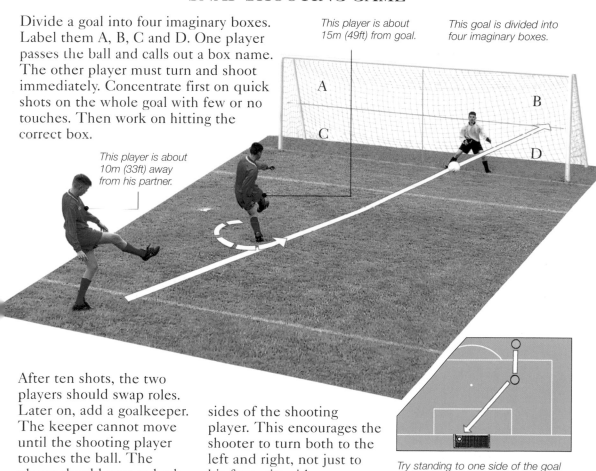

This player is about 15m (49ft) from goal.

This goal is divided into four imaginary boxes.

This player is about 10m (33ft) away from his partner.

After ten shots, the two players should swap roles. Later on, add a goalkeeper. The keeper cannot move until the shooting player touches the ball. The player should pass to both sides of the shooting player. This encourages the shooter to turn both to the left and right, not just to his favourite side.

Try standing to one side of the goal to work on more angled shots.

SET PIECE TACTICS IN ATTACK

Set pieces are moves planned in training by a team, usually from restarts such as free kicks, throw-ins and corners. Many goals are scored from set pieces. They should be rehearsed frequently so that you and your team-mates know exactly what you are doing.

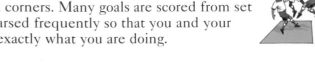

FREE KICKS

Choose just a few free kick moves to work on. Don't make them too elaborate. You may end up confusing yourselves, not the opposition.

Ball passed to the right of the row of defenders.

WORKING ON CROSSES

Many goals come from quick, accurate crosses, both from corners and in open play. All players should practise crossing the ball. In the game below, you need at least three outfield players and a goalkeeper.

The attacker should come to meet the ball. He must get there first before the defender.

The crosser should vary the types of crosses he sends in. This cross is to the feet of the attacker.

This far post cross is met by the attacker who has moved back to get behind his marker.

This cross is into space in front of the attacker. It's a hard ball to defend and a bad tackle can mean a penalty.

After some time, add more pairs of attackers and defenders. This demands more accurate crosses and tighter defending.

If you're first to the ball, then you have a better chance of getting a header or strike at goal. The defender has to think about both ball and player. If he just watches the ball, the attacker can feint and get clear of the defender.

BEATING AN OFFSIDE TRAP

An attacking team must be patient. Even the best offside trap can break down and the attack can be given a clear run at goal.

Remember, a player is not offside if he is level with the last outfield defender on the pitch. Here are some more helpful tips.

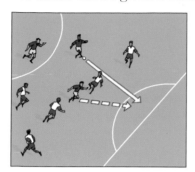

Time your run. This attacker has delayed his run long enough to stay onside until the ball is eventually played.

Disguise your play. This attacker faked a pass, but instead, dribbled through the defence which pushed up for offside.

Think quickly from a restart. You cannot be offside if you receive the ball directly from a throw-in, goal kick or corner.

ATTACKING THROW-INS

Throw-ins can be a great attacking weapon. Long throws are as good as a cross, while quick throws can catch a team out. As with all restart situations, always be aware of the quick move. Here's a simple throw-in move down the line which involves drawing a defender to create space for a full back to receive the ball.

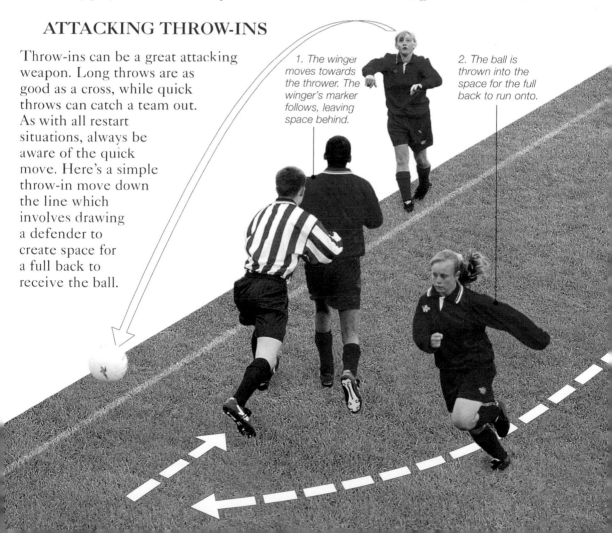

1. The winger moves towards the thrower. The winger's marker follows, leaving space behind.

2. The ball is thrown into the space for the full back to run onto.

SET PIECE TACTICS IN DEFENCE

With so many goals scored from set pieces, defenders must concentrate. Teams should quickly organize their defence as soon as a corner, free kick or throw-in is given.

DEFENDING AT CORNERS

For corners and free kicks within scoring range, defenders should listen to their goalkeeper as he organizes a free kick wall or positions defenders.

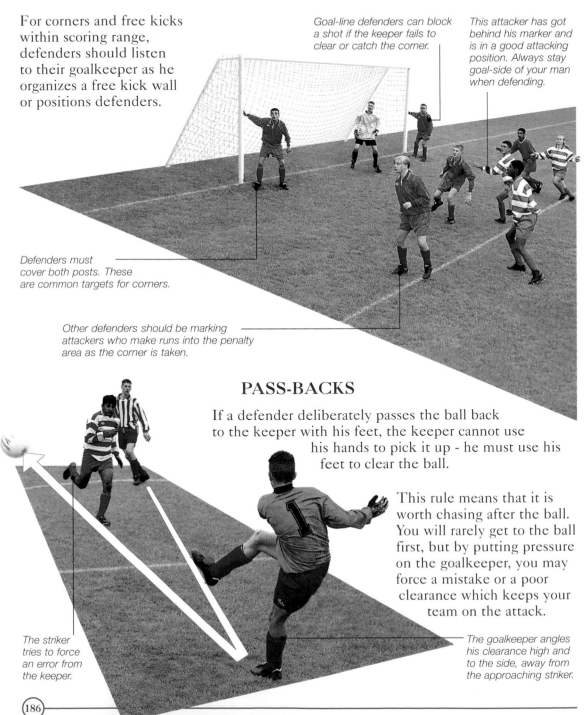

Goal-line defenders can block a shot if the keeper fails to clear or catch the corner.

This attacker has got behind his marker and is in a good attacking position. Always stay goal-side of your man when defending.

Defenders must cover both posts. These are common targets for corners.

Other defenders should be marking attackers who make runs into the penalty area as the corner is taken.

PASS-BACKS

If a defender deliberately passes the ball back to the keeper with his feet, the keeper cannot use his hands to pick it up - he must use his feet to clear the ball.

This rule means that it is worth chasing after the ball. You will rarely get to the ball first, but by putting pressure on the goalkeeper, you may force a mistake or a poor clearance which keeps your team on the attack.

The striker tries to force an error from the keeper.

The goalkeeper angles his clearance high and to the side, away from the approaching striker.

COMBINATION MARKING

A mixture of both man-to-man and zonal marking is often used at set pieces. This is known as combination marking. The picture on the right shows combination marking being used to defend a long free kick. The defence is zonally marking with one defender man-marking the opposition's dangerous striker, who may make a late run.

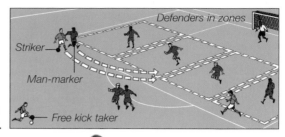

Defenders in zones

Striker

Man-marker

Free kick taker

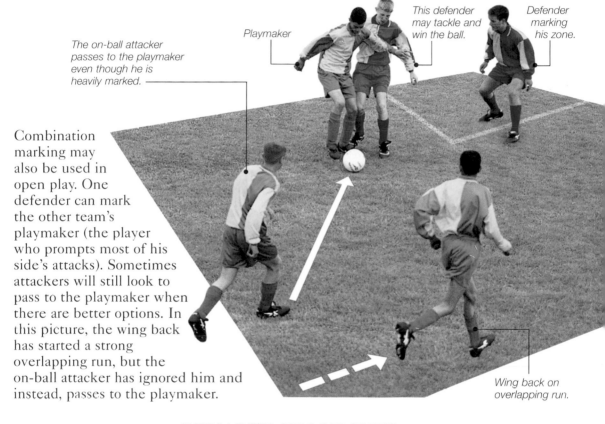

The on-ball attacker passes to the playmaker even though he is heavily marked.

Playmaker

This defender may tackle and win the ball.

Defender marking his zone.

Combination marking may also be used in open play. One defender can mark the other team's playmaker (the player who prompts most of his side's attacks). Sometimes attackers will still look to pass to the playmaker when there are better options. In this picture, the wing back has started a strong overlapping run, but the on-ball attacker has ignored him and instead, passes to the playmaker.

Wing back on overlapping run.

PENALTY SHOOT-OUTS

More and more games are being decided by penalty shoot-outs with five penalties per side and 'sudden death' penalties if the scores are level. The coach chooses penalty-takers. Each coach has his own theory of the best order for his penalty-takers to play. Some prefer to save their best penalty-taker to last when the pressure is greatest. Others prefer to send him in first to put pressure on the other team. Whatever the order your team decides upon, if you are likely to be included, practise taking penalties often.

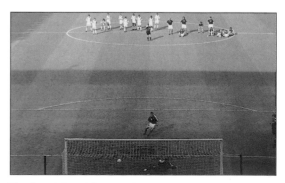

The Czech Republic score in a penalty shoot-out against France during Euro '96. See how the other players stand in the centre circle as the penalties are taken.

COMMUNICATION

Communicating with your team on the pitch is essential. Many defensive mix-ups and breakdowns in attack are due to a lack of communication. Calls should be clear, concise and calm. Calling for the ball is a special skill. Only call when you're free. You can work on this by playing a five-a-side game where you can only receive a pass if you've called for it. If you don't call, but receive the ball, possession passes to the other side.

SOME COMMON CALLS AND SIGNALS

Always use the player's name when shouting 'leave', 'mine', 'time' or 'man-on'. Not doing so is considered 'ungentlemanly conduct' and the referee can call a foul.

'Man-On!' – tells the on-ball player that an opposing player is approaching. Adding which side the player is coming from is even more helpful.

'Leave' or 'Mine' – tells a team-mate that you will take the ball.

Some signals are non-verbal. Here you can see a player signalling to his defence to push up quickly.

'Time' – tells a player about to receive or on the ball that he is unmarked and has space to turn and view the situation.

'Force him outside' – is a defensive order meaning stay inside the attacker forcing him towards the touchline.

A team may have a range of free kicks which they have worked on in training. This player is signalling to his team-mates which sort of free kick he intends to take.

HEAD UP

Communication is not just about what you say or signal, it's also about being in a position to see what your team-mates are doing and saying. For this, you need to have your head up and be aware of the game around you at all times. This is especially important when you are the player in control of the ball.

French international Didier Deschamps has the ball at his feet, but is looking up to spot where his team-mates are placed and what passes are possible.

FIVE V TWO MINI GAME

This fun game helps communication skills. A team of two players act as defenders. They must try to get the ball from the team of five. The team with the ball are each numbered from one to five. One can only pass to two, two to three and so on. If player five manages to pass to player one, the team scores a point. Swap the defenders over once the side has scored three points.

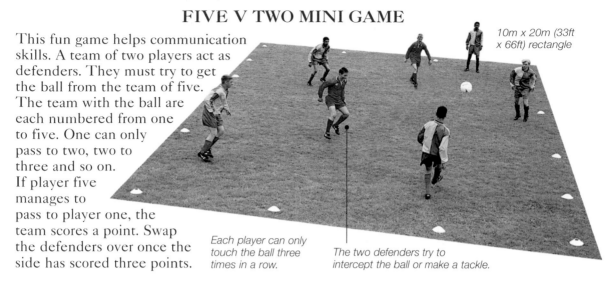

10m x 20m (33ft x 66ft) rectangle

Each player can only touch the ball three times in a row.

The two defenders try to intercept the ball or make a tackle.

THE REFEREE'S SIGNALS

The referee and his two assistants are in charge of the game. Don't argue with them. It doesn't help you or your team. Talking back may earn a yellow, or even a red card. Play until you hear the whistle.

Don't assume that a referee has seen a foul and stop playing. In the noise of a big game, it's not always possible to hear what the referee has said, so it's useful to know his signals.

Hand ball foul — Awarded for deliberate hand or arm contact.

Stand back ten yards — For the opposition team at a free kick.

Play on — The referee lets the play continue.

Indirect free kick — Given for obstruction.

Kicking foul — Player deliberately kicked.

Pushing foul — Player pushed off ball.

Foul throw-in — Feet over side-line.

Tripping foul — Player deliberately tripped.

PRE-MATCH TACTICS

Be prepared for your match early. If possible, check out the pitch conditions beforehand. Make sure every player knows his role, especially new players or ones that have been out of the side for some time. Your team's formations and tactics may have changed since a player previously played.

WARMING UP AND STRETCHING

Warming up before a match is a vital tactic. Stretching your muscles means you're less likely to get injured. Warming up exercises also help to make you more alert and ready for the match.

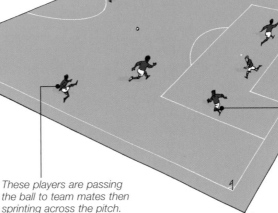

These players have just started warming up. They're jogging round the pitch gently stretching their legs and back muscles.

Pack long and short studs and clothes to keep you warm and dry before and after the game. Goalkeepers should also take a towel to keep their gloves dry.

These players are passing the ball to team mates then sprinting across the pitch.

These players are warming up with some sprints across the pitch.

HAMSTRING STRETCH

Stand upright with one leg straight, a little in front of you. Slowly reach down. Don't bounce or move sharply. Hold for a count of ten, rise slowly and repeat.

GROIN STRETCH

Keep your feet pushed together.

Use your elbows to push your legs down gently.

Sit down with the soles of your feet pressing together and your hands on your knees. Press your knees down gently and hold this position for a count of ten.

CALF STRETCH

Extend your leg while keeping your other foot flat on the floor.

Bend one knee, stretching your other leg out behind you. Slowly push yourself down towards the ground and hold. Stand up and repeat with other leg.

CONCENTRATION

Concentration is important right from the moment just before the match starts. Watch how the opposition team line up. Don't get caught by a quick break at the start.

From kick-off, this team has attacked down the wing. The speed of the attack catches the defending team out.

Always think about your positioning. Be especially aware when the ball goes out of play or there's a free kick. You may be tempted to relax and rest, but the opposing team may choose just this time to strike.

The red team have taken a quick free kick which creates a shooting chance.

Concentration wavers most when you're tired at the end of each half. Statistics show that this is also the time when goals are most likely to be scored. Make an extra special effort to concentrate at these times.

CONFIDENCE

Confidence is vital. If a player is nervous, he's more likely to make a mistake. Players lacking confidence are unlikely to carry out the team's tactics.

For example, a defender may be told to, 'attack when possible.' If the defender lacks confidence, he may decide that there is no opportunity to do so.

This attacker spotted that the defender looked nervous so he decided to try and go past him.

This player is unconfident and believed he couldn't tackle the attacker. As a result he hasn't closed him down or made a challenge as quickly as he should have done.

This player is chasing back to do his team-mate's job. As a result he's let the attacker he was marking go free.

KEEPING CONFIDENCE

You can't win every game you play. Nor can you score in every game or be the man of the match every time. Even top players make mistakes and have poor runs of form. The secret of success is not to get upset, but to train hard and never stop trying your best on the pitch.

Before Euro '96, Alan Shearer hadn't scored in 12 England games. In Euro '96 he was top scorer.

WORLD SOCCER QUIZ

78. What happened to the World Cup Jules Rimet Trophy in 1970?

a. Some thieves stole it and melted it down
b. It was badly damaged when the car that was carrying it crashed
c. Brazil became the first nation to win the World Cup three times, so kept the Trophy

79. 2002 World Cup hosts South Korea play in which of these colours?

a. Red and blue
b. Yellow and white
c. All green

80. Which of these former World Cup winners did not qualify for the 1998 World Cup in France?

a. Argentina
b. Uruguay
c. Italy

81. At which World Cup did the famous phrase 'total football' come into use for the first time?

a. 1974
b. 1978
c. 1982

82. In 1998, the number of teams playing in the World Cup Finals was increased from 24 to how many?

a. 28
b. 32
c. 36

83. The four British nations, England, Scotland, Northern Ireland and Wales have qualified together for the World Cup only once. In which year?

a. 1958
b. 1962
c. 1966

84. In 1994, German player Stefan Effenberg was sent home early from the World Cup. Why?

a. He had food poisoning
b. He made rude gestures at fans
c. He was caught taking drugs

85. When were the World Cup rules changed to allow teams to make substitutions?

a. 1954
b. 1962
c. 1970

86. When England won the World Cup in 1966, who did they defeat in the final at Wembley Stadium?

a. Germany
b. Brazil
c. Italy

87. The first official women's FIFA World Cup took place in 1991. Which was the host country?

a. Germany
b. USA
c. China

88. The 1934 World Cup Final was between Italy and Czechoslovakia. What did the two team captains have in common?

a. They were both injured during the match
b. They both got married after the Final
c. They were both goalkeepers

89. Why was the kick-off delayed just before the start of the 1974 World Cup Final between West Germany and Holland?

a. The groundstaff had forgotten to put the corner flags out
b. One of the players was approached by a fan as he ran out of the tunnel
c. The referee had left his whistle behind

90. Which European Footballer of the Year dedicated his award to politician Nelson Mandela?

a. Ruud Gullit, 1987
b. Lothar Matthäus, 1990
c. George Weah, 1995

91. Belgium beat Argentina in the first match of the 1982 World Cup Finals. Why was this a surprise?

a. Argentina was the host nation
b. Argentina were the World Cup holders
c. Belgium had never qualified before

SOCCER QUIZ ?

PART SEVEN

GOALKEEPING

CONTENTS

GOALKEEPING BASICS

The goalkeeper is one of the most important players in a soccer team. All successful teams have a good goalkeeper as well as a strong defence. A keeper's main job is to protect the goal, but he also helps organize the defence, and his kicks and throws can lead to sudden or gradual attacks. This part of the book shows how to develop the skills and qualities you need to be a good keeper.

WHAT MAKES A GOOD KEEPER?

Decisiveness – you need to be able to think quickly every time there is an attack on your goal (see page 206).

Agility – you will often have to jump, fall and dive as you try to stop a shot at goal (see page 202).

Courage – you will have to dive and jump in crowded penalty areas with many legs, elbows and boots around you (see page 206).

A cool head – if you make a mistake or are faced with a high pressure situation, you need to be able to keep calm and focus on the game (see page 207).

You can find out how to do acrobatic diving saves, like this one, on page 202.

STAR KEEPER

Good co-ordination – sometimes you will need to change direction very quickly and make fast reflex saves (see page 221).

Good communication – your defence will want to hear clear instructions at 'set piece plays' (see pages 214 and 216).

Positional sense – you will need to be able to vary your position in the goal to make it harder for attackers to shoot (see page 204).

Many soccer experts believe that Danish keeper Peter Schmeichel has played a big part in Manchester United's success.

GOALKEEPING LAWS

There are a number of laws of the game which you will need to know about as a keeper. Soccer laws can change quite often, so you will need to keep up to date with them. Breaking a law is 'foul play' and a free kick may be given against you.

★ When you have the ball in your hands, you can only take up to four paces before you must release it.

★ After you have taken hold of the ball, you must get it out to your team-mates in no more than five or six seconds.

★ You can only handle the ball inside your own penalty area. If you come out of the area, use your feet or head when you touch the ball. Breaking this law is very serious, and you might get sent off.

★ If a team-mate passes the ball back to you, or throws a throw-in directly to you, you cannot use your hands to control the ball. You can handle headers and passes that come off the chest or thigh.

USEFUL KICKING TERMS

This book uses a number of special terms to describe the parts of the foot and the stages in kicking a ball.

Your **backswing** is when you swing your leg back before you kick the ball.

Your **follow-through** is when you swing your leg up after kicking the ball.

The **inside** of your foot stretches from your big toe back to your ankle.

Your **instep** is the flat area over your laces, but not including your toes.

PARTS OF THE PITCH

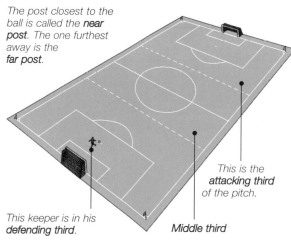

The post closest to the ball is called the **near post**. The one furthest away is the **far post**.

This is the **attacking third** of the pitch.

This keeper is in his **defending third**.

Middle third

You will spend most of your time in your team's defending third of the pitch. When your team is attacking, then play is in your attacking third. The area in-between is called the middle third.

READY TO SAVE

When you think you've got what it takes to be a goalkeeper, then the next step is to get hold of the right equipment and learn the vital goalkeeping skills of quick movement around the goal area and reliable handling of the ball.

GOALKEEPER'S STANCE

When you're waiting to make a save, you should stand in a set position. This allows you to react quickly to attacks on the goal.

This is the typical stance used by goalkeepers. It shows you are alert and ready.

Try to lean forwards slightly so you are ready to make quick and sudden falls or jumps.

Your legs should be slightly bent, and about a shoulder width apart.

Your weight should be equally balanced on the balls of your feet.

Keep your head still and your eyes on the ball.

Your hands should be at around waist height with palms facing outwards.

WHAT TO WEAR

A cap or visor keeps the sun out of your eyes when dealing with high balls.

Wear loose, comfortable clothes. Diving and bending isn't easy in tight clothes.

A shirt with padded elbows and shoulders helps to protect you when you dive.

Gloves with latex palms help to give you much more grip on the ball.

On hard ground, wear tracksuit bottoms to protect your knees.

MOVING AROUND THE GOAL AREA

When you are comfortable with the keeper's stance, you can practise moving quickly around the goal area. If you can move well, catches are much easier to take, as you get more of your body behind the ball. Try moving in the set position, taking small sideways steps. Don't cross your feet as it can slow you down. Then ask a team-mate to move backwards and forwards across the penalty area. Try to mirror his movements.

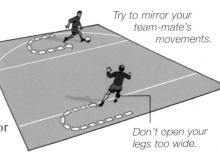

Try to mirror your team-mate's movements.

Don't open your legs too wide.

THE W SHAPE

For shots or headers that come towards you at chest or head height, the most effective catching technique is the W shape. The palms of your hands face outwards and your index fingers and thumbs form a 'W' around the back of the ball. Your fingers need to be spread wide and thumbs should be about an inch or two (2-5cm) apart.

As the shot approaches, you need to keep your eyes on the ball. If you look away from the ball, this could mean a dropped catch and a rebound to an opponent.

Keep your hands well in front of your body, so you can watch the ball as you catch it.

Make sure your fingers are relaxed and flexible so that they absorb the impact of a shot. The ball might bounce out of rigid, tense hands.

This is how your hands should look when you catch using the W shape.

CATCHING AND MOVING

This game will help you to practise combining your sideways movement in the set position with taking catches at chest or head height.

Lay out a zigzag pattern of sports markers on a pitch with a gap of about 2m (6ft) between each one. Weave through the markers, staying in the set stance.

After you catch, bring the ball close in to your body, so that it cannot slip out of your hands.

Ask a team-mate to throw or kick shots at chest or head height. He should vary the direction of the throws, aiming to your sides as well as straight ahead.

GOOD HANDLING

The W shape is a useful basic catching technique, but because the ball comes at many different heights and angles, you also need to get to know other ways of handling it. No matter where the ball is coming from, good footwork will make handling a lot easier.

CRADLING THE BALL

Scooping the ball into your body is the best method to use with balls that come at waist or stomach height. It is a very safe way of catching and some keepers use the scoop with chest high balls too.

Cradle the ball with your hands and arms.

As the shot arrives, angle your hands downwards, giving the ball a clear path to travel into your body.

As the ball comes into contact with your chest or stomach, wrap your hands and forearms around the back of the ball. Your body will cushion the impact of a shot. Try not to step back as you catch.

USEFUL TIPS

★ Always try to lean into a shot. This makes it much easier to scoop the ball into your body.

★ You may need to take a small jump to get your upper body behind a slightly higher shot.

★ It's very risky to use the W shape with a waist high shot, as you can't get your eyes behind the flight of the incoming ball.

STAR SCOOP

This Derby County keeper makes a good scoop while under pressure in an English Premier League game.

THE BARRIER POSITION

The barrier is the safer of the two methods you can use for ground level shots. It takes time to get down into this position, so it's best to use the barrier when you have a clear view of the ball or can see the shot early.

Place one knee on the ground, with your leg in the position shown in the picture. Put the foot of your other leg lengthwise alongside it, so that you make a long barrier.

Your hands should be in front of the barrier, covering any gap between your foot and knee, and ready to scoop up the ball.

Your leg and foot provide extra protection behind your hands.

THE BENDING SCOOP

It isn't easy to get into the safer barrier position quickly, so with faster ground shots it's better to use the bending scoop. This position relies upon good footwork and close attention to the movement of the ball.

As the shot approaches, bring your feet close together. Then bend down and scoop the ball into your hands.

It's risky to use this method on uneven playing surfaces and in bad weather conditions. An unexpected deflection of the ball can cause serious problems.

HIGH AND LOW SHOT PRACTICE

This game will help you practise catching shots aimed at different heights. You will need two other players.

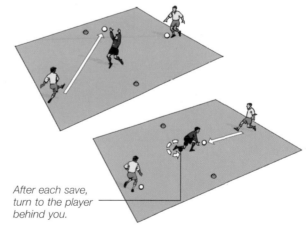

After each save, turn to the player behind you.

Mark out a goal 3m (10ft) wide, and place two team-mates 5m (16ft) away on either side of it, each with a ball. One player provides chest and head high shots, the other player hits ground shots. This is a tiring drill, so swap around regularly.

SHOTS NEAR THE KEEPER

Some shots come too quickly for you to have time to do a kneeling or bending save. When you need to get down to the ball as fast as possible, falling to the ground is the best solution. Practising falling saves will help you get ready to try diving saves later on.

THE COLLAPSING SAVE

When a ball is aimed close to you, there is no need to dive for it. What you should do instead is move quickly out of the set stance and collapse onto the shot. When you do a collapsing save, swing your legs to one side and drop down to the ball hands first. Your body will act as a barrier behind your hands. Try not to land on your elbows (see page 202).

Notice how the goalkeeper above is already looking to position his hands behind the ball. Although he has begun to swing his legs to one side, the top half of his body is steady and focused on the ball.

The keeper puts both hands on the ball. One hand wraps around the back of the ball, while the other is on top.

The wrapping hand acts as a barrier. The hand on top grips the ball to his body.

Once the shot has been stopped, the keeper pulls the ball in close to his chest. He then curls himself around the ball to help protect his body in a crowded goal area.

COLLAPSING TIPS

★ You should practise collapsing saves regularly, because many keepers find them very difficult to do.

★ Don't overdo your collapsing movement. It shouldn't involve any jumping or acrobatic leaps.

★ The ball will be moving fast, so get your hands down in time, otherwise the ball will squeeze under your body.

This keeper didn't move fast enough.

SAVING WITH YOUR FEET

When a shot is fired in from very close range, you will need to react fast to make a save. If you don't have time to get your hands to the ball, you'll have to save with your feet and legs.

As the ball approaches, keep your weight well balanced and turn your feet outwards. Watch the ball very closely and try to use your legs as a barrier.

Saving with your feet should only be attempted as a final option. This type of save is instinctive and you have no control over where the ball rebounds to.

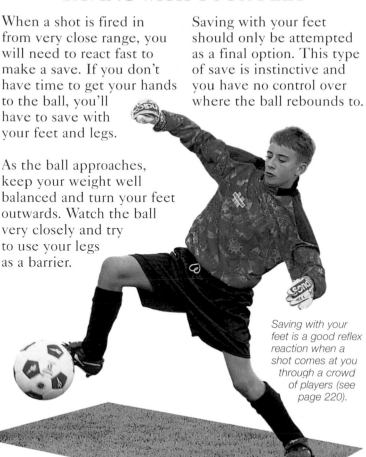

Saving with your feet is a good reflex reaction when a shot comes at you through a crowd of players (see page 220).

PREPARING FOR DIVING SAVES

Diving saves involve a lot of falling on the ground. Here are two games to give you more practice in this, before you learn how to dive. It's best to practise with another keeper, who can also get used to falling.

1. Your team-mate rolls the ball through your legs. Turn around quickly and fall on the ball before it is out of your reach.

2. Your team-mate throws balls a metre (3ft) either side of you. Crouch down to catch them, falling on your side as you catch.

HANDS AND FEET PRACTICE

Mark out a goal about 4m (13ft) wide within the goal area. Place two more markers the same distance apart about 3m (10ft) out from goal. Do the same again about 6m (20ft) out.

Ask a team-mate to stand on a line level with either set of markers and take shots at goal. Swap with your team-mate when you feel tired. Use your hands to save whenever possible.

Practise collapsing saves for longer shots.

Save with your feet and legs for closer, faster shots.

DIVING SAVES

When attackers fire wider shots at goal, you'll need to attempt a diving save. Successful acrobatic diving saves give goalkeepers a lot of satisfaction and can make the difference between winning or losing a match. However, there is much more to a diving save than simply leaping into the air. The right jumping and landing techniques are essential.

A DIVING CATCH

When you spot the 'flight', or direction, of the ball, take a few quick sideways paces to reduce your diving distance. Stay focused on the ball in the set stance.

Just before you are about to dive, quickly transfer your weight onto the foot nearest the incoming ball. Push down hard on this foot and then begin to leap up.

Try to get as much thrust or 'spring' from your leg as possible. As you leap up, keep your eyes on the ball and dive slightly forwards to attack the shot.

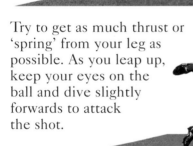

Use the W shape catching technique, letting your hands absorb the power of the shot. Grasp the ball tightly so that it doesn't bounce out of your hands when you land.

A SAFE LANDING

It's vital to learn a safe landing technique. When you hit the ground, try to land on your side, as this is a well cushioned part of the body. Don't come down on your elbows or your stomach.

Keep your body relaxed as you land.

If you are playing on an artificial surface or on hard ground, tracksuit bottoms can help prevent painful grazes to the knees.

THE CAT

Many diving saves require impressive agility and suppleness.

In the 1960s and '70s, Peter Bonetti of Chelsea and England became known as 'The Cat', because of his quick reflexes and diving technique.

TIPPING THE BALL

You should aim to catch most diving saves, but if a shot is too powerful or too well-placed to catch, you should still try to get a touch on the ball as it goes by.

A slight deflection, or tip, of the ball can be enough to push it off target. When the shot touches your hand, make sure your palm is open and your fingers are spread wide. Try to push or flick the ball away.

Use only one hand to deflect the ball.

Keeping your palm open makes a bigger target for the ball to hit.

When you deflect the ball away, try to tip it over the bar or around the post.

PLAY SAFE

If you push the ball straight out in front, you could give it to an opposing striker.

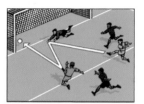

The safest option is putting it out of play for a corner. You can tip the ball with either hand as you dive, but try to use the hand nearest the ball. Use your upper hand for tipping over the bar, and your lower hand for pushing the ball around the post.

DIVING TIPS

★ It is better to use swift footwork to get closer to the ball and make an easier save than to attempt a difficult diving save.

★ All keepers have a favourite diving side but you should be a strong diver on both sides. Spend extra time building up your weaker spring.

IMPROVING YOUR DIVES

This game helps you get used to the hard impact with the ground that follows a diving save. It can also strengthen your spring off the ground. Ask a team-mate or another keeper to shoot or throw the ball just inside either post of a full size goal. Stand in the middle of the goal before each shot and as the ball approaches, leap up off the foot nearest the ball. Swap around after four or five diving saves.

Try to catch every shot. Only tip the ball away if you have to.

Be careful that you don't collide with the posts. Always watch your position.

POSITIONING

In goalkeeping, good positional sense is as important as sound handling skills, especially when the ball is in the defending third of the pitch. Good positioning involves skilful footwork and getting your body behind the ball. This makes a lot of saves easier for you and also makes shooting at goal harder for your opponents.

GETTING IN LINE

Keepers like to position themselves somewhere on an imaginary line between the ball and the centre of the goal. This is known as being in line with play.

This keeper is in line with play and so as a shot comes in, he can get his body behind the ball and make a simple save.

Here the keeper hasn't managed to keep in line with play. As a shot approaches, he is at full stretch and has to make a much more difficult save.

NARROWING THE ANGLE

Good keepers not only need to be in line but off their goal-line too. By coming off the goal-line, keepers reduce the view of the goal for attackers and 'narrow' the shooting angle. Shots become much easier for the keeper to reach.

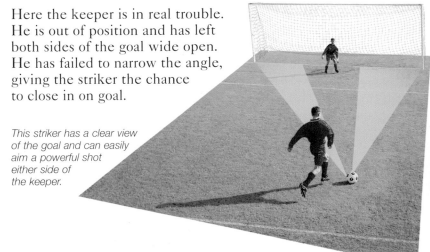

The striker has a small target area.

Here the goalkeeper is in the perfect position. He is in line with play and has come off his goal-line to narrow the angle. He can handle shots to his left or right.

Here the keeper is in real trouble. He is out of position and has left both sides of the goal wide open. He has failed to narrow the angle, giving the striker the chance to close in on goal.

This striker has a clear view of the goal and can easily aim a powerful shot either side of the keeper.

IN THE DEFENDING THIRD

You should always be in line when the ball is in your defending third of the pitch. How far off your goal-line you should be depends on where play is taking place, and if you think that your goal area is under threat of attack from a sudden shot or cross.

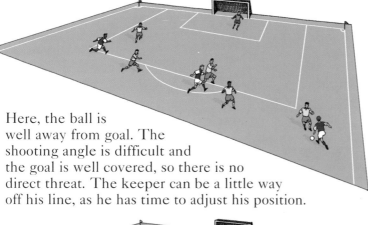

Here, the ball is well away from goal. The shooting angle is difficult and the goal is well covered, so there is no direct threat. The keeper can be a little way off his line, as he has time to adjust his position.

Here, the attack is inside the penalty area and the striker will soon be in a position to shoot. The keeper must not be too far off his goal-line as he is directly involved in play. He must be well in line with the ball.

THE CHIP SHOT

A keeper should be well off his line and in touch with play when the opposition are on the attack, but he mustn't rush out too fast.

This keeper is rushing out to narrow the angle.

If a striker is nearing the goal and sees the keeper off his line, he may try to lob, or chip, the ball over his head (see page 220).

The striker lobs the ball into the unguarded goal.

RECOVERING POSITION

You must always be ready to change your position quickly. A sudden sideways pass near or inside the penalty area will leave you well out of line. You need to get in line again fast, before an attacker can shoot into the open space.

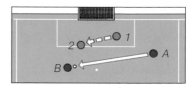

Here, player A passes to player B. The keeper should move from position 1, where he was covering player A, to position 2 to line up against player B. By making a direct diagonal movement, he will get into position sooner.

THE ANGLES GAME

This game helps you practise getting in line with play and narrowing shooting angles. Ask two team-mates, each with a ball, to stand on either side of the penalty area about 14m (46ft) out from goal.

Get into line, shout 'ready' and then save from player A.

Do the same with player B. A and B should vary their positions before each shot.

ONE-ON-ONES

A defensive mistake or a great pass can lead to a striker being through on goal, with only the keeper to beat. These 'one-on-one' situations are a real test of technique and temperament for any goalkeeper.

FORCING THE ATTACKER WIDE

You need to position yourself well and react quickly and positively if you are to have any chance of stopping an attacker's run on goal. Don't commit yourself too early to rushing out, but try to narrow the shooting angle and force the attacker wide away from goal. This will make it more difficult for him to shoot and will give defenders a chance to get back and support you. Be ready for a sudden shot.

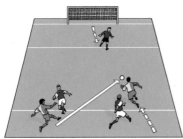

1. As the striker is running onto a pass but has not yet touched the ball, get quickly off your line and narrow the shooting angle.

2. Once the striker has the ball, slow down, and watch out for a shot. Get into the set stance and block the route to goal.

3. As the striker tries to take the ball around you, stay in line and force him wide. It is now much harder for him to score.

DIVING AT AN ATTACKER'S FEET

When a striker attempts to dribble the ball around you, try to gain possession by diving at the player's feet.

This type of save is difficult and you need a lot of courage and a cool head. Only dive if you feel sure you will win possession. Be positive and attack the ball.

The best time to make your move is when the ball is slightly ahead of the attacker and not totally under control.

Go in hands first for the ball. By keeping them in front of your face, you help to protect your head.

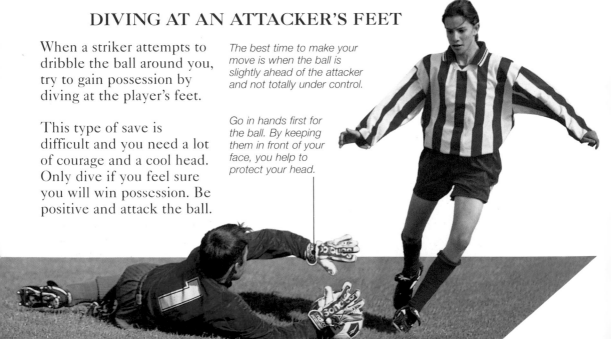

SPREADING YOURSELF

As you go down to save at an attacker's feet, try to 'spread yourself' on the ground, making a long barrier between the ball and the goal. This will also help narrow the angle.

Get down low, trying not to leave any gaps between your body and the ground. Once you have claimed the ball, wrap your body around it for extra security.

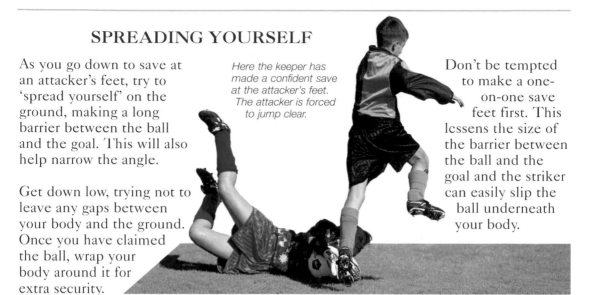

Here the keeper has made a confident save at the attacker's feet. The attacker is forced to jump clear.

Don't be tempted to make a one-on-one save feet first. This lessens the size of the barrier between the ball and the goal and the striker can easily slip the ball underneath your body.

SPREADING PRACTICE

This drill helps you to judge the moment when to dive at an attacker's feet. Mark out a pitch about 10m (33ft) square. Ask two teammates to keep possession of the ball as you move about in the set stance, diving at their feet. Don't be tempted to save feet first.

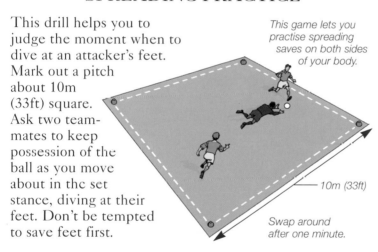

This game lets you practise spreading saves on both sides of your body.

10m (33ft)

Swap around after one minute.

STAYING COOL

One-on-ones are very pressurized situations. You should try to stay calm and not make any rash decisions. Remember that the striker is under more pressure than you are. He is expected to score and has to decide very quickly how to get the ball past you, and into the net.

If you know your opponent has one weaker shooting foot, force him to take the ball on that side.

Looking big and confident can unsettle a striker – so don't crouch down too far in your stance. Waving your hands or arms around quickly can also affect a striker's concentration.

STAR BLOCK

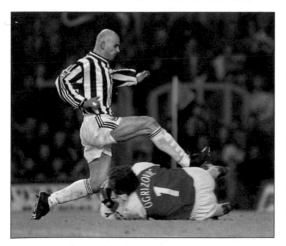

Here Coventry City goalkeeper Steve Ogrizovic shows a lot of courage and prevents an almost certain goal, by making an impressive spreading save.

He bravely dives at the feet of Newcastle United's Georgian international midfielder Temur Ketsbaia and wins possession of the ball.

HANDLING CROSSES

Many goals come from high crosses aimed deep into the penalty area. Every cross is different, and you need to decide whether to come for a cross or leave it for your defence to clear. Catch a cross if you can, but punch or tip if you have to. If you decide to deal with a cross, be positive and go for the ball.

POSITIONING FOR CROSSES

Where you stand for a cross depends on where the crosser is. Half turn your body towards the crosser so that you can watch movements in the area as well as the ball.

Here, the ball is near the wing and a long way out from goal. The keeper is positioned in the centre of the goal so that he won't be left stranded by a cross over his head. Moving backwards and catching a ball under pressure isn't easy.

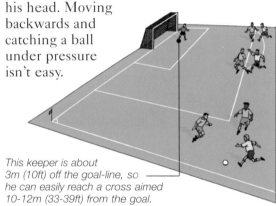

This keeper is about 3m (10ft) off the goal-line, so he can easily reach a cross aimed 10-12m (33-39ft) from the goal.

Play has now moved away from the wing and well into the attacking third of the pitch. The keeper is moving closer to the near post to narrow the angle. He must still be alert to the chance of a far post cross.

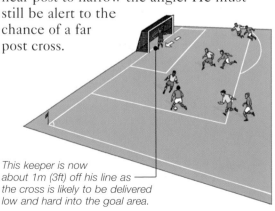

This keeper is now about 1m (3ft) off his line as the cross is likely to be delivered low and hard into the goal area.

A CLEAN CATCH

You need good communication with your defence (see page 214) when dealing with a cross. If you decide you can reach an incoming cross and can make a clean catch without other players getting in your way, then clearly shout 'Keeper's ball!' as you take a running jump for it.

Jump off one leg and catch the ball about 30cm (1ft) in front of your face, using the W shape.

Lift up the leg nearest to the opposition to protect your lower body against challenges.

As you jump, turn sideways on to the opposition and face the ball. Try to catch a cross when the ball is at its highest point. This makes it harder for strikers to get up and reach the ball. When you have dealt with a cross, be ready to make a quick throw (see page 210) to start an attack.

TWO-HANDED PUNCHES

Sometimes other players can get in your way or put you under so much pressure that you are unable to catch the ball. In this case, try to punch it away instead. A good punched clearance needs height and distance to give you enough time to recover your position if the ball goes straight to an opponent.

This is how you clench your fists for a two-handed punch.

Aim for the lower half of the ball.

Take a running jump at the ball and shout 'Keeper's ball!' To get maximum power in your punches you need to use two clenched fists. This also offers a larger surface area for the ball to hit. Keep your fists together and strike the ball firmly with the part of your hands between the knuckles and the finger joints.

ONE-HANDED PUNCHES

If you can't get two hands to the ball, you may have to use a less powerful one-handed punch.

One-handed punches are quite difficult to do because you only have a small punching surface.

When the ball is drifting over your head, and you have to move backwards quickly, a one-handed punch will strike the ball out of danger towards the opposite wing.

TIPPING

If an inswinging cross is aimed deep into the goal area and you are under a lot of pressure, you could try tipping the ball over the bar for a corner (see page 203).

When you tip the ball out for a corner, you are giving possession straight back to the opposition. A catch or strong punch is safer.

Use the hand which is furthest from the goal, to get a much bigger swing at the ball.

CROSSES GAME

This game should get you used to handling under pressure and timing your jumps. Stand in the centre of a goal and ask two team-mates, each with a ball, to supply crosses from the wings.

Ask your team-mates to vary the height and pace of the crosses.

This team-mate acts as an opposing striker, trying to beat you to the ball. Team-mates could swap roles regularly.

THROWING

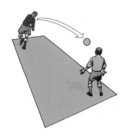

Accurate and reliable distribution of the ball to your team-mates is an essential skill for a keeper. Well placed throws or kicks can lead to dangerous attacks on your opposition's goal. There are three main types of throw and each can be effective in opening up space for an unmarked team-mate.

THE UNDERARM ROLL

For an underarm throw, start by swinging your throwing arm back.

You use the underarm roll when you are aiming for a team-mate no more than 8m (26ft) away. As he will be positioned near the goal, use this throw when no opponents are close by. Don't use this type of throw on muddy pitches, as the ball might get stuck.

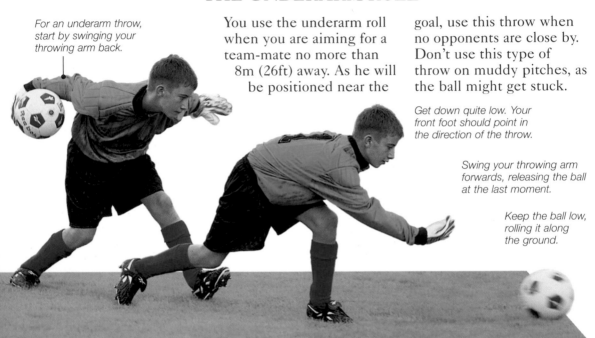

Get down quite low. Your front foot should point in the direction of the throw.

Swing your throwing arm forwards, releasing the ball at the last moment.

Keep the ball low, rolling it along the ground.

THE JAVELIN THROW

Use the javelin throw to cover distances of up to 15m (49ft). Your target might be a team-mate who has moved into space on the wing or who has dropped back from midfield. Javelin throws should be delivered low and fast to their target, so try not to throw the ball too high in the air.

Bend your knees slightly to help keep the ball low as you release it.

Bend your throwing arm back and bring the ball up level with your shoulder. Aim your non-throwing arm at the target and point your front foot in the same direction.

Swing your throwing arm forwards quickly and release the ball. Flicking your wrist will help keep the ball low. For extra distance on your throw, follow through powerfully.

THE OVERARM THROW

Use the overarm throw to cover distances of 15m (49ft) or more. When your technique is well developed, the overarm throw can travel nearly as far as a kick. This throw is very good for getting the ball upfield quickly once an opposition attack has broken down. A fast, well placed throw can leave opponents badly out of position and can turn defence into attack.

Bring your throwing arm back behind your body. Keep it straight. Point your non-throwing arm and your front foot at the target.

Swing your throwing arm powerfully upwards and over your shoulder.

Transfer your weight onto your front foot. To get height on the throw, release the ball when your arm is at its highest point.

WHEN TO THROW

★ Use a throw after cutting out a cross. You can change the direction of play while opponents are still in your defending third.

★ If the opposing team has a tall defence, low throws are a lot better than high kicks for keeping possession.

★ When you are playing in a strong wind, use throws rather than kicks, as they are easier to direct and control.

★ Stick to throwing if you are not a strong kicker. Good throws are better than weak kicks.

WHERE TO THROW

Most throws should be aimed towards the sides of the pitch, where a team-mate may be able to find some space to run into.

Aim for the safest part of the pitch.

A throw aimed into the crowded centre of the pitch will be difficult to control and could be easily intercepted. As most throws travel quite low through the air, you shouldn't try to throw over the heads of opponents.

THROWING GAME

Ask two keepers to help you with this game so you can all practise your throwing skills. Form a triangle, 6m (20ft) apart, and roll the ball underarm to each other first.

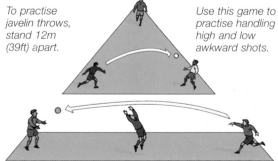

To practise javelin throws, stand 12m (39ft) apart.

Use this game to practise handling high and low awkward shots.

For overarm practice, two throwers stand about 15m (49ft) apart. The other keeper stands in the middle and tries to intercept the throws.

KICKING

Place kicks, volleys and half-volleys give you an opportunity to send the ball a long way upfield, changing defence into attack. Keepers need to be strong accurate kickers, so practise regularly.

THE PLACE KICK

A place kick is a kick taken when the ball is stationary, such as a goal kick or free kick. Long, powerful place kicks help ease pressure on your defence. If your kicks don't travel very far, make sure they are accurate.

Take an angled run-up and put your non-kicking foot to the side of the ball. Your kicking foot swings forwards quickly.

As you kick, lean back slightly and keep your eyes fixed on the ball.

Strike the lower half of the ball with your instep. Follow through powerfully.

THE VOLLEY

To do a volley, you drop the ball from your hands and kick it before it hits the ground. When you are holding the ball, you can take four steps as a run-up before you kick (see page 195). The higher you aim a volley, the longer it will take to reach its target.

As you run, hold the ball in front of you at waist height. Take a good backswing as the ball drops.

Place your non-kicking leg behind the ball. Leaning back slightly will help to get lift on the kick.

Keeping your head steady, kick the bottom of the ball with your instep. Follow-through smoothly.

THE HALF-VOLLEY

When you do a half-volley, the ball bounces once before you kick it. Use half-volleys in windy conditions, as they do not travel as high through the air as volleys. It's risky to try them on muddy or uneven pitches.

Drop the ball from about waist height. It should land just in front of your non-kicking foot.

As the ball bounces, swing your kicking leg forwards, leaning back as you kick.

Watching the ball carefully, strike the bottom half of it with your instep.

WHICH KICK TO CHOOSE

Think carefully about what type of kick to use and don't take any chances. Aim all place kicks to the sides of the pitch, and never kick across the penalty area. Only kick over your opponents' heads with high volleys or half-volleys.

If you are a strong kicker, you might be able to reach the attacking third with a powerful volley.

Half-volleys travel more quickly than volleys and so are good for starting fast, unexpected attacks.

Place kicks aimed to the sides of the pitch are safer and might find team-mates in space.

If your strikers are not good at heading the ball, a short kick to a defender is better than a kick upfield.

TARGET PRACTICE

You will need five or six balls for this game which will improve the accuracy and distance of your kicks. Ask another keeper to help you. Take turns at kicking and retrieving the balls.

For place kicks, kick alternately from either corner of the goal area, aiming inside two markers 6m (20ft) apart on the halfway line.

For volleys, position markers level with the circle in the other half of the pitch.

For place kicks, position the markers equally between the centre circle and the touchline.

For half-volleys and volleys, kick from the edge of the penalty area. Try to clear the markers in the opposition's half of the pitch.

HELPING THE DEFENCE

Although as a keeper you have your own important job to do, you should remember that you are part of the defensive unit. A good keeper will communicate with his team-mates and be on-hand to receive back passes and cut out through balls.

TALKING TO YOUR DEFENCE

From the goal area, you have a good view of the pitch and can see how play is developing. This allows you to advise your defenders about what they should do and warn them about possible dangers. You should shout clear, short instructions. Decide with your team-mates before a game what you will shout in different situations. There are several well-known, regular shouts.

KEEPING UP WITH PLAY

Try to stay in line with play even when the ball is not in your defending third. If you are always in touch with the game, you might be able to offer some support to your team-mates in tricky situations.

'Keeper's ball!' – shout this to claim possession in any situation, and especially for crosses (see page 208).

'Peter, pick him up!' – tells a specific team-mate to mark an opponent who is unmarked.

'Push up!' – gets your defence to move upfield, possibly catching opponents offside (see page 215).

Here play is in the attacking third. The keeper is on the edge of the penalty area, ready to deal with long clearances and through balls.

'Time!' – tells a team-mate with the ball that no opposing players are near enough to challenge him.

'Played!' – congratulates a team-mate for some good play. It's good to encourage your team-mates.

'Man on!' – warns a team-mate with the ball who is unaware that an opponent is about to tackle him.

Play is now in the middle third and the keeper has moved back slightly. He can cut out through balls or long-range shots as well as receive back passes.

PLAYING AS A SWEEPER

A good keeper will be ready to act as a defensive 'outfield' player when needed. All players except the keeper are known as outfield players as they are able to move freely about the pitch.

If a team-mate wants to pass the ball back to you, stand a few metres back from him, in case he overhits or misdirects the pass.

Be ready to take on the role of 'sweeper', a spare man at the back of the defence. You can clear up any loose balls and can be on-hand to receive back passes from defenders.

When you receive a back pass, remember that you can only use your hands with headers, not with passes from feet.

THE OFFSIDE RULE

All keepers need to know about the offside rule. You can often stop dangerous attacks by catching opposing attackers offside. Your team is then awarded an indirect free kick.

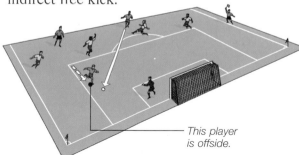

This player is offside.

A player is offside when, just as a pass is made to him, there are less than two opponents between him and the goal. No player can be offside in his own half or if he receives the ball directly from a corner, throw-in or goal kick. Asking your defence to push up to catch strikers offside is risky. If an attacker gets past a defender who has pushed up, he is through on goal.

CLEARANCE KICKS

You will sometimes be in position to intercept dangerous through balls with a powerful one-touch clearance which aims to force the ball well upfield or out of play.

Accuracy is not so important with these kicks, but you must react quickly and kick powerfully while under pressure. Only come out of your area if you are sure you will get to the ball first.

Try to make good, strong contact with the ball for a powerful clearance kick.

CORNERS AND THROW-INS

Corners and throw-ins in your defending third give your
opponents the chance to use a 'dead', or stationary, ball to carry
out some pre-planned moves, called 'set piece plays'. The fact
that no player can be offside if he receives the ball directly from
a throw-in or corner makes these moves very dangerous.

ORGANIZING CORNER DEFENCE

As keeper, you are responsible for making
sure that your defenders are in a good
position and that no opposing attackers are
unmarked. Most players in your team will
have a particular job to do at a corner,
whether marking opposing players or
covering different parts of the penalty
area. Shout clear instructions to your team-
mates and take charge of the situation,
making quick, confident decisions.

One or two players
should cover the far post
and the area in front of it.

One player should
guard the area around
the near post, with
another player
nearby to cover a
very short corner.

Other players should mark
opponents who have come
forward for the corner.

You should stand in the
centre of the goal, about
1m (3ft) off your line, so
you can deal with a near or
far post delivery.

One defender
should stand on the edge
of the goal area to give the
keeper extra support.

No defender can come any
nearer than 9m (30ft) to
the corner taker.

THE NEAR POST MOVE

One of the most dangerous and commonly
used set piece plays at a corner is the three
touch move which involves an inswinging
corner to the near post.

The aim of this move is to get the ball
into the goal using just three touches.
An attacker swings the corner in to
the near post where a tall opponent
tries to flick on a header towards
the far post. Another player tries to
get in front of his marker to meet
the flick-on with a header or shot.

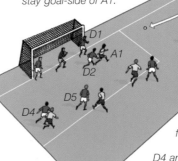

Here, to deal with a near post
move, D1 and D2 must
stay goal-side of A1.

The keeper
should be
positioned centrally
to deal with any
flicked-on headers.

D4 and D5 must stay
close to their markers.

THE OUTSWINGER

The outswinging corner is aimed at players on the edge of the penalty area who will run in and head the ball at goal.

An outswinging cross

To catch an outswinging cross, come out fast as the ball will be moving away from you. It might be better to let defenders deal with it, so be ready to make a save.

THE SHORT CORNER

Short corners allow opponents to keep possession of the ball while they decide whether to cross or try a long-range shot.

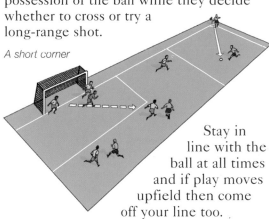

A short corner

Stay in line with the ball at all times and if play moves upfield then come off your line too. Your defenders should keep marking in case of a sudden cross.

LONG THROW-INS

Long throw-ins are becoming very popular as a way of getting the ball into the goal area. Most teams will have a player who can easily throw the ball deep into the penalty area. Treat long throw-ins like near post corners, as your opponents will try to use a three touch move.

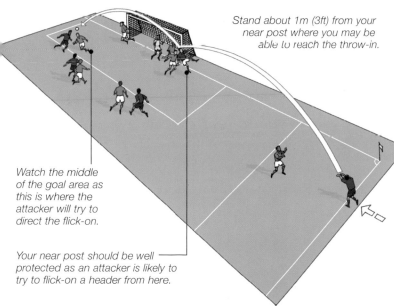

Stand about 1m (3ft) from your near post where you may be able to reach the throw-in.

Watch the middle of the goal area as this is where the attacker will try to direct the flick-on.

Your near post should be well protected as an attacker is likely to try to flick-on a header from here.

SET PIECE TIPS

★ Stand near the middle of the goal at corners, so you can cover any part of your goal area. Watch the kicker, but be aware of movements in the penalty area.

★ Don't get blocked on your line by players crowding in front of you. Move around on your line to make some space.

★ You should treat corners in the same way as crosses (see page 208). If you think you can safely deal with the ball, then be positive and go for it. Try to take charge of your goal area and be decisive.

★ Short throw-ins in your defending third can be dangerous. Defenders should mark the attackers in and around the penalty area and you should be ready for a cross.

You should be able to tell when a long throw-in is about to happen. The thrower will take a long run-up before throwing and your opponents will push taller players into your penalty area.

FREE KICKS AND PENALTIES

Penalties and direct free kicks, where the taker of the kick can shoot straight for goal, give your opponents a good scoring opportunity. You can organize defensive cover at free kicks, but penalties are a challenge for you alone. They give you the chance to pull off a great save.

CENTRAL FREE KICKS

To reduce the chances of a goal from a central direct free kick, you need to form a defensive wall. You and your team-mates should work out in practice where everyone is positioned for free kicks and who will organize the wall.

In a match, if you are organizing the wall, then you need to do it quickly before your opponents catch you out of position. The wall must be at least 9m (30ft) away from the kick. It should be lined up slightly past the near post to make swerve shots more difficult.

The wall covers the near post, and the keeper covers the far post.

To see the kicker clearly, the keeper stands well to the side of the wall.

There should be about five players in a wall. One player runs out to block a sideways pass.

The player in line with the near post must be quite tall to make chip shots harder.

If a chip or swerve shot gets past the wall, you may have time to move across and save it.

WIDE FREE KICKS

There is less chance of a shot from a wide free kick, so the wall does not need so many players in it. A two or three player wall can block a deep cross into the goal area. Stand in the centre of your goal about 2m (6ft) off your line.

A small wall allows other players to mark opponents.

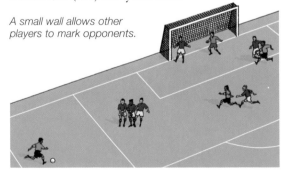

KICKS INSIDE THE AREA

Indirect free kicks, where the ball has to touch another player before it enters the goal, can be awarded in the penalty area. These can occur in very dangerous positions, so bring as many players behind the ball as possible.

For central kicks, the keeper should rush out as the kick is taken.

SAVING PENALTIES

The outcome of a penalty kick can decide the result of a game, but all the pressure is on the penalty-taker, because the whole of his team will expect him to score. Before the kick is taken, move from side to side if you want to. You can't move forwards until after the ball has been kicked.

Moving from side to side along your goal-line may help distract the penalty-taker before he takes the kick.

Watch to see if the taker keeps looking at one particular side of the goal before he kicks. But don't assume he's definitely going to shoot in that direction – he may be trying to trick you. Try to delay your dive until the kick has actually been taken. Don't try to anticipate a shot – react to one.

Use any technique to save a penalty. Fall slightly forwards as you dive to put more power behind a tip and keep the ball out of the goal.

DUMMY TACTIC

A 'dummy' is a way of fooling your opponents by pretending to move in one direction but then actually going in the other. You can use, or 'sell', a dummy to try to make a penalty-taker shoot at a particular part of the goal.

WATCH THE RUN-UP

Watching the penalty-taker's run-up may tell you which side of the goal he is aiming for. Straight run-ups are difficult to predict, because the kicker may choose either side or may kick straight ahead.

Angled run-up – left-footed shot goes to the left.

Curved run-up – right-footed shot goes to the left.

1. As the taker runs up to kick, sell a dummy left or right, as if you are about to dive to this side.

2. Dive to the opposite side. The taker may be fooled into shooting where you want him to.

Angled run-ups can result in shots aimed at the same side of the goal as the kicking foot.

Curved run-ups often lead to shots into the opposite side of the goal to the kicking foot.

RECOVERY SAVE PRACTICE

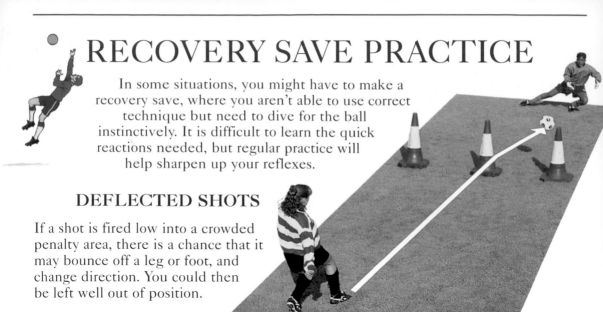

In some situations, you might have to make a recovery save, where you aren't able to use correct technique but need to dive for the ball instinctively. It is difficult to learn the quick reactions needed, but regular practice will help sharpen up your reflexes.

DEFLECTED SHOTS

If a shot is fired low into a crowded penalty area, there is a chance that it may bounce off a leg or foot, and change direction. You could then be left well out of position.

To practise saving deflected shots, put a row of three heavy 1m (3ft) high markers 6m (20ft) out from goal, with a gap of 60cm (2ft) between each one. Ask a team-mate to stand 5m (16ft) further back and fire shots at goal. Some shots will deflect off the markers.

You have to react very fast to save a deflected shot. If you are wrong-footed by a deflection, try to save with your feet (see page 201).

Only move after the shot has been made.

Keep your weight well balanced and don't dive too early.

OVERHEAD LOBS

If you are caught out of position, an attacker may lob, or chip, the ball over you. As lob shots travel slowly, you have the chance to recover your position with quick footwork and make a save.

To practise this, place a marker 6m (20ft) from the centre of the goal and ask a team-mate to stand on the penalty spot with a ball. Run out and touch the marker.

As you touch it, your team-mate throws the ball over your head. Step back quickly and leap up. Try to tip the ball over the bar (see page 203).

This game should improve your jumping technique.

As you step back, turn sideways slightly so that you are facing the ball more.

THE REFLEX SAVE

When there are many players in front of you, blocking your view of play, you might have to react very quickly to deal with a shot that you only see at the last moment. To practise reflex saves, stand in the centre of the goal with your back to a team-mate who stands about 12m (39ft) out from goal.

When your team-mate shouts 'Turn!' he shoots at goal while you turn around and try to make a save.

You will need to react fast and make a reflex, or instinctive, save.

Your team-mate shouldn't aim too far away from your body and should vary his position before each shot.

Don't worry about your technique. Catch a shot if you can, but if not, try to block or tip it. When you see a low shot very late, saving with your feet may be the best option (see page 201). Practise regularly to speed up your reflexes.

THE FOLLOW-UP SAVE

Whenever you make a save but do not keep possession of the ball, always get back into position quickly, so that you are able to deal with a follow-up shot.

This game will help you practise getting in line with the ball, making a save and then rapidly recovering your position.

This game is very tiring, so rest after each pair of saves or swap around with another keeper.

Stand in the centre of the goal and ask four team-mates, each with a ball, to position themselves an equal distance apart, 15m (49ft) out from goal. Get in line and save from the player furthest to the right. Then save from the next player along who shoots just as you complete the first save. Repeat the exercise with the players on the left.

Your coach could number each striker from 1 to 4 and then shout out one of the numbers. You then save from this player.

221

PRE-MATCH PREPARATION

It's important that you develop a regular routine before a game, so that you are well prepared, both physically and mentally. You should approach a game with a positive attitude, feeling fit and confident. Just before a game, make sure you do a proper warm-up and some handling practice.

PRE-MATCH TIPS

★ Try to get a good night's sleep before a game and don't do anything too energetic the day before. It's best to be well rested and alert.

★ Be careful about what you eat before a game. You need to eat well to give yourself energy, but don't eat a large meal just before exercising.

★ Spend time sorting out your kit. Take kit, such as tracksuit bottoms and a cap, which will be useful in different types of weather.

★ When you arrive at the pitch, check the quality of the playing surface and keep an eye on the weather conditions, as these might affect the game.

★ Try not to get too nervous in the build-up to a game. Getting worried and stressed wastes a lot of energy, so stay calm and relaxed.

★ Before you warm up, discuss defensive tactics with your team-mates, to make sure everyone knows what to do at set piece plays and corners.

STRETCHING AND LOOSENING EXERCISES

Warming up before a game is essential. If you don't loosen up your muscles, you could get injured. Exercise for about ten minutes until you feel warmer, but don't tire yourself out. After finishing these exercises, do some gentle jogging.

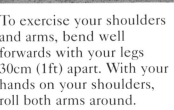

To loosen your neck muscles, gently roll your head around in a circle ten times. Then do the same the other way around. This is a very relaxing exercise.

To exercise your shoulders and arms, bend well forwards with your legs 30cm (1ft) apart. With your hands on your shoulders, roll both arms around.

To loosen your hamstring muscles, lift up one leg and bend the knee back until you can hold your ankle in your hand. Then do the same with your other leg.

BALL WORK

Getting the feel of the ball will help your handling during a game. Basic routines will improve your timing and get you focused.

Some of the exercises earlier in the book such as high and low shot practice (see page 199) would be ideal, as are the ones below.

Move the ball in a circle around your body, passing it from one hand to the other behind your back. Start at waist height and move up to chest level.

Lie on your stomach with your arms in front of you. Ask a team-mate to throw catches to you from about 2m (6ft) away. Raise your legs as you catch.

To sharpen your reflexes, ask a team-mate to stand 2m (6ft) away holding a ball at chest height. When he drops the ball, catch it before it hits the ground.

STAY FOCUSED

During a game you may not touch the ball for long periods, but stay focused at all times, or you may start making mistakes. Always use good technique and never get casual about making saves.

This keeper stopped concentrating for a moment and is now unable to get to this long-range shot.

BE CONFIDENT

As the last line of defence for your team, you need to seem confident at all times.

American keeper Kasey Keller shows his confidence by claiming a catch early on in a game.

If you appear nervous, the opposing team might think your technique is weak and could try to pressurize you. Believe in your own ability to play well and remember that you are a crucial player in your team.

WORLD SOCCER QUIZ

92. 1994 World Cup runners-up Italy struggled to qualify for a place in the 1998 Finals. Who did they finally beat in a play-off to get through?

a. Russia
b. Poland
c. Georgia

93. In which year did Sweden host the World Cup?

a. 1934
b. 1938
c. 1958

94. What is Silvio Gazzaniga's claim to fame?

a. He designed the FIFA World Cup which replaced the Jules Rimet Trophy
b. He was the Italian team manager in the 1960s
c. He was the referee in the 1990 World Cup Final

95. Which famous player refused to play in the 1978 World Cup?

a. Grzegorz Lato, Poland
b. Johan Cruyff, Holland
c. Jairzinho, Brazil

96. Which nation won the World Cup for the second time in 1950?

a. Italy
b. Uruguay
c. West Germany

97. Morocco was the first African nation ever to qualify for the World Cup Finals. In which year did this happen?

a. 1958
b. 1966
c. 1970

98. Which member of the 1978 winning Argentinian World Cup team was also playing for a European club at the time?

a. Mario Kempes
b. Leopoldo Luque
c. Daniel Passarella

99. Which German player scored in the World Cup Final in both 1974 and 1982?

a. Gerd Müller
b. Paul Breitner
c. Franz Beckenbauer

100. Which Brazilian player was nicknamed 'The White Pele' and became South American Footballer of the Year in 1977, 1981 and 1982?

a. Jairzinho
b. Socrates
c. Zico

101. Three nations have hosted the World Cup twice. France and Mexico are two. Which is the third?

a. Argentina
b. Italy
c. Uruguay

102. The 2002 World Cup is unique for which of these reasons?

a. It is the first time for the World Cup to be hosted in Asia
b. It is the first time for 32 nations to go through to the Finals
c. It is the first time for all the matches to be played on an artificial surface

103. Who beat Bulgaria 4-0 to come third in the 1994 World Cup?

a. Romania
b. Holland
c. Sweden

104. Up until 1998, which national team had only won the World Cup once?

a. Uruguay
b. England
c. Italy

105. Which player won both the European and World Footballer of the Year titles in 1997?

a. Ronaldo
b. Matthäus Sammer
c. Alessandro del Piero

106. Which nation was banned from entering the 1994 World Cup for cheating in a 1990 qualifying match?

a. Bolivia
b. Greece
c. Chile

SOCCER QUIZ ?

PART EIGHT
TRAINING AND FITNESS

CONTENTS

TRAINING BASICS

To be a good soccer player, you must be fit. The best way to develop a high level of fitness is to do regular training sessions. Training can be tough, but it is also very rewarding and it helps you improve your soccer skills, too.

GETTING AN EDGE

An unfit team has no chance of winning against a fit one. Regular training can improve your all-round ability and can make your team difficult to beat. It gives you the edge over opponents in the following key areas:

Speed – you can get past opponents more easily and be first to the ball.

Stamina – you have enough energy to play a whole game at your best.

Strength – you can win the ball in tough challenges to turn defence into attack.

Quick reactions – you can anticipate play and punish opposition mistakes.

TRAINING AND ENERGY

Your body has two ways of producing the energy that you need when you exercise – the aerobic energy system, and the anaerobic energy system. These terms appear throughout this part of the book. This is how each system works.

The anaerobic system provides a lot of energy quickly but can only work for short periods of time.

The aerobic energy system is what you use when you do steady activities such as walking or jogging. It uses your food and the oxygen you breathe in to create energy in your muscles. The harder you exercise, the more oxygen your muscles need. You breathe deeper to take more oxygen in, and your heart beats faster to pump it to your muscles.

The aerobic system can provide energy for long periods of time.

You use the anaerobic energy system for sudden, 'explosive' exercise such as sprinting and jumping, when your body needs more energy than it can get aerobically. This system does not need oxygen to produce energy, so it only uses your food.

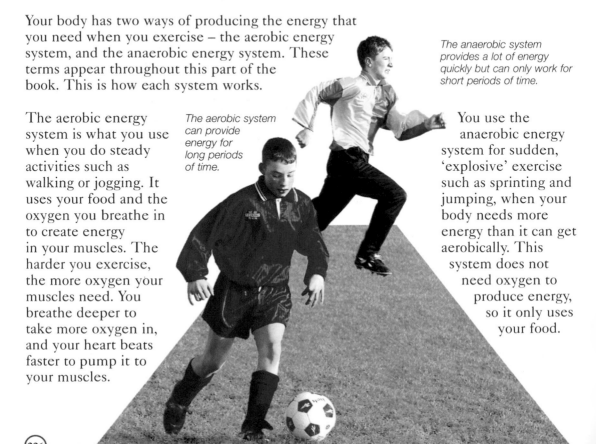

KIT AND EQUIPMENT

If you have the right kit, you can train in all weather conditions and on different surfaces. Wherever you train, it's important to keep warm.

Sports markers, such as those shown here, are useful but not essential. You could use bags or sweaters instead.

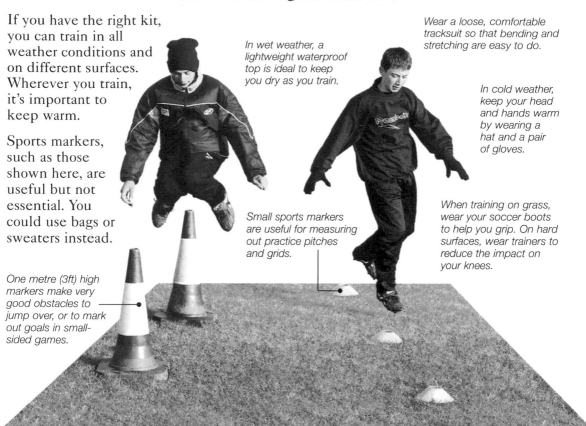

In wet weather, a lightweight waterproof top is ideal to keep you dry as you train.

Wear a loose, comfortable tracksuit so that bending and stretching are easy to do.

In cold weather, keep your head and hands warm by wearing a hat and a pair of gloves.

Small sports markers are useful for measuring out practice pitches and grids.

When training on grass, wear your soccer boots to help you grip. On hard surfaces, wear trainers to reduce the impact on your knees.

One metre (3ft) high markers make very good obstacles to jump over, or to mark out goals in small-sided games.

PLANNING A TRAINING SCHEDULE

Plan to train about twice a week, but avoid very hard training in the day or two before a game. Here is an outline of how to structure a session:

Try to make each session varied and interesting. A good training schedule should include aerobic and anaerobic exercise as well as skills work.

10 minutes	First, loosen up for about 5 minutes (see pages 230 and 232), then do some stretches (see pages 231, 232 and 233).
10 minutes	For the next 30 minutes, do a variety of games and exercises. Spend about 10 minutes on each one. There are plenty to choose from in this book. For example: ★ Running games (pages 236-237) ★ Skills training (pages 242-243) ★ Quick reaction games (pages 244-245) Rest briefly between each exercise.
10 minutes	
10 minutes	
25 minutes	Play a game of soccer (a small-sided game if there are only a few of you).
5 minutes	Warm down for 5 minutes with some gentle jogging and stretching exercises.

This team is doing a variety of activities.

These players are working on their sprinting speed.

Some players are stretching their muscles.

These two players are working on their ball control.

MUSCLES FOR SOCCER

Your body has over 600 muscles. Whenever you do a different activity, such as walking around or running, you use a different set of muscles. Playing soccer uses a wide variety of them. If you know how your muscles work, it will help you to understand how to look after them and how to make them stronger.

WHAT MUSCLES ARE MADE OF

Muscles are made up of lots of long, thin cells or fibres. There are two types of fibre. One is used in aerobic exercises which need stamina, such as jogging. These are called 'slow' fibres. The other type, 'fast' fibres, work anaerobically and provide short bursts of energy. The number of fast and slow fibres in each muscle varies from person to person.

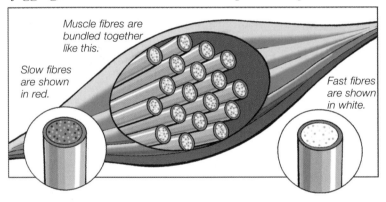

Muscle fibres are bundled together like this.

Slow fibres are shown in red.

Fast fibres are shown in white.

BUILDING STRENGTH

To build up the strength of a muscle, it needs to be worked at full capacity. As you exercise the muscle, its fibres become bigger to cope with the extra work. See page 234 for some strengthening exercises.

Most top professional players, such as Colombia's Faustino Asprilla, have very strong leg muscles.

HOW MUSCLES WORK

Muscles are attached to your bones by flexible cords called tendons. As you use a muscle, the tendon pulls on the bone and makes it move.

Muscles are also very flexible and can contract, or shorten, to half their normal length. A muscle becomes firmer and thicker when it is contracted.

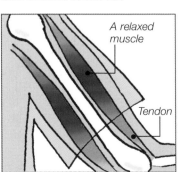

A relaxed muscle

Tendon

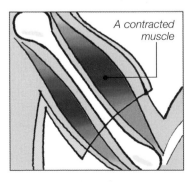

A contracted muscle

KEY MUSCLES

When you are playing soccer, you use many different muscles to run, kick, head or catch. Here are some of the key muscles you use, and what you use them for.

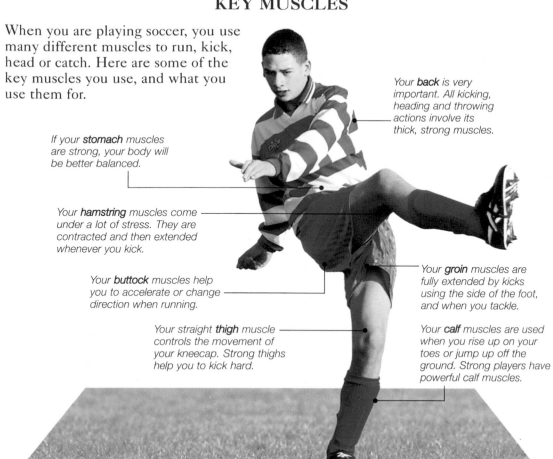

*Your **back** is very important. All kicking, heading and throwing actions involve its thick, strong muscles.*

*If your **stomach** muscles are strong, your body will be better balanced.*

*Your **hamstring** muscles come under a lot of stress. They are contracted and then extended whenever you kick.*

*Your **buttock** muscles help you to accelerate or change direction when running.*

*Your **groin** muscles are fully extended by kicks using the side of the foot, and when you tackle.*

*Your straight **thigh** muscle controls the movement of your kneecap. Strong thighs help you to kick hard.*

*Your **calf** muscles are used when you rise up on your toes or jump up off the ground. Strong players have powerful calf muscles.*

INJURY RISKS

Most muscles are arranged in pairs which work together when you move. For instance, when you sprint, your hamstrings contract as your thigh muscles extend. If one muscle contracts too quickly, the opposite muscle may be pulled or strained.

In any soccer game, you have to make sudden twisting and stretching movements. This makes it likely that you will get injured from time to time. There are many different ways of injuring yourself, but you can help reduce the chances of this happening (see page 253).

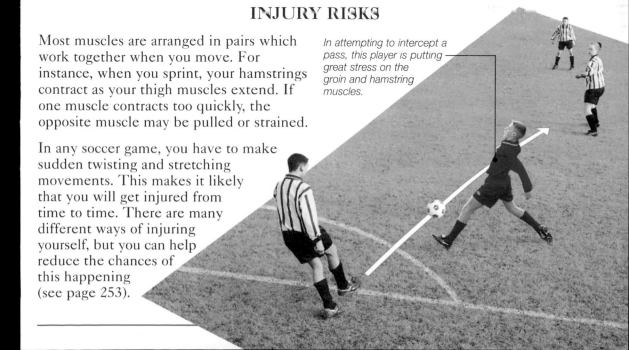

In attempting to intercept a pass, this player is putting great stress on the groin and hamstring muscles.

LOOSENING AND STRETCHING

Every training session should begin with loosening up exercises, because cold, stiff muscles can easily be injured. You should then move on to more demanding muscle stretches. Regular stretching sessions will help you to stay flexible and supple.

GETTING LOOSE

Loosening routines should involve gentle body movements and should raise the temperature of your muscles. It is really important to loosen up your whole body, not just your legs. Once you are warm, you are then ready to try out other exercises and stretching positions which make your muscles work harder. Any loosening session need only last for about five minutes.

Stand with your legs 60cm (2ft) apart and put your hands on your hips. Slowly swing your hips around in a circle five times.

Stand with your feet 30cm (1ft) apart and gently swing your right arm over your shoulder ten times. Repeat with your left arm.

Lie down and raise your right leg up towards your chest. Then lower it and do the same with your left leg. Try not to lift your head up.

JOG AND PASS

To complete a loosening up session, gently work your lower body muscles with some basic ball work.

Jog across a pitch, and back again, with a couple of your team-mates. As you run, turn and pass a ball to each other.

As you jog, try to maintain a gentle, even pace. Don't sprint or make sudden movements.

UPPER BODY STRETCHING

Stretching routines do more than just warm up your muscles. By stressing and extending your muscles, they also increase your flexibility. Only attempt stretching positions after loosening up.

The position shown here stretches your stomach, back and arms. Lie face down and place your hands in line with your shoulders. Use your arms to push the top half of your body up.

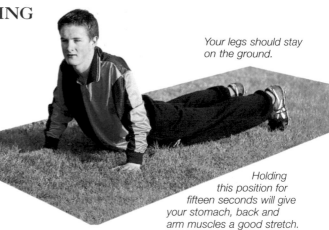

Your legs should stay on the ground.

Holding this position for fifteen seconds will give your stomach, back and arm muscles a good stretch.

CATCH AND THROW

This game is a good way of stretching your stomach. Stop if you feel any tightness in your muscles.

Raise your legs as you catch.

Sit on the ground with your legs slightly bent. Ask a team-mate standing about 2m (6ft) away to throw you a high catch. Rock back as you catch the ball above your head.

Throw the ball straight back, pushing yourself forwards as you throw. Try to work quickly, swapping over regularly.

STRETCH AND BEND

This is a fast-moving game that stretches your lower back, stomach muscles and the backs of your legs.

Stand back-to-back with a team-mate, about 60cm (2ft) apart. Raising your arms right up, pass a ball back over your head to your team-mate.

Your team-mate should take the ball and then bend forwards, passing the ball back to you through her legs. Bend your knees as you take the ball.

A SIDE STRETCH

To stretch the muscles in your sides, swivel round to pass the ball behind you using both hands. Twist one way to pass and the other to receive.

LEG MUSCLE STRETCHING

You use the muscles in your legs for every aspect of soccer, so it is important you pay particular attention to stretching your lower body. Concentrate on working your hamstrings, groin, thigh and calf muscles.

LEG LOOSENER

Always remember to loosen up before stretching. You can use this varied jogging routine as an alternative to 'jog and pass' (see page 230). Place four markers on the ground about 20m (66ft) apart, then start jogging slowly from the first marker to the second. Turn sideways and sidestep to the third marker. Then do another half turn and jog backwards until you reach the final marker.

20m (66ft)

Slow jog   Sidestep   Jog backwards

Once you reach the end marker, repeat the stages back again to complete the circuit.

Do about three circuits, but don't tire yourself out.

HAMSTRING STRETCH

It's easy to pull your hamstring muscles, so use this routine to help keep them supple and flexible.

If you are really supple, you may be able to roll the ball right down to the ground.

With your feet together, hold a ball against your chest. Begin to roll it down slowly towards your toes. Bend as the ball moves down, then roll it back up to your chest. If you feel a tightness in the back of your legs as you bend, don't stretch any further.

FIGURE-OF-EIGHT MOVE

This tricky ball passing routine is ideal for working your groin muscles.

The ball should make a figure-of-eight pattern as it passes around your legs.

Lean over to your left and right as the ball moves between your legs.

Stand with your knees bent and your legs well apart. Swing your right hand around the outside of your right leg to pass a ball to your left hand in between your legs. Then swing your left hand around your left leg to pass the ball back again.

HOPPING GAME

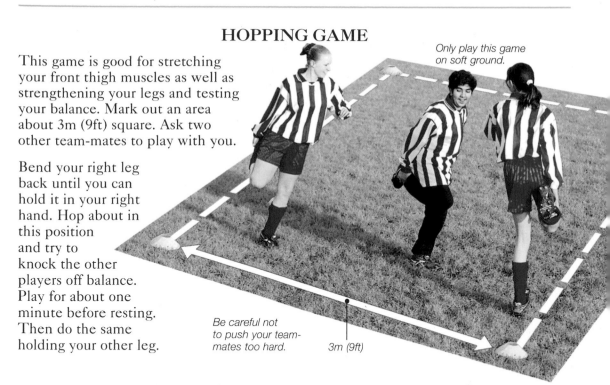

Only play this game on soft ground.

This game is good for stretching your front thigh muscles as well as strengthening your legs and testing your balance. Mark out an area about 3m (9ft) square. Ask two other team-mates to play with you.

Bend your right leg back until you can hold it in your right hand. Hop about in this position and try to knock the other players off balance. Play for about one minute before resting. Then do the same holding your other leg.

Be careful not to push your team-mates too hard.

3m (9ft)

CALF MUSCLE PUSH

You can either do this simple stretching position with a team-mate or on your own against a wall.

Push against your team-mate for up to twenty seconds, then swap legs.

Place one foot about 60cm (2ft) in front of the other and point both feet forwards. Put your hands on the shoulders of your team-mate and as he leans his weight forward, push against him. You will feel a stretch in the calf of your back leg.

ANKLE AGILITY

Your ankle joints get a lot of use during a match. They are put under particular stress when you tackle or shoot. Improving the flexibility and movement in your ankles can be achieved with some simple ball control exercises.

Place two markers 1m (3ft) apart, and drag a ball across from one marker to the other using the inside of your foot.

When you reach the other marker, use the outside of your foot to drag the ball back again. Try to work quickly.

To exercise your calf muscles as well as your ankles, rise up on your toes and do quick passes between your feet.

STRENGTH AND POWER

To make tackles or firm challenges for the ball, or to produce sudden, explosive pace, you need to be strong and powerful. When working on your strength and power, make sure you focus on your upper body as well as your legs.

LEG AND BODY LIFTS

This game will strengthen your stomach muscles. Play with a friend and concentrate on working well together, so that you co-ordinate your movements properly. As it is tiring, stop regularly for a rest.

Your team-mate must keep his legs bent.

Lie down flat and hold the ankles of a team-mate lying behind you with his feet on your shoulders and his arms stretched out.

With a ball between your feet, raise your legs up. Your team-mate does a sit-up at the same time and takes hold of the ball.

He then lies down again before sitting up. Lower your legs almost to the ground before raising them to get the ball.

WHEELBARROW WALKING

This strengthens your arms and shoulders. Lie face down with your hands on the ground and ask a team-mate to lift up your legs. Walk along on your hands with your team-mate supporting your lower body.

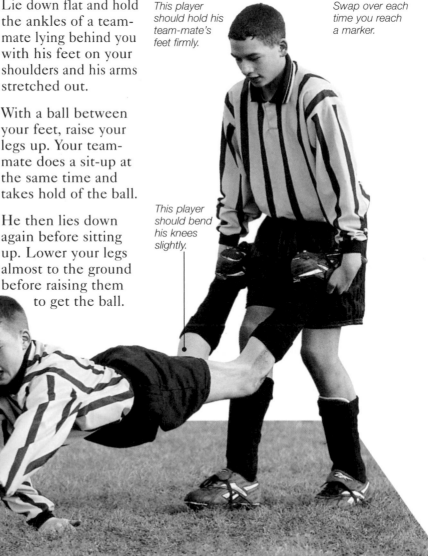

This player should hold his team-mate's feet firmly.

Swap over each time you reach a marker.

This player should bend his knees slightly.

Race against other teams over a short distance. Markers can show the finishing line.

HOP AND JUMP CHALLENGE

Hopping, jumping and skipping are good ways of improving the strength and power in your legs. To increase your power, do this exercise as fast as you can, with only a very short time on the ground between hops and jumps. Put a marker on the ground. 5m (16ft) away, put four low markers in a line, 1.5m (4.5ft) apart. Another 5m (16ft) away, line up four 60cm (2ft) high markers, 1.5m (4.5ft) apart. A friend should stand by the final high marker with five balls.

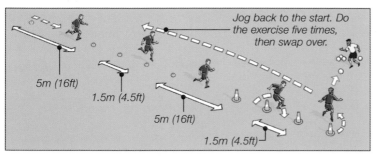

Jog back to the start. Do the exercise five times, then swap over.

5m (16ft)

1.5m (4.5ft)

5m (16ft)

1.5m (4.5ft)

Jog from the first marker to the low markers. Hop between the low markers, changing your hopping leg each time.

Jog to the high markers and leap over them using both feet. Once over the last marker, head a ball thrown by your friend.

When you reach the high markers, bring your knees right up as you jump over them.

Keep your eyes on the ground as you land.

ROPE SKIPPING

This is an enjoyable way of warming up your muscles and building up strength in your legs. Try a variety of skipping styles to exercise one or both of your legs.

When you jump over the rope, like this, try swaying from side to side as you skip to develop a rhythm.

When you step over the rope, swap your front leg regularly to give both your legs an equal workout.

JUMPING TIPS

★ As jumping and hopping are quite strenuous activities, it is vital that you warm up properly first.

★ Always use a soft surface such as grass or matting when jumping and hopping, to reduce the impact on your knees.

★ Try using trainers on very dry grass as you may slip over if you wear your soccer boots.

★ Make sure that this part of your training session doesn't last too long. One ten minute jumping session a week is enough.

SPEED AND STAMINA

While power in your legs is important, as a soccer player you also need to develop speed and stamina. All players must work on their running skills, but depending on what position you play in, you may need to give extra time to speed or stamina work.

SPRINTING TECHNIQUE

There are times when you will have to run as fast as you can, whether you play in defence or attack, so knowing how to 'sprint' (run fast over a short distance) is essential. Sprinting uses your strength and power and fully extends your leg muscles.

Swing your arms backwards and forwards in time with your strides.

Keep your neck and shoulders relaxed and steady.

Your aim is to maximise your stride length. Lift the heel of your back leg up high.

Move your back leg forward quickly, lifting your knee right up. Keep breathing deeply.

Drive your front leg forward and fully extend your back leg. Your stride is now very wide.

Keep your feet and knees facing forwards. For extra power, swing your arms vigorously.

CIRCLE SPRINT

The piggy-back position is good for strengthening your leg muscles.

This game improves your sprinting. You need an even number of players. Get into pairs, piggy-back style, and form a circle 6m (20ft) wide.

On a given signal, the player being lifted jumps down, races around the circle, and gets back onto his partner's back. Swap positions with your partner after three races.

DISTANCE RUNNING

To build up your stamina, you need to run longer distances at a constant, steady speed. This sort of running can be quite boring, so it is good to run with other team-mates so that you can encourage each other. Put two markers about 40m (130ft) apart.

40m (130ft)

Run at about half your fastest pace.

Stand next to one of the markers with two team-mates. One player runs between the markers seven times and then rests while the others run. Next, each player runs six times. Carry on until each player only makes one run.

FOLLOW THE MOVING TARGET

This game is a tough and challenging way of doing steady speed running. Mark out an area about 30m (98ft) square. One player, the 'moving target', stands on the opposite side of the square to the other runners, who are the 'chasers'.

Everyone starts running. The chasers try to catch up with the target runner. If they succeed, rest, then change the target runner. If they don't, stop after five minutes anyway and rest, then change the target.

This is not a sprinting game, so both target and chasers should run at a steady pace.

WHO NEEDS TO RUN FAST?

Most attacking players, such as strikers and wingers, need pace and acceleration over short distances to get away from defenders and to run on to through balls.

Here, French international Youri Djorkaeff uses his speed to launch a dangerous attack.

WHO NEEDS STAMINA?

Central midfield players who link defence with attack have to work particularly hard and need a good level of stamina. Full backs and wing backs also cover a lot of ground up and down the wings, supporting attacks and then tracking back to mark opponents.

This full back has covered a lot of ground to get back and tackle his marker.

INTERVAL TRAINING

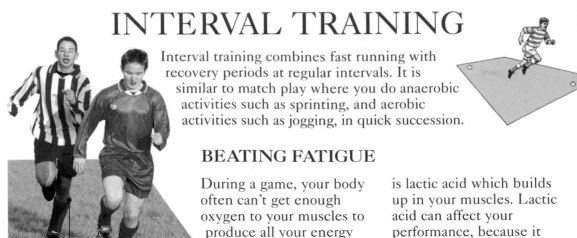

Interval training combines fast running with recovery periods at regular intervals. It is similar to match play where you do anaerobic activities such as sprinting, and aerobic activities such as jogging, in quick succession.

BEATING FATIGUE

During a game, your body often can't get enough oxygen to your muscles to produce all your energy aerobically. This means it has to produce some energy anaerobically (see page 226). A by-product of the anaerobic system is lactic acid which builds up in your muscles. Lactic acid can affect your performance, because it makes you feel tired (fatigued) and makes your muscles feel heavy. Interval training helps you get used to tolerating the build-up of lactic acid.

This player has been badly affected by fatigue and is unable to beat his opponent in this race to the ball.

MARKER SPRINT

This game includes sprinting with recovery periods of slow jogging. Mark out a 20m (66ft) square and put five randomly-spaced markers inside.
A few friends should train with you. Each choose a number and slowly start jogging around the square.

20m (66ft)

Four players jogging

When you or your coach shouts a number, that player should sprint into the square and touch all the markers, then rejoin the back of the jogging group. End the game when you have all sprinted three times.

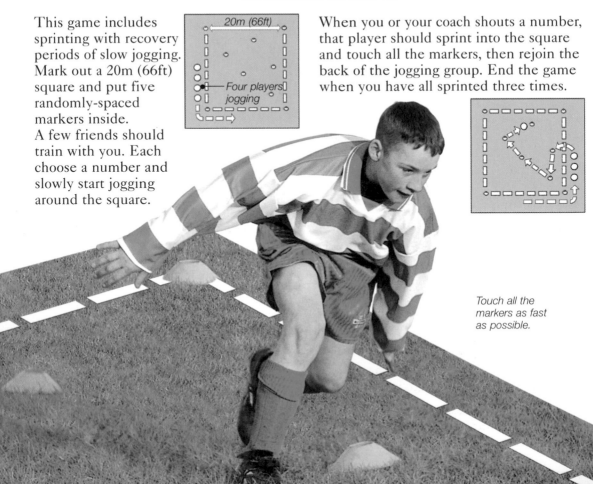

Touch all the markers as fast as possible.

SHOOTING RACE

This interval training game also provides dribbling and shooting practice. Play with three or four team-mates and your team's keeper if possible. Play on half a full-size pitch, or use a marker as a starting point and mark out a goal 6m (20ft) wide, about 25m (80ft) away.

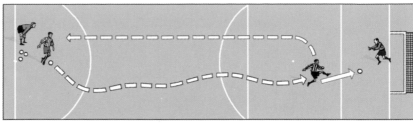

One player goes in goal. The others go to the centre circle with a ball each. One player runs at the goal and shoots, and then sprints back. The second player starts once the first has had his shot. Award one point for each goal.

Use collecting the balls as your recovery period.

This player has had a shot at goal and is about to sprint back to the centre circle.

This game gives your keeper a good practice session, but if you can't play with your keeper, take turns in goal.

INTERVAL TRAINING TIPS

High intensity training makes your heart beat fast, to supply extra oxygen to your muscles (see page 226). If you make your heart work hard on a regular basis, it gradually becomes stronger. As a result, the time you need for recovery decreases.

★ Always give yourself a good recovery period between anaerobic exercise sessions. Although interval training can be hard work, you shouldn't tire yourself out.

★ If you do some interval training about once a week, your body will adjust more quickly to the pace of a game.

STAR FITNESS

It is important for top players to have the same level of energy throughout a game. Here Argentinian striker Gabriel Batistuta moves forward energetically even though it is close to the end of the game.

BALL GAMES

Getting fit is hard work. To make it more interesting, it helps if you include several ball games in your training programme as well as basic running routines. These ball games will give you a good but enjoyable workout.

RELAY GAME

This relay race is played in pairs. It combines some ball work with some fast running. Place one marker on the ground, then mark out a circle about 6m (20ft) away from it all the way around. Split into pairs. Each pair should have a ball and stand around the circle.

Spread out around the circle.

Try not to kick the ball too far ahead of you.

Dribble the ball towards the marker, aiming to go as fast as possible. When you reach it, turn around and start running back towards your partner.

As you run, focus on speed rather than ball skills.

When you get close, pass the ball quickly to your partner who then runs to the marker. The winners are the first to complete five relays.

PRESSURE PASSING

This is a fast game and can give you an intensive workout. Play with about six of your friends. Form a circle 8m (26ft) wide around one central player. Two players around the circle should have a ball.

One of the players with a ball passes it towards the centre of the circle. The player in the middle collects it and passes to a different player. Just as this pass is made, the player with the second ball passes into the middle.

Keeping two balls on the move is hard work.

The central player has to run quickly backwards and forwards to provide passes to the rest of the circle. He should swap with another player after one minute.

POSSESSION GAME

This game involves a circle of players, with one in the middle. The idea is to make the central player work hard at gaining possession of the ball. No-one should be in the middle for more than a minute. Players should swap over once they feel tired.

Accurate passes are needed in this game.

Form a circle about 10m (33ft) wide and start passing a ball to each other. Try not to let the player in the middle touch it. If this player intercepts your pass or manages to tackle you, then you must take over in the middle.

ONE AGAINST ONE

This attacker is trying to keep the ball under close control.

This is a competitive and intensive game for two players. Mark out a pitch 5m (16ft) square with two goals 1m (3ft) wide. One player starts with the ball and has to try to get it into his opponent's goal. The other player defends. Return the ball to the attacker if it goes out of play or if the defender gains possession. After one minute has passed, swap roles. Rest after playing both ways.

This defender is watching the ball very closely and is careful not to give the attacker too much space.

SKILLS TRAINING

A good training session should include some skills practice, and there are many ball games which can help improve your playing technique. Concentrate on different skills each time you train.

PASS AND FOLLOW

This game involves quick, accurate passing and some sprinting. Play with at least five team-mates and line up in two groups behind two markers, about 8m (26ft) apart.

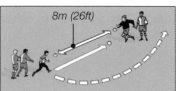

8m (26ft)

One player passes to another at the front of the opposite group. He then sprints after his pass and joins the back of the other group. Each player carries on this pattern. Everyone rests after five minutes.

This player is running to the back of the opposite group.

This player is waiting for her turn.

THREE SKILLS GAME

This game needs at least six or seven players. It is useful because it covers throw-ins, ball control, dribbling and some running. Put three markers in a triangle 15m (49ft) apart. Divide the players into two groups, A and B. Group A stands at marker 1 and group B at marker 2. Each player in group A has a ball.

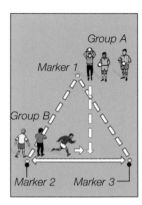

Group A

Marker 1

Group B

Marker 2   Marker 3

A player from group A does a throw-in. A player from group B runs and controls it.

The group B player dribbles around marker 3, as shown, then runs to the back of group A.

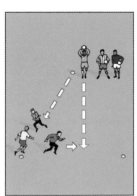

The thrower runs to the back of group B. Meanwhile, the next two players repeat the game.

TWO GOAL CHALLENGE

This game tests your shooting skills. You need two other players and three balls. Mark out two goals facing each other, 6m (20ft) wide and 18m (59ft) apart.

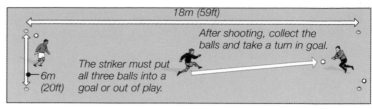

18m (59ft)

After shooting, collect the balls and take a turn in goal.

The striker must put all three balls into a goal or out of play.

6m (20ft)

One player is the striker and has a ball at his feet. The other two players are keepers. Each has a spare ball by one of his posts.

The striker can shoot at either goal at any time. If he scores or shoots wide, the keeper throws his spare ball out to him.

If the keeper catches the shot, he throws the same ball out again. If the ball rebounds out, the striker shoots until it is out of play.

HEAD VOLLEYBALL

This game is good heading practice. Mark out a 6m (20ft) square with a row of markers halfway across it. Play with a friend who stands opposite you. One player throws a ball to the other, who heads it back. Keep heading until the ball falls to the ground. As well as trying to beat your opponent, aim to have good rallies some of the time.

6m (20ft)

You get a point if your opponent heads the ball outside the grid, or if it drops on his side. The winner is the first player to ten points.

This player is practising powerful headers by trying to head the ball over his opponent.

The other player is watching the flight of the ball closely and is ready to move back quickly.

MENTAL AGILITY

All good soccer players need to be able to make quick decisions and be alert at all times, so it is important to spend some time strengthening your mental agility. Your reactions are like any other skill – they improve with practice.

SHADOWING GAME

This game helps to develop your powers of concentration. Put ten markers an equal distance apart in a 6m (20ft) wide circle.

Play in threes. Two players stand at opposite markers, while the third player stands nearby, ready to give instructions.

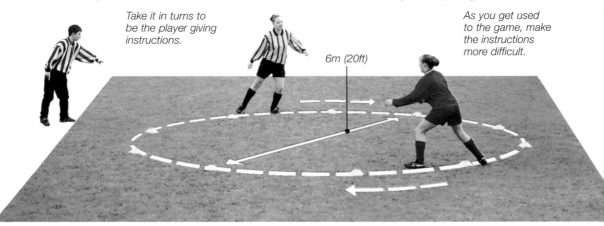

Take it in turns to be the player giving instructions.

As you get used to the game, make the instructions more difficult.

6m (20ft)

The third player shouts out instructions such as 'Move two markers to the right!' The other players follow these instructions quickly. If the players in the circle get the instructions right, they will always be opposite each other. The first one to make a mistake must run around the circle before continuing the game.

DIAMOND GAME

This game tests your mental agility as you need to do the opposite of what is asked. Four players form a diamond. Each is given a name, either 'up', 'down', 'right' or 'left', as shown. One player stands in the middle and another is 'spare'.

Up

Play this game quickly and rest after five minutes.

Left

Right

Down

The spare player shouts out the names of some of the players. The middle player touches the opposite players – if the spare player shouts 'right, up', the middle player touches 'left, down'. If the middle player gets the instructions right, she swaps with the last player touched. If not, she stays in the middle.

Spare player

QUICK RESPONSE RUNNING

This game improves your response times. The faster you can react, the more likely you are to win a race to the ball in a match.

Stand by a row of markers with some team-mates, facing a second set of markers 15m (49ft) away. Another player, or your coach, stands nearby and gives instructions.

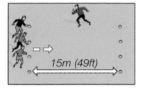

15m (49ft)

Stand in a straight line with your team-mates.

1. When your coach shouts 'Now!', start jogging towards the far markers.

Don't set off too quickly and jog quite slowly.

2. When your coach shouts 'Down!', sit down as quickly as you can.

Be ready to react to the second shout.

Try to anticipate the final shout, so that you can get slightly ahead of your team-mates.

3. As your coach shouts 'Go!', jump up and sprint to the markers. Repeat the race five times, then rest.

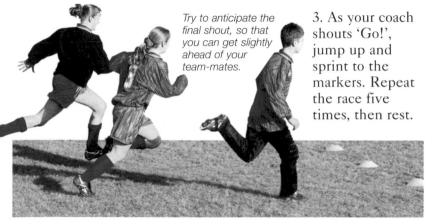

REACTION TIPS

★ In the hour or so before a match, try to keep your mind focused on the game ahead.

★ Keep an eye on what is going on around you. Staying alert will help you anticipate play.

This quick-thinking player has intercepted a pass.

★ Once you are focused, you should try to concentrate for the whole game. A brief lapse in concentration can cost your team a goal or the match.

STAR REACTIONS

Here, Italian defender Paulo Maldini is very alert and is quick to challenge an opponent.

GOALKEEPER TRAINING

If you are a goalkeeper, you have a special job to do and a lot of your training needs to be centred around improving your handling, flexibility and strength. Keepers should also have a good level of fitness and need to do running work with their team-mates.

ARM AND SHOULDER WORK

This exercise is good for stretching and strengthening your arm and shoulder muscles. If you have strong upper body muscles, it helps improve your catching and punching.

Put one leg slightly in front of you for balance.

A friend stands opposite you about 1m (3ft) away. Lean forwards and hold each other's forearms firmly. To loosen and stretch your muscles, both of you rotate your arms, as shown above, slowly building up speed. To strengthen your muscles, take it in turns to push against the movement of the other's arms. This makes rotating your arms around much harder to do.

LEG BUILDER

Powerful leg muscles are vital for a keeper, as you often have to jump for crosses and make acrobatic dives. You have to move fast to do this exercise, but it is very effective at building up your leg muscles. You can do this on your own with a ball.

Keep your eyes on the ball all the time.

Stand with your legs 60cm (2ft) apart. Hold a ball in front of you at knee level.

Throw the ball as high as possible into the air and then quickly sit down.

Stand up again before you catch the ball. Do this ten times and then rest.

QUICK PASS GAME

This game works on your basic handling skills and sharpens your reflexes. Holding a ball, stand between two friends who are about 4m (13ft) apart. One of these friends should also have a ball.

Play with other keepers if you can.

Swap over after one minute in the middle.

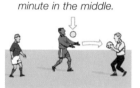

Throw your ball right up into the air, then turn to the friend with a ball.

Catch a throw from this player and quickly turn to your other friend.

Throw the ball to him, and then get ready to catch your own ball again.

MOVE AND DIVE

This game should improve your movement around the goal area and works on your reflexes and flexibility. Mark out a 6m (20ft) wide circle and put six balls an equal distance apart around it. Number them one to six. Stand in the middle of the circle and ask a friend or another keeper to stand nearby and shout out a number. When your friend shouts, run and dive at this ball. Get up quickly and run back to the centre while your friend shouts another number for you to run to.

6m (20ft)

As this game involves a lot of impact with the ground, play on a soft surface. Swap with your friend after six saves.

Move around quickly, keeping on your toes.

ON MATCH DAYS

On the day of a game, you need a routine for before and after the match. Warm up properly and make sure you keep your muscles warm during and after the game. This helps to prevent injury and stiffness.

A BASIC WARM-UP ROUTINE

A warm-up routine should last ten or fifteen minutes. Start with loosening and stretching exercises. Then do some ball work to give you a feel for the ball and to get you moving around. If you are an attacker, spend some time warming up your keeper by practising your shooting.

You could use this warm-up routine with a team-mate. Put two markers 8m (26ft) apart and stand between them. Each of you has a ball. Both start dribbling towards different markers. Continue around your markers and pass each other in a figure-of-eight movement.

Three minutes of this exercise is enough to warm you up. If you have time, practise passing the ball to each other, too.

Do this routine at a steady pace, with the ball under close control.

RUNNING ROUTINES

The final part of the warm-up should be the most intensive. Spend about five minutes going through a variety of running routines.

Start off with some light jogging, before moving on to the techniques shown here. Once you are feeling warm and your muscles are loose, end your warm-up with a couple of fast sprints to get your heart pumping and deepen your breathing.

Both these routines are used by top players in their pre-match warm-ups.

To work your calf and hamstring muscles, run with your hands held out in front of you. Bring your knees up high so that they touch your hands.

This exercise works your thighs. Run with your hands facing outwards behind your back. Bring your heels up high and try to touch your hands.

WHAT TO DO AT HALF-TIME

At half-time, go into the changing room to rest and keep warm. Have a drink to replace lost fluids and keep doing gentle loosening exercises so you don't get stiff. If you have to spend half-time on the pitch, you must keep moving about and stretching.

This team is spending half-time on the pitch. Each player is doing regular muscle stretches.

SUBSTITUTES

If you are one of your team's substitutes, warm up before a game with your team-mates in case you need to replace another player soon after the start. During the game, warm up every ten minutes so that your muscles don't get cold and stiff.

These substitutes are doing a warm-up routine at the edge of the pitch, in case they are called on to play.

WARMING DOWN AFTER THE MATCH

After the match, you should spend a few minutes doing an easy and relaxing warming down session. If you stop exercising suddenly, lactic acid (see page 238) can get trapped in your muscles and can make them feel tired and sore the next day.

Gentle jogging and stretching cools your muscles down slowly and helps to get rid of any lactic acid that has built up.

These players have put on warm clothing and are going through a light warming down session.

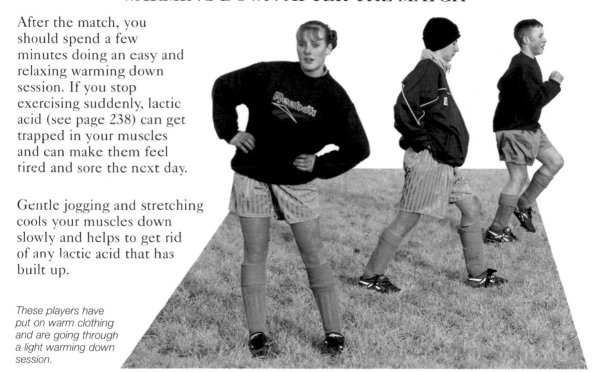

PRE- AND POST-MATCH TIPS

★ Arrive at a game early so that you have plenty of time to get physically and mentally prepared.

★ Do your warm-up twenty minutes before the start of a game. If you do it too early, your muscles will get cold again and you will have wasted valuable energy.

★ Always build up the intensity of your warm-up gradually. Remember that cold muscles are easily injured, so avoid sudden, explosive movements early on.

★ After a game, have a warm shower. This is good for relaxing your muscles, as well as giving you the chance to get clean.

FOOD AND DRINK

Food plays a vital part in providing you with all the energy you need. It also helps you to grow, keep warm and recover from injuries. To play soccer at your best, you need a healthy diet which contains plenty of energy-giving foods.

DIFFERENT KINDS OF FOODS

All food contains some 'nutrients'. Each nutrient helps the body to develop and function in a different way. Carbohydrates, fats, proteins, vitamins and minerals are all nutrients. These are found in different foods in varying amounts.

Most of your energy comes from carbohydrates. Bread, pasta, potatoes, rice and cereals are good carbohydrate sources. Carbohydrate is stored in your liver and muscles as glycogen, or in your blood as glucose.

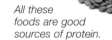

All these foods are good sources of protein.

Carbohydrate is the main nutrient in these foods.

Protein is used to build and repair your body and can also give you energy. Many foods contain some protein but meat, fish, milk, nuts and beans are particularly good sources of it.

Sweets also provide you with carbohydrate in the form of sugar (but see opposite page).

Many fruits and vegetables contain vitamins and minerals.

Foods containing fat provide energy but you need to do a lot of exercise before you make use of it. Fried foods contain a lot of fat. Meat and dairy products can also contain a high amount of fat.

Your body needs vitamins and minerals in small amounts. Many foods contain them. Vitamin C, for instance, which repairs damaged cells and keeps your skin healthy, is found in citrus fruits and green vegetables.

Butter is almost pure fat. Cakes tend to contain a lot of fat, and red meat can be fatty, too.

WATCHING WHAT YOU EAT

If you eat a balanced diet containing plenty of fresh foods, you should obtain the necessary amounts of protein, vitamins and minerals your body needs each day. Some foods, though, can be bad for you if you eat a lot of them.

Sugar is often added to packaged and tinned foods.

Try not to eat too much fatty food as this can lead to heart disease later in life and can make you put on a lot of weight.

Although sugar can give you energy, it contains no other nutrients. A lot of sugar can rot your teeth and may cause spots.

Packaged snacks and fast foods contain a lot of salt. Too much can cause high blood pressure and blood circulation problems.

WHAT TO DRINK

In a game, sweating makes you lose a lot of fluid. Make sure you replace this fluid quickly or you may become dehydrated. This can lead to cramp (see page 252) and fatigue. Try to drink at regular intervals during play, and also at half-time.

You can buy isotonic sports drinks if you don't want to make your own.

Drinks such as tea and coffee are good for making you feel awake and alert but can also dehydrate you. It's best not to drink them just before or after a game.

Water is a good basic drink to have before, during and after a game to keep your fluid levels up. Avoid fizzy water as the gas may make you feel bloated.

As you sweat, you lose salt as well as water. 'Isotonic' drinks give you energy and help your body to replace salt. Water mixed with fruit juice is a good isotonic drink.

EATING TIPS

★ In the two or three days before a game, try to eat more carbohydrate-based food. This helps build up your glycogen and glucose stores and so provides you with more energy when you play.

★ Make sure you have a carbohydrate-based pre-match meal about three or four hours before the game. You need to allow enough time for the food to be digested, or you may feel sick and uncomfortable.

★ Eat another carbohydrate-based meal within a few hours of finishing a game. You will have used up a lot of energy, and you need to replace it as soon as possible. Isotonic drinks will help too.

★ Try to eat a balanced diet all the time to improve and maintain your general health. To get the maximum benefit from your training, it's important you don't eat too much junk food.

DEALING WITH INJURIES

All soccer players get injured sometimes, whether in a game or as a result of doing a lot of training. Most injuries are not very serious and only take a short time to heal, but you need to know how to treat them, otherwise a small problem can become a big one.

TREATING YOUR OWN INJURIES

Common minor injuries include bruises, cuts or grazes, slight muscle strains and 'sprains' of joints or ligaments (flexible cords that support your joints). If you are not bleeding too much and can still walk, you can treat these yourself. After the game, use an ice pack on bruises, sprains and strains to lessen swelling and pain. Support the injury with a bandage and raise it up on a cushion to keep reducing the swelling.

Use a pain relieving spray during the game.

If the pain is too bad, ask your coach to substitute you.

Wash small cuts and grazes and then apply antiseptic to prevent infection. Put a dressing or plaster on the cut once it is dry. Cushioned plasters or bandages give the wound protection.

Cover a wound with a plaster after cleaning it thoroughly.

DEALING WITH CRAMP

Cramp is one of the most common soccer injuries. It involves the sudden, painful contraction of a group of muscles. It may be caused by too much lactic acid in your muscles (see page 238) or by dehydration, so try to drink plenty of fluids during the game.

For cramp in your calf muscle, ask a team-mate to straighten your knee and then to gently push your foot up towards your shin.

For cramp in your foot, a team-mate gently pushes your toes back. It also helps to stand on the front part, or 'ball', of your foot.

For cramp in your thigh, lie down. Ask someone to straighten your knee and pull your leg up, then push your knee down.

PREVENTING INJURIES

Although there is no guaranteed way of avoiding injury, there are some simple precautions you can take to reduce the chances of it happening. It is important you look after your body before, during and after a game (see pages 248-249).

You must wear shin pads during a game to protect the lower part of your legs from injury.

Warming up before a game will greatly reduce the risk of pulling a muscle in the first few minutes.

Too much kicking and jumping can damage your knees, so try not to overdo your soccer playing.

SERIOUS INJURIES

When a serious injury occurs, stay calm and get help at once from adults. If a player is in a lot of pain he may have badly pulled or torn a muscle or sprained a joint. Don't try to move him in case he has actually fractured or dislocated a bone or joint. Keep him relaxed, and cover him with a blanket or coat to help him to stay warm.

When a bad injury occurs, stop the game and inform the referee.

The referee should call for medical help.

MAKING A FIRST AID KIT

It is essential for your team to have a bag at every game containing medical products to treat any injuries that occur. Include painkillers to relieve the pain of minor injuries.

Some important things to keep in your bag are a pair of scissors, some plasters and dressings, antiseptic cream or wipes and pain relieving spray. Remember to replace anything you use before the next game.

STAYING FIT AND HEALTHY

Try to stay fit all the time, and not just during the soccer season. Being fit can make you feel good and can improve the way you look. Regular exercise, a balanced diet and taking care of your body help to maintain your health.

FITNESS AND YOUR BODY

If you are fit and active, your body becomes stronger and works more efficiently. You are more resistant to certain illnesses and medical problems such as colds, flu and other infectious diseases. Also, a strong heart can help improve your resistance to heart disease later in life.

Regular exercise can make you feel more relaxed as it is an effective way of relieving stress and tension.

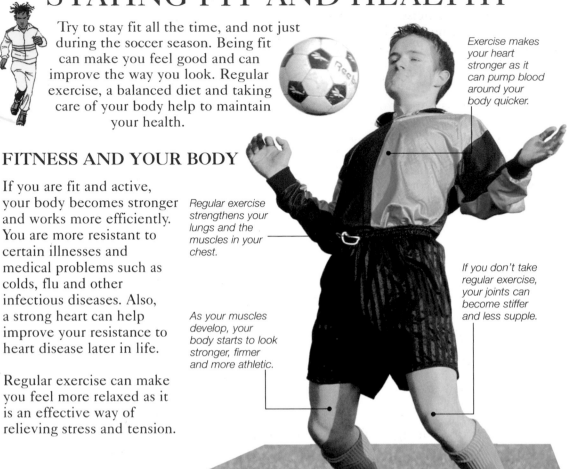

Exercise makes your heart stronger as it can pump blood around your body quicker.

Regular exercise strengthens your lungs and the muscles in your chest.

As your muscles develop, your body starts to look stronger, firmer and more athletic.

If you don't take regular exercise, your joints can become stiffer and less supple.

FEELING CONFIDENT

Getting fit can really improve your self confidence. Every time you play a match, you will know that you are as fit, if not fitter, than your opponents. You will be more prepared to attempt difficult challenges and make attacking runs.

Even if you haven't been selected for a team, keep working at your fitness and stay confident. You have a much better chance of being included if you are one of the fittest players in the squad.

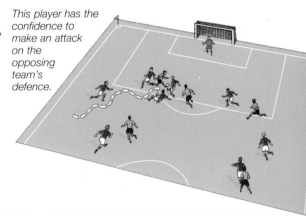

This player has the confidence to make an attack on the opposing team's defence.

LOOKING AFTER YOURSELF

Although regular exercise is very good for improving your fitness and health, you also need to get plenty of rest. If you make your body do too much work, you may get injured or ill.

Use a bandage to support a muscle or joint that has been injured.

If you get a serious injury, you must follow medical advice and take time off to recover. You need to be patient and resume your training schedule slowly. If you do hard physical exercise when you are still injured, you may make the injury even worse.

PRE-SEASON TRAINING

When the soccer season ends, do some form of exercise to maintain your level of fitness. There are many activities to pick from and playing other sports can be fun. You could work out a training schedule including several different sports.

Cycling builds up your leg muscles as well as your stamina. Cycling up hills is particularly hard work.

Tennis is a fun and competitive game. It includes short sprints and works your upper body.

Swimming exercises all your muscles and is excellent for your stamina, strength and suppleness.

STAR PLAYER

Brazilian star Ronaldo is the complete soccer player. He has superb ability and also a high level of fitness.

HEALTH TIPS

★ Keep to a balanced diet, eating plenty of fresh food and fibre and avoiding too much fatty food and sugar.

★ Try to get a good night's sleep every night. Sleep helps your body grow, repair and refresh itself. You need to spend time relaxing your mind and muscles.

★ Avoid addictive substances such as alcohol and cigarettes. These can have a bad effect on your health and can cause serious problems later in life.

★ Once the soccer season is over, try to do a good exercise session three times a week.

INDEX

SOCCER QUIZ ANSWERS

SOCCER QUIZ
?

Answers to the offside quiz on page 119:
1) Offside (the offside player receives the ball indirectly from the throw-in) 2) Not offside (the offside player is not interfering with play) 3) Offside (he is in a position which gives him an advantage) 4) Not offside (he dribbles through).

If you would like to improve your soccer by attending a soccer course in your holidays, you can find out about different courses from Bobby Charlton Soccer Schools Ltd, Hopwood Hall, Rochdale Road, Middleton, Manchester M24 6XH. Tel: 0161 643 3113.

Library photographs: Action Images, Allsport UK, Empics

With special thanks to soccer players Osman Afzal, Brooke Astle, Sajid Aziz, Kevin Better, Botlme Bolotete, Carl Brogden, Nathan Brooks, David Buckley, Nicola Burton, John Cox, Ben Dale, Leanne Davis, Deps Gabonamong, James Peter Greatrex, Gemma Grimshaw, Mohammed Gulfam, Alicia Hardiker, Rachel Horner, David Hughes, Moynul Islam, John Jackson, Lindsey Jamieson, Michael Jones, Sarah Leigh, Andrum Mahmood, Nathan Miles, Otlaadisa Mohambi, Andrew Perkin, Leanne Prince, Matthew Rea, Peter Riley, Daniel Savastano, Mohammad Usman Shafiq, Christopher Sharples, Ciaran Simpson, Jody Spence, John Tabas, Ben Tipton, Mark Travis, Joe Vain, Christopher White, Neil Wilson, David Wood, and to their coaches, Dave Benson, Alex Black, Bryn Cooper, Warren Gore and Gavin Rhodes.